Dear visitors of the Ahl al-Bayt.

This booklet is intended to provide you with the information, supplications, and visitations you need in your personal and spiritual journey through the Holy Shrines. We pray that it is of benefit to you.

This booklet was compiled from the pages of duas.org.

This booklet is provided to you for the purposes of this journey ONLY, and is not meant for public distribution.

If you find any mistakes, please email info@mainstay.us with the page number and correction.

We appreciate your cooperation.

And as always, keep us in your prayers. You are in ours.

-The Mainstay Foundation

Title: The Calling

Printed in the United States.

ISBN: 978-1-943393-86-2

IN THIS BOOKLET

About the Shrines

THE HOLY CITY OF NAJAF

The Shrine of Imam Ali (a)

The Shrine of the Commander of the Faithful (a), Prophet Adam, and Prophet Noah

Imam al-Ṣādiq (a) said,

> *God Almighty revealed to Noah while he was in the ark to encircle the House [of God (i.e., the Kaʿbah)] for a week. He did as God revealed to him. He then went down in the water to his knees and drew up a coffin which contained Adam's bones. He carried the coffin inside the ark, then encircled the House so long as God willed. He then reached the Gate of Kufa and the center of its mosque. There, God said to the earth, 'Swallow your water.' So it swallowed its water from the Kufa mosque just as the water started from its mosque, and the crowd that was with Noah in the ark dispersed.*
>
> *Noah took the coffin and buried it in Gharī, which is a piece of the mountain where God spoke to Moses directly, sanctified Jesus a great sanctity, took Abraham as a friend, took Muhammad (s) as a beloved, and made a home for prophets. By God, none lived there after his pure fathers Adam and Noah who was greater than the Commander of the Faithful. If you journey to the side of Najaf, visit the bones of Adam, the remains of Noah, and the body of Ali ibn Abī Ṭālib (a). Surely, you are visiting the first forefathers, Muhammad (s) the Seal of Prophets, and Ali (a) the Master of Vicegerents. Surely, his visitor will have the gates of the heavens be opened to them while supplicating. Do not be negligent of goodness.*

Position of the Two Fingers

There was a disbelieving tyrant whose name was Murrah ibn Qays who was once speaking about his tribe and forefathers. He asked the elders of the tribe about those who had passed away from his family. They said that Ali ibn Abī Ṭālib (a) had killed thousands of them. He asked where Imam Ali (a) had been buried and was told that he was buried in Najaf. Murrah set out with a great army to attack Najaf. After six days of defending their city, the people of Najaf were defeated. Murrah entered the city and came to the shrine. He entered the courtyard and said, "O' Ali, you killed my fathers and grandfathers!" He wanted to exhume the purified grave. However, two fingers came out of the grave, as if they were the tongues of his sword Dhu al-Fiqār. They struck the cursed Murrah, and he was cut in half. The two halves became black stones, which were placed behind the city gates. Thus, whoever visited that holy land, the burial place of the Commander of the Faithful (a), would kick that stone with his foot.

Some of the Prominent Scholars Buried in the Holy Shrine

Shaykh al-Ansari

One of the most prominent scholars of the modern age (d. 1281 AH/1865 CE). Due to his great impact on the Islamic disciplines, he became known in the seminary as "al-Shaykh al-Aʿẓam" ("The Greatest Shaykh"). The seminary greatly benefitted from his books – especially "Fawāʾid al-Uṣūl" and "al-Makāsib," which have been adopted as textbooks in the highest level of seminary teaching.

Sayyid Abūlqāsim al-Khoei

The leader of the seminary in his time (d. 1413 AH/1992 CE). He enriched the seminary with scholarship and teaching for decades until hundreds of prominent scholars graduated from his seminars. In addition to lessons on fiqh and uṣūl, he held seminars on the interpretation of the Noble Quran which produced his book "The Prolegomena to the Quran" (al-Bayān fī Tafsīr al-Quran).

He also authored "Muʿjam Rijāl al-Ḥadīth," which is the product of extensive work that brought together the conditions of the narrators and what was mentioned about them in previous sources. In addition, the book includes numerical analyses of their narrations and other important details in investigating their status.

Sayyid Muhammad Saeed al-Hakeem

One of the great contemporary marājiʿ (d. 1443 AH/2021 CE). He enriched the seminary with scholarship and teaching, and many of the seminary's high-ranking professors were his students. He authored important books on fiqh and uṣūl, discussing the latest theories in those disciplines. He also contributed to the seminary through writings on theology and historical analysis of the biographies of Ahl al-Bayt (peace be upon them).

He and his family were imprisoned by the tyrannical Baath regime for a period of more than 8 years, during which he suffered the most severe forms of injustice and torture. As a marjiʿ, his office had an active presence in Shia society due to the high concern he had for believers all over the world.

The Valley of Peace Cemetery and the Shrine of the Prophets Hūd and Ṣāliḥ

The largest cemetery in the world and included in the World Heritage List. It has received wide attention among the believers because of the great spiritual merit to being buried in it. It was narrated that the Commander of the Faithful (a) said, "If it was revealed to you, you would have seen the souls of the believers in this outskirt [of Kufa], visiting and talking. Surely, in this outskirt [of Kufa] is the soul of every believer."

It was also narrated that he looked at this area and said, "How beautiful is your land and how sweet is your bottom. O' God, make my grave here."

This soil gathered the bodies of the saints, the righteous, and the worshipers. Chief amongst them are the two great prophets, Hūd and Ṣāliḥ (peace be upon them both).

Al-Hindī Mosque

It is one of the centers of knowledge in the Holy City of Najaf, where students of the Islamic disciplines gather throughout the day to form study circles in various subjects and at different academic levels. Congregational prayers are also held here throughout the day. This congregation was historically led by a many different scholars and righteous people.

It is reported that a man from India came to establish this mosque more than 200 years ago, so the scholars of Najaf gathered to lay the foundation stone. He said to them, "I want the one who laid the foundation stone to be a person who never missed the morning prayer in his life." Everyone abstained, so he set the stone himself. Thus, the mosque was founded on piety from the first day. It was expanded by the great marjiʿ of his era, Grand Ayatollah Sayyid Muḥsin al-Hakeem.

Al-Khaḍrāʾ Mosque

It is one of the ancient mosques of Najaf, adjacent to the Shrine of Imam Ali (a). Its foundation is likely to date back to the 10th century AH (16th century CE).

The last renovation of its building was in the year 1384 AH by the order of the leader of the religious seminary, His Eminence Grand Ayatollah Sayyid Abulqāsim al-Khoei. After that, he used it as a center to deliver his lessons and lectures. He also used to conduct congregational prayers in it. When his health deteriorated and he stopped teaching, his son-in-law Grand Ayatollah Sayyid Nasrallah al-Mustanbiṭ took his place. After Sayyid al-Mustanbiṭ passed away, Grand Ayatollah al-Khoei assigned His Eminence Grand Ayatollah Sayyid Ali al-Sistani to teach there and lead the prayer.

Al-Ṭūsī Mosque

It is located to the north of the Shrine of Imam Ali (a). It was the house of the leader of the Shia sect at his time, Abū Jaʿfar Muhammad ibn al-Ḥasan al-Ṭūsī (known as al-Shaykh al-Ṭūsī). Before his death in the year 460 AH, he instructed that the house be rebuilt as a mosque after him. When he passed away, he was buried in it. Today the visitors find the tomb of al-Shaykh al-Ṭūsī in the middle of the mosque's courtyard. The great scholar and jurist, Sayyid Muhammad Mahdī Baḥr al-ʿUlūm (d. 1212 AH) and many scholars from his descendants were also buried in another side of the mosque. This mosque has become a center of learning in the seminary of Najaf.

Library of al-Rawḍah Al-Ḥaydariyyah

This library holds the books found in the Holy Shrine of Imam Ali (a). It is considered the mother of libraries in Najaf, as it dates back to the beginning of the fourth century AH after the emergence and growth of the city and its seminary. One historian said, "In the courtyard of this shrine is a library that was established long ago. Numerous sultans, princes, ministers, scholars, and well-to-dos were concerned with the order of this library and enriching it with precious written books. Among the most famous of them was ʿIḍd al-Dawlah al-Buwayhī (d. 372 AH/982 CE).

Unfortunately, in 755 AH/1354 CE the building of the Holy Shrine burned, and the library burned with it. Ibn ʿInabah said, "In the Holy Shrine [of Imam Ali (a)], there was a Quran in three volumes handwritten by the Commander of the Faithful (a). It burned when the shrine burned in the year 755."

But with the passage of time and with the efforts of great scholars and esteemed benefactors, generation after generation, this library has flourished. Today, it contains three hundred thousand books in addition to theses and university treatises. It is constantly increasing with the blessings of its owner, the Commander of the Faithful (a).

Imam al-Hakeem Library

It was founded in the year 1377 AH/1957 CE by the supreme religious authority of his time, Grand Ayatollah Sayyid Muḥsin al-Hakeem. It consists of five floors: the bottom floor contains a storehouse for books and binding; the one above it houses manuscripts and their administrative needs; the ground floor contains the library's administration, the men's reading hall, and the index room; the first floor contains publications and a hall for women; and the second floor is also for publications.

During the Iraqi uprising of 1991 CE, the library was partially destroyed by the Iraqi army. Some of the soldiers used to burn books to make food or tea. However, God Almighty sent some believers who saved valuable manuscript, buying them from whoever stole them and returning them to the library. This service is worthy of remembrance and gratitude.

The founder, Grand Ayatollah al-Hakeem, had a vision to spread learning to all communities, regardless of location or development of their cities. He strived to open branches of the library in Iraqi cities, whether they were townships, districts, or governorates. More than seventy branches were opened since the year 1960 CE, distributed over all regions of Iraq, including branches opened in some Islamic countries such as Pakistan, Iran, Lebanon, and others.

It is worth noting that most of the branches during the time of the Baathist regime were subjected to bombing, burning, and confiscation, while the rest of them were closed. More than 115 branches were re-opened, and work is still underway to open the rest of the branches, as well as to open new branches in various Iraqi cities.

Al-Amīnī Library

The Commander of the Faithful (a) Public Library is one of the most prominent and most valuable libraries in Najaf. It was founded in 1952 by His Eminence, ʿAllāmah Abdulḥusayn al-Amīnī, author of the famous al-Ghadīr Encyclopedia. He established the library while searching for reliable sources for his well-known encyclopedia.

ʿAllāmah al-Amīnī used to travel a lot in search of books and writings that mention the incident of Ghadīr and what is related to it, in addition to the various sources of Islamic thought. His journey included destinations in Iran, Pakistan, India, countries of the Levant, Egypt, and others. By 1972, he collected more than 15,000 books in various fields and Islamic disciplines, such as books on history, hadith, interpretation, and others. This formed the core of the existing library.

Kāshif al-Ghiṭāʾ Library

It was founded in the days of Shaykh Jaʿfar al-Kabīr (d. 1228 AH). It included personal books belonging to him, including several manuscripts. It was inherited generation after generation in the Kāshif al-Ghiṭāʾ family, and the library began to expand its books and manuscripts as it passed down from scholar to scholar. The library is now open the public, and it receives many readers every day.

The number of topics through which the library books were classified reaches about 38 subjects. The number of printed books in the library has reached more than 12,000 titles. The library is distinguished by the presence of rare books that were printed in the fifties of the last century or before, as there are rare first editions for widely circulated books.

Al-Jawāhirī Mosque

The great jurist and eminent scholar, Grand Ayatollah Shaykh Muhammad Ḥasan al-Najafī, was one of the sect's leading scholars and references of his time. He is famous for authoring the complete jurisprudential encyclopedia titled "Jawāhir al-Kalām fī Sharḥ Sharā'i' al-Islām," which exceeded all previous encyclopedias in terms of capacity and information about the sayings of previous scholars and their evidence.

The students were attracted to his lessons due to the brilliance of his statements, his skillful teaching, the abundance of his knowledge, and his diligent research. Attendance in his seminars included more than sixty mujtahids. He passed away in 1850 CE in the Holy City of Najaf and was buried in his cemetery adjacent to his famous mosque, near Holy Shrine of Imam Ali (a).

Shrine of Ṣāfī Ṣafā

Whenever the Commander of the Faithful (a) wanted to be alone, he would go to the outskirts of al-Gharī (modern day Najaf). One day a man came from the desert riding on a camel and a funeral procession was in front of him. When he saw the Imam (a), he approached him and greeted him.

The Imam (a) replied, "From where [do you hail]?"

The man said, "From Yemen."

The Imam (a) said, "What is this funeral that you have with you?"

The man said, "My father's funeral, I came to bury it in this land."

The Imam (a) said to him, "Why did you not bury him in your land?

The man said, "He asked me to do so in his. He said, 'A man who will intercede for [a great number] the like of Rabī'ah and Muḍar will be buried there.'"

The Imam (a) said, "Do you know that man?"

The man said, "No."

The Imam (a) said, "By God, I am that man. By God, I am that man. Get up and bury your father." And so, the man buried his father in that spot.

Al-Ḥannānah Mosque

Al-Ḥannānah Mosque is in the north of the old town of Najaf. It is the location of the pillar which leaned and bowed in sorrow and grief when the funeral procession of the Commander of the Faithful (a) passed by. The leaning pillar remained until the end of the 8th century AH.

This mosque was also a stopping point for the caravan of Ahl al-Bayt when they were taken captive after the tragedy of Karbala. The cursed Ibn Ziyad kept them there so that they do not rile the people of Kufa against him. During their stay, sounds of grief would emanate from the mosque in sorrow for their tragedy. Therefore, it was called Masjid al-Ḥannānah, or "the grieving mosque."

Shrine of Kumayl ibn Ziyād

The shrine of Kumayl ibn Ziyād is located close to the al-Ḥannānah Mosque. It is the place where the companion Kumayl ibn Ziyād al-Nakhaʿī al-Kufī was buried after he was killed by al-Ḥajjāj al-Thaqafī.

Kumayl ibn Ziyād is considered a great companion who lived 18 years alongside the Messenger of God (s). He is one of the companions of Imam Ali (a) and was his guardian over the city of Hit and the surrounding areas. He is also the narrator of his famous supplication known as Duʿāʾ Kumayl.

Dār al-Ḥikmah School

It was founded by the supreme religious authority in his era, Grand Ayatollah Muḥsin al-Hakeem, on a 1,250 m^2 plot of land. It was inaugurated in the year 1391 AH/1971 CE, and it continued to receive students and provide services until the tyrannical Baath Party destroyed it completely without allowing what was inside it to be removed, especially important books. After the fall of the tyrannical regime, the late Grand Ayatollah Sayyid Muhammad Saeed al-Hakeem decided to restore it in a manner commensurate with the present era.

Dār al-ʿIlm School

A school and library founded in 1973 by the leader of the seminary, Grand Ayatollah Sayyid Abulqāsim al-Khoei. Its location is only 30 meters away from the Holy Shrine of Imam Ali (a). The Baathist regime, under the pretext of urban expansion, decided to demolish the large, populous school in 1990. Divine will did not allow for the school building be built again during the lifetime of its founder.

The land of the school remained unbuilt until the darkness of the Baath was lifted from the face of Iraq, and the Holy City of Najaf returned to its splendor. The sons of the founder, may God bless his soul, began to rebuild the school into two 11 floor buildings, with a new urban image and distinguished services. Praise be to God, the first section was completed and opened in 2017, and work is continuing to complete the remaining sections.

Imam Ali (a) School (al-Madrasah al-ʿAlawiyyah)

It was founded by the supreme religious authority Sayyid Ali al-Sistani. The school is part of the ʿAlawī complex, which includes a residential neighborhood designated for students of the seminary in Najaf.

The school was built on an area of 5000 m2, and it consists of three main buildings. The middle building includes three wings and four levels, which include seminar halls, library, mosque, and administrative offices. It has been adorned with the names of great scholars such as Shaykh al-Ṭūsī, al-Sayyid al-Murtaḍā, Shaykh al-Mufīd, and others. It is also adorned with names of a number of distinguished men of ḥadīth such as Ṣafwān ibn Yaḥyā, Muhammad ibn Abī ʿUmayr, Jamīl ibn Darrāj, and others. The building includes 233 small halls and offices.

Each of the two other buildings consists of three floors and has been allocated for student housing. The number of rooms in them is 464, accommodating approximately 500 students with various necessary facilities. The school was inaugurated in a joyful ceremony attended by a number of scholars and distinguished people on the anniversary of the birth of Lady Fāṭimah al-Zahrāʾ (a) in the year 1437 AH/2016 CE.

THE CITY OF KUFA

The Grand Mosque of Kufa

It was narrated on the authority of al-Aṣbagh ibn Nabātah that one day, while the Commander of the Faithful (a) and his companions were in the Grand Mosque of Kufa mosque, the Imam (a) said,

> *O' people of Kufa! God has favored you with something with which He did not favor anyone else. It is the favor of your mosque, which was the house of Adam, Noah, and Idrīs. It was the mosque of Abraham the Friend of God, the mosque of my brother al-Khiḍr, and my mosque. This mosque of yours is one of four mosques which God Almighty chose for its people.*
>
> *It is as if I see [this mosque] coming on the Day of Judgement [in the form of a man] wearing two white garments - just like one in a state of iḥrām. It will intercede for its people and for those who pray in it. Surely, it's intercession will not be rejected. The days and nights will not pass [for long] until the Black Stone is set in it. Surely, a time will come over it when it will be the mosque of the Mahdī (a) from amongst my children - and the mosque of every believer. Every believer on earth will either be in it, or will long for it. Do not abandon it. Seek closeness to God by praying in it. Seek it for the fulfillment of your needs. Surely, if people knew the blessings in it, they would come to it from the corners of the earth, even if they had to come crawling on ice.*

Hānī ibn ʿUrwah

Hānī ibn ʿUrwah al-Murādī was one of the most prominent and honorable citizens of Kufa, and one of the close companions of Imam Ali (a). He participated alongside the Imam (a) in the Battle of the Camel and the Battle of Ṣiffīn. His house was also the center of political activity in Kufa when ʿUbaydullāh ibn Ziyād came to it. Hānī played a prominent role in supporting the movement of Muslim ibn ʿAqīl, the ambassador of Imam al-Ḥusayn (a) to Kufa.

Hānī ibn ʿUrwah was a prominent member of his tribe and had thousands of followers. When ʿUbaydullāh ibn Ziyād accused him of sedition against the Umayyads, he denied the allegations. Ibn Ziyād was so angered by Hānī's response that he began to hit him on the face with a rod until he broke it. Soon after Muslim ibn ʿAqīl was martyred, Ibn Ziyād ordered Hānī's execution. Hānī ibn ʿUrwah's tomb is adjacent to the Grand Mosque of Kufa.

Maytham al-Tammār

Maytham ibn Yaḥyā al-Tammār al-Asadī al-Kufī was one of the closest companions of the Commander of the Faithful (a). Imam Ali (a) had taught him the hidden knowledge of calamities and bereavements.

He was the preacher of the Shia in Kufa. He would say to Ibn ʿAbbās, "Ask me whatever you want about the interpretation of the Quran. Surely, I was taught its meanings by the Prophet (s) and its interpretations by the Commander of the Faithful (a)."

Imam al-Kāẓim (a) said, "On the Day of Resurrection a caller will call out, 'Where are the disciples of Ali ibn Abī Ṭālib (a), the successor of the Messenger of God, Muhammad ibn ʿAbdullāh (s)?' There, 'Amr ibn al-Ḥamaq al-Khuzāʿī, Muhammad ibn Abī Bakr, Maytham ibn Yaḥyā al-Tammār the freed slave of Banū Asad, and Uways al-Qaranī will stand up."

When ʿUbaydullāh ibn Ziyād took governorship of Kufa and learned of Maytham's allegiance to Imam Ali (a), he ordered his execution. Maytham would say to Ibn Ziyād, "By God, my master had told me that I would be killed by a callous and baseborn person who will sever my arms, legs, and tongue and crucify me!"

Ibn Ziyād wanted to prove Imam Ali (a) wrong, so he ordered the severing of Maytham's limbs and his crucifixion, but ordered that his tongue be left in place. When Maytham was crucified on a palm tree, he began to speak the merits of the Hashemites and he shames of the Umayyads. His words were so heavy on Ibn Ziyād that he ordered Maytham's tongue to be cut out. Thus, Maytham was martyred in the exact state which Imam Ali (a) had foretold. That was on the 22nd of Dhu al-Ḥijjah, 60 AH, ten days before the arrival of Imam Ḥusayn (a) to Karbala.

Al-Sahlah Mosque

Abū Baṣīr narrated on the authority of Imam al-Ṣādiq (a) that he said,

O' Abū Muhammad, it is as if I see the Awaited One (a) with his family and dependents finding residence in al-Sahlah Mosque.... It was once the house of Idrīs and the house of Abraham. God has not sent a prophet except that he prayed in it. It is the dwelling of al-Khiḍr. The one who resides in it is like the one who resides in the tent of the Messenger of God (s). There is no believer, male or female, except that their heart yearns for it.... It is one of the spots from which God loves to be called upon. Not a day or night passes except that the angels visit this mosque and worship God in it. If I were near you, I would not pray except in it.

Shrine of Prophet Yūnus

Among the blessed mosques mentioned by the Commander of the Faithful (a) is the al-Ḥamrā' Mosque, which is located on the Euphrates River. It is also known as the shrine of the Prophet Yūnus.

The Commander of the Faithful (a) is narrated to have said, "The al-Ḥamrā' Mosque is the mosque of Yūnus ibn Mattā. A spring will erupt in it that will appear in al-Sabkhah and its surroundings."

Some believe this site is a place related to him and not his grave, and that Prophet Yūnus had traveled at the end of his life to Palestine, died there, and was buried in a village called Ḥalḥūl.

THE CITY OF KARBALA

The Shrines of Imam Ḥusayn (a) and his brother al-ʿAbbās (a)

There are countless traditions about the merits of visiting Imam al-Ḥusayn (a). The state so much about that the rewards of his visitors that it boggles minds. We will mention here a few examples of such narrations.

Imam al-Ṣādiq (a) said,

> *Four thousand angels are at the grave of al-Ḥusayn (a), dusty and unkempt. They weep for him until the Day of Resurrection. Their leader is an angel called Manṣūr. No visitor visits him except that they greet him. No [visitor] says farewell except that they follow him [until he reaches home]. No [visitor] falls ill except that they visit him. No [visitor] dies except that they pray on him and his funeral procession and seek forgiveness for him after his death.*

He also said,

> *If one of you had performed ḥajj [every year] his entire life, but did not visit al-Ḥusayn ibn Ali (a), he would be deemed negligent of one of the rights of God and the rights of the Messenger of God (s). Surely, the right of al-Ḥusayn (a) is an obligation from God, required of every Muslim.*

He said in another tradition,

> *Whoever visits the grave of [Imam al-Ḥusayn (a)] has connected with the Messenger of God (s) and has connected with us [the Ahl al-Bayt (a)]. Backbiting him is forbidden and his flesh is forbidden for Hellfire. God will give him for every [penny] spent a thousand cities [in Paradise] in a safeguarded book. God will be there for him for his needs, and will protect everything he left behind. He will not ask God anything except that God will give and answer him – either expediting it [in this world] or delaying it for him [to receive its rewards in the hereafter].*

Imam al-Ṣādiq (a) also said,

> *If you wish [to visit] the tomb of al-Ḥusayn (peace be upon him), visit it while you are solemn, sad, disheveled, and dusty. Surely, al-Ḥusayn (a) was killed while he was solemn, sad, disheveled, dusty, hungry, and thirsty.*

Zaynabī Hill

It is the place where Lady Zaynab (a) stood when she left the camp. She would place her hands on her head and look for her brother, the Master of Martyrs Imam al-Ḥusayn (a). She would see him covered in his own blood and cry, "O' Muhammad (s)! O' father! O' Ali (a)! O' Jaʿfar! O' Ḥamzah! This is Ḥusayn in the open, fallen in Karbala. I wish the sky had fallen on the earth! I wish the mountains had collapsed into the valleys!" She then raced towards Imam al-Ḥusayn (a). ʿUmar ibn Saʿd and his companions had surrounded the Imam (a) as he was taking his last breaths.

She called, "O' ʿUmar! Will Abū ʿAbdullāh (a) be killed while you are looking at him?!" ʿUmar turned his face away with tears were running down his beard. She said, "Woe to you! Is there not a Muslim among you?" But no one answered her.

Imam al-Ḥusayn's Camp

The place where the tents of Imam al-Ḥusayn (a) and his family and companions were erected during the Battle of Karbala. It is visited to seek blessings from their relics and to remind the visitor of the tragedy that befell them.

THE CITY OF BAGHDAD

Shrine of Imam al-Kāẓim (a) and Imam al-Jawād (a)

Imam Mūsā al-Kāẓim (a) faced a great deal of tyranny and oppression at the hands of the Abbasids. In fact, he became known as al-Kāẓim – or the one who represses his rage – because of the severity of the oppression and terror he experienced and yet remained patient. He was imprisoned by the Abbasid authorities for long periods of time – historians disagree how long, but some state that it was up to 14 years. He was martyred with poison while in prison and buried in Baghdad.

Imam al-Kāẓim's (a) grandson, Imam al-Jawād (a), also suffered a great deal of harassment and oppression at the hands of the Abbasids. He would be summoned into the Abbasid courts as a teenager and asked to debate Muslim and non-Muslim scholars. While this was an attempt to humiliate a young member of the Ahl al-Bayt (a), Imam al-Jawād always proved his preeminence in knowledge and piety. He was poisoned at the young age of 25 and buried in Baghdad alongside his grandfather Imam al-Kāẓim (a).

There are numerous traditions concerning the merit of visiting the Holy Shrine in Kāẓimiyyah. In one tradition, Imam al-Riḍā (a) said, "One who visits the grave of my father in Baghdad is like one who visits the grave of the Messenger of God (s) and the grave of the Commander of the Faithful (a). However, the Messenger of God (s) and the Commander of the Faithful (a) have their merit."

In another narration, Imam al-Riḍā (a) said, "Visiting of the grave of my father [Imam al-Kāẓim (a)] is like the visiting the grave of al-Ḥusayn (a)." When Imam al-Riḍā (a) was asked about the reward of one who visits his father's grave, he responded, "Paradise. Go and visit it."

Burāthā Mosque

It is one of the oldest mosques in Iraq and was a Christian monastery in the past.

At the present time, the Burāthā area includes a large mosque with two minarets built in the year 1375 AH, an old library, a sanctuary, a prayer hall, a wide courtyard, an old cemetery, and a water well known as the well of Imam Ali.

The area was visited by Imam Ali (a) while he was returning to Kufa from one of his battles. A monk from the nearby monastery came down and asked about the army's leader. He said that he had read in the scriptures that a prophet or the successor of a prophet would lead a large group in prayer in this exact area. When he saw Imam Ali (a), he embraced Islam.

The Four Ambassadors

They are the ambassadors of the Awaited Imam Mahdī (a) to his Shia during the time of the minor occultation, which lasted 69 years (260-329 AH). All four ambassadors resided in Baghdad, and each one of them has a widely visited shrine.

The four ambassadors are:

1. ʿUthmān ibn Saʿīd al-ʿUmarī. He served as ambassador from 260 AH to 265 AH.
2. Muhammad ibn ʿUthmān al-ʿUmarī. He served as ambassador from 265 AH to 305 AH.
3. Al-Ḥusayn ibn Rūḥ al-Nubakhtī. He served as ambassador from 305 AH to 326 AH.
4. Ali ibn Muhammad al-Samarī. He served as ambassador from 326 AH to 329 AH.

Before the fourth ambassador passed away, a signed letter came from Imam al-Mahdī (a) with the following text:

> *In the name of God, the Most Gracious, the Most Merciful. O' Ali ibn Muhammad al-Samarī, may God reward your brethren in your death, which is going to take place in six days' time. Take care of your affairs and do not appoint anyone in your place, as the complete occultation has taken place. I will not appear until God permits me to do so (may His name be exalted) and that will be after a long time and after the hearts become hard and the earth is filled with wickedness. There will be those who will come my followers claiming to have seen me. Beware, those who claim*

this before the rise of al-Sufyānī and the [hearing of the] call [from the sky] are liars. And there is no power except in God, the All-exalted, the All-supreme.

Al-Mutanabbī Street

Al-Mutanabbī Street is in the center of Baghdad and is considered the cultural market for the people of Baghdad where bookstores flourish. The street houses a printing press dating back to the 19th century. It also contains several libraries that include rare books and manuscripts in addition to some old Baghdadi buildings.

On March 5, 2007, a car bombing struck the busy street, killing at least 30 shoppers and destroying many libraries and buildings. The oldest library in the street, which was established in 1908, was completely demolished. The Shābandar Café, which is one of the ancient landmarks of Baghdad, was also destroyed.

THE CITY OF SAMARRA

The Shrine of Imam al-Hādī (a) and Imam al-ʿAskarī (a)

Imam al-Hādī (a) came from Medina to Samarra in 234 AH at the behest of the Abbasid caliph al-Mutawakkil. He bought a spacious house where he lived with his family and dependents who he brought from Medina with him. Imam al-Hādī (a) passed away from the poison that the caliph al-Muʿtaz planted for him on the 3rd of Rajab, 254 AH. He was buried in one of the rooms of his house.

Imam al-Ḥādī's (a) son, Imam al-Ḥasan al-ʿAskarī (a), was martyred in the same way. He had been poisoned by Abbasid caliph al-Muʿtamid. He passed away on the 8th of Rabīʿ al-Awwal, 260 AH, and was buried next to his father.

In the same year, Lady Narjis, the mother of Imam al-Mahdī (a), passed away. She was buried behind the tomb of the two Imams a short distance away. In 274 AH, lady Ḥakīmah, daughter of Imam al-Jawād (a), died, and she was buried next to her brother Imam al-Hādī (a).

In 289 AH, and after the death of the caliph al-Muʿtaḍid, a window was erected in the wall of the house, from which passers-by in the street overlooked those graves inside. The house remained unchanged for nearly forty-one years. Samarra lost its splendor and many of its citizens when the Abbassid capital was moved to a different city. As the city became mostly empty, it was necessary for some of the notables amongst the Shia of Baghdad to undertake the maintenance of this shrine. These individuals used to organize convoys on occasions and accompany the visitors to Samarra, and then return them to Baghdad.

In February 2006, the Holy Shrine of Imam al-Hādī (a) and Imam al-ʿAskarī (a) was the target of a terrorist bombing which destroyed its dome and three-quarters of the building. The Holy Shrine was attacked again in June 2007, and its two minarets were destroyed. Following the attacks, Grand Ayatollah Sayyid Ali al-Sistani issued a statement of condemnation and called the Shia to "exercise self-restraint and avoid any vengeful act." The wise actions of the religious leadership in Najaf is credited with avoiding increased sectarian violence in Iraq following the horrible incidents.

The Shrine of Sayyid Muhammad

Sayyid Muhammad is the son of Imam al-Hādī (a) and older brother to Imam al-ʿAskarī (a).

When Imam al-Hādī (a) left Medina for Samarra, he left his son Muhammad in Medina as a child. In the year 252 AH, Muhammad intended to perform Hajj, then join his father from Mecca and stay with him in Samarra for some time. He fell ill on his return to Medina in the city of Balad, close to Samarra. He passed away there at the age of about twenty.

The shrine of Sayyid Muhammad is located in the city of Balad, 85 km north of Baghdad and about 50 km south of Samarra. The shrine was subjected to a terrorist attack in 2016.

The Spiral Minaret

A minaret of the Great Mosque which was founded by the Abbasid caliph al-Mutawakkil in 237 AH on the western side of Samarra. The mosque was designed by the Christian architect Dalīl ibn Yaʿqūb and was considered at the time one of the largest mosques in the Islamic world.

The Spiral Minaret got its name from its cylindrical, spiral shape. It is built with clay bricks with a total height of 52 meters and is located 27.25 meters from the northern wall of the mosque. The minaret's exterior consists of a spiral staircase with a width of 2 meters that wraps around the body of the minaret in a counterclockwise direction.

Specific Supplications

Asking Permission

Taking the permission to enter any of the shrines, you recite the following:

اَللَّهُمَّ إِنِّي وَقَفْتُ عَلَىٰ بَابٍ

allahumma inni waqaftu `ala babin

O Allah, I am standing at one of the doors

مِنْ ابْوَابِ بُيُوتِ نَبِيِّكَ

min abwabi buyuti nabiyyika

of Your Prophet's Houses—

صَلَوَاتُكَ عَلَيْهِ وَآلِهِ

salawatuka `alayhi wa alihi

may Your blessings be upon him and his Household.

وَقَدْ مَنَعْتَ ٱلنَّاسَ انْ يَدْخُلُوٓاْ إِلاَّ بِإِذْنِهِ

wa qad mana`ta alnnasa an yadkhulu illa bi'idhnihi

And You have prevented people to enter there before they obtain his permission.

فَقُلْتَ: "يَا ايُّهَا ٱلَّذِينَ آمَنُواْ

faqulta ya ayyuha alladhina amanu

You have thus said, "O ye who believe!

لاَ تَدْخُلُواْ بُيُوتَ ٱلنَّبِيِّ إِلاَّ انْ يُؤْذَنَ لَكُمْ"

la tadkhulu buyuta alnnabiyyi illa an yu'dhana lakum

Enter not the Prophet's houses until leave is given you."

اَللَّهُمَّ إِنِّي اعْتَقِدُ حُرْمَةَ صَاحِبِ هٰذَا ٱلْمَشْهَدِ ٱلشَّرِيفِ فِي غَيْبَتِهِ

allahumma inni a`taqidu hurmata sahibi hadha almashhadi alshsharifi fi ghaybatihi

O Allah, I believe in the sanctity of the owner of this holy shrine in his absence

كَمَا اعْتَقِدُهَا فِي حَضْرَتِهِ

kama a`taqiduha fi hadratihi

as same as I believe in it in his presence.

وَاعْلَمُ انَّ رَسُولَكَ وَخُلَفَاءَكَ عَلَيْهِمُ ٱلسَّلاَمُ

wa a`lamu anna rasulaka wa khulafa'aka `alayhimu alssalamu
I also know for sure that Your Messenger and Your Representatives—peace be upon them—

احْيَاءٌ عِنْدَكَ يُرْزَقُونَ

ahya'un `indaka yurzaquna
are live, finding their sustenance in the presence of You;

يَرَوْنَ مَقَامِي

yarawna maqami
they can see my place,

وَيَسْمَعُونَ كَلاَمِي

wa yasma`una kalami
hear my words,

وَيَرُدُّونَ سَلاَمِي

wa yarudduna salami
and respond to my greetings,

وَانَّكَ حَجَبْتَ عَنْ سَمْعِي كَلاَمَهُمْ

wa annaka hajabta `an sam`i kalamahum
but You have prevented my hearing from receiving their words

وَفَتَحْتَ بَابَ فَهْمِي بِلَذِيذِ مُنَاجَاتِهِمْ

wa fatahta baba fahmi biladhidhi munajatihim
and You have opened the door of my understanding to taste the fine flavor of my confidential speech with

وَإِنِّي اسْتَاذِنُكَ يَا رَبِّ اوَّلاً

wa inni asta'dhinuka ya rabbi awwalan
I thus ask Your permission—O my Lord—first of all,

وَاسْتَاذِنُ رَسُولَكَ صَلَّىٰ ٱللَّهُ عَلَيْهِ وَآلِهِ ثَانِياً

wa asta'dhinu rasulaka salla allahu `alayhi wa alihi thaniyan
the permission of Your Prophet—peace be upon him and his Household—secondly,

وَاسْتَاذِنُ خَلِيفَتَكَ ٱلإِمَامَ

wa asta'dhinu khalifataka al'imama
the permission of Your Representative, the Imam

ٱلْمَفْرُوضَ عَلَيَّ طَاعَتُهُ...

almafruda `alayya ta`atuhu
the obedience to whom is incumbent upon me...

You may now mention the name of the Imam that you are visiting his holy shrine and mention the name of his father.

For instance, if you are visiting the holy shrine of Imam al-Husayn ('a), you may say, "al-Husayn ibn `Ali—peace be upon him."

And if you are visiting the holy shrine of Imam al-Rida ('a), you may say, "`Ali ibn Musa al-Rida—peace be upon him" and so on. You may then say:

وَٱلْمَلاَئِكَةَ ٱلْمُوَكَّلِينَ بِهٰذِهِ ٱلْبُقْعَةِ ٱلْمُبَارَكَةِ ثَالِثاً

walmala'ikata almuwakkalina bihadhihi albuq`ati almubarakati thalithan
...and the permission of the angels whom are commissioned to supervise this blessed area, thirdly.

اادْخُلُ يَا رَسُولَ ٱللَّهِ

a'adkhulu ya rasula allahi
May I enter, O Messenger of Allah?

اادْخُلُ يَا حُجَّةَ ٱللَّهِ

a'adkhulu ya hujjata allahi
May I enter, O Argument of Allah?

اادْخُلُ يَا مَلاَئِكَةَ ٱللَّهِ ٱلْمُقَرَّبِينَ

a'adkhulu ya mala'ikata allahi almuqarrabina
May I enter, O angels of Allah—the intimate,

ٱلْمُقِيمِينَ فِي هٰذَا ٱلْمَشْهَدِ

almuqimina fi hadha almashhadi
the residing in this shrine?

فَاذَنْ لِي يَا مَوْلاَيَ فِي ٱلدُّخُولِ

fa'dhan li ya mawlaya fi alddukhuli
So, (please do) permit me to enter, O my Master,

افْضَلَ مَا اذِنْتَ لاِحَدٍ مِنْ اوْلِيَائِكَ

afdala ma adhinta li'ahadin min awliya'ika
in the best way of permission that you have ever conferred upon any of your intimate adherents.

فَإِنْ لَمْ اكُنْ اهْلاً لِذٰلِكَ

fa'in lam akun ahlan lidhalika
If I do not deserve such permission

فَانْتَ اهْلٌ لِذٰلِكَ

fa'anta ahlun lidhalika
then you are worthy of conferring it upon me.

You may then kiss the holy doorstep (of the shrine) and enter, saying

بِسْمِ ٱللَّهِ وَبِٱللَّهِ

bismi allahi wa billahi
In the Name of Allah (I begin), in Allah (I trust),

وَفِي سَبِيلِ ٱللَّهِ

wa fi sabili allahi
on the way of Allah (I proceed),

وَعَلَىٰ مِلَّةِ رَسُولِ ٱللَّهِ

wa `ala millati rasuli allahi
and on the norm of the Messenger of Allah,

صَلَّىٰ ٱللَّهُ عَلَيْهِ وَآلِهِ

salla allahu `alayhi wa alihi
may Allah bless him and his Household.

اَللَّهُمَّ ٱغْفِرْ لِي

allahumma ighfir li

O Allah, (please do) forgive me,

وَٱرْحَمْنِي وَتُبْ عَلَيَّ

warhamni wa tub `alayya

have mercy upon me, and accept my repentance,

إِنَّكَ انْتَ ٱلتَّوَّابُ ٱلرَّحِيمُ

innaka anta alttawwabu alrrahimu

for You are verily the Oft-Returning, the All-Merciful.

IMAM ALI IBN ABI TALIB (A)

The Visitation

اَلسَّلاَمُ عَلَيْكَ يَا اَمِيْنَ اللهِ فِيْ اَرْضِهِ

alssalamu `alayka ya amina allahi fi ardihi

Peace be upon you, O trustee of Allah on His lands

وحُجَّتَهُ عَلَى عِبَادِهِ

wa hujjatahu `ala `ibadihi

and argument of Allah against His servants.

اَلسَّلاَمُ عَلَيْكَ يَا اَمِيْرَ الْمُؤْمِنِيْنَ

alssalamu `alayka ya amira almu'minina

Peace be upon you, O Commander of the Faithful.

اَشْهَدُ اَنَّكَ جَاهَدْتَ فِيْ اللهِ حَقَّ جِهَادِهِ

ashhadu annaka jahadta fi allahi haqqa jihadihi

I bear witness that you strove for the sake of Allah as it ought to be striven,

وعَمِلْتَ بِكِتَابِهِ

wa `amilta bikitabihi

acted upon His Book,

واتَّبَعْتَ سُنَنَ نَبِيِّهِ

wattba`ta sunana nabiyyihi

and followed the instructions of His Prophet,

صَلَّى اللهُ عَلَيْهِ وآلِهِ

salla allahu `alayhi wa alihi

peace of Allah be upon him and his Household,

حَتَّى دَعَاكَ اللهُ اِلَى جِوَارِهِ

hatta da`aka allahu ila jiwarihi

until Allah called you to be in His vicinity.

فَقَبَضَكَ اِلَيْهِ بِاِخْتِيَارِهِ

faqabadaka ilayhi bikhtiyarihi
So, He grasped you to Him by His will

وَ اَلْزَمَ اَعْدَآئَكَ الْحُجَّةَ

wa alzama a`da'aka alhujjata
and put your enemies under the claim

مَعَ مَالَكَ مِنَ الْحُجَجِ الْبَالِغَةِ عَلٰى جَمِيْعِ خَلْقِهِ

ma`a ma laka min alhujaji albalighati `ala jami`i khalqihi
although you have inclusive claims against all of His creatures.

اَللّٰهُمَّ فَاجْعَلْ نَفْسِيْ مُطْمَئِنَّةً بِقَدَرِكَ

allahumma faj`al nafsi mutma'innatan biqadarika
O Allah, (please do) cause my soul to be fully tranquil with Your decrees,

رَاضِيَةً بِقَضَآئِكَ

radiyatan biqada'ika
satisfied with Your acts,

مُوْلَعَةً بِذِكْرِكَ وَ دُعَآئِكَ

mula`atan bidhikrika wa du`a'ika
fond of mentioning and praying to You,

مُحِبَّةً لِصَفْوَةِ اَوْلِيَآئِكَ

muhibbatan lisafwati awliya'ika
bearing love for the choicest of Your intimate servants,

مَحْبُوْبَةً فِيْ اَرْضِكَ وَ سَمَآئِكَ

mahbubatan fi ardika wa sama'ika
beloved in Your lands and heavens,

صَابِرَةً عَلٰى نُزُوْلِ بَلَآئِكَ

sabiratan `ala nuzuli bala'ika
steadfast against the affliction of Your tribulations,

شَاكِرَةً لِفَوَاضِلِ نَعْمَآئِكَ

shakiratan lifawadili na`ma'ika

thankful for Your graceful bounties,

ذَاكِرَةً لِسَوَابِغِ الآئِكَ

dhakiratan lisawabighi ala'ika

always bearing in mind Your incessant gifts,

مُشْتَاقَةً اِلىٰ فَرْحَتِ لِقَآئِكَ

mushtaqatan ila farhati liqa'ika

longing for the gladness of meeting You,

مُتَزَوِّدَةً التَّقْوٰى لِيَوْمِ جَزَآئِكَ

mutazawwidatan alttaqwa liyawmi jaza'ika

supplied with piety for the day of Your rewarding,

مُسْتَنَّةً بِسُنَنِ اَوْلِيَآئِكَ

mustannatan bisunani awliya'ika

pursuing the morals of Your intimate servants,

مُفَارِقَةً لِاَخْلَاقِ اَعْدَآئِكَ

mufariqatan li'akhlaqi a`da'ika

quitting the conducts of Your enemies,

مَشْغُوْلَةً عَنِ الدُّنْيَا بِحَمْدِكَ وَ ثَنَآئِكَ۔

mashghulatan `an alddunya bihamdika wa thana'ika

and distracted from this world by praising and thanking You.

اَللّٰهُمَّ اِنَّ قُلُوْبَ الْمُخْبِتِيْنَ اِلَيْكَ وَالِهَةٌ

allahumma inna quluba almukhbitina ilayka walihatun

O Allah, the hearts of those humbling themselves to You are fascinated,

وَ سُبُلَ الرَّاغِبِيْنَ اِلَيْكَ شَارِعَةٌ

wa subula alrraghibina ilayka shari`atun

the paths of those desiring for You are open,

وَ اَعْلَامَ الْقَاصِدِيْنَ اِلَيْكَ وَاضِحَةٌ

wa a`lama alqasidina ilayka wadihatun
the sings of those directing to You are evident,

وَ اَفْئِدَةَ الْعَارِفِيْنَ مِنْكَ فَازِعَةٌ

wa af'idata al`arifina minka fazi`atun
the hearts of those having recognition of You are resorting to You,

وَ اَصْوَاتَ الدَّاعِيْنَ اِلَيْكَ صَاعِدَةٌ

wa aswata aldda`ina ilayka sa`idatun
the voices of those beseeching You are mounting up to You,

وَ اَبْوَابَ الْاِجَابَةِ لَهُمْ مُفَتَّحَةٌ

wa abwaba al-ijabati lahum mufattahatun
the doors of responding to them are wide open,

وَ دَعْوَةَ مَنْ نَاجَاكَ مُسْتَجَابَةٌ

wa da`wata man najaka mustajabatun
the prayer of him who speaks to You confidentially is responded,

وَ تَوْبَةَ مَنْ اَنَابَ اِلَيْكَ مَقْبُوْلَةٌ

wa tawbata man anaba ilayka maqbulatun
the repentance of him who turns to You modestly is admitted,

وَ عَبْرَةَ مَنْ بَكٰى مِنْ خَوْفِكَ مَرْحُوْمَةٌ

wa `abrata man baka min khawfika marhumatun
the tear of him who weeps on account of fear from You is compassionated,

و وَ الْاِغَاثَةَ لِمَنِ اسْتَغَاثَ بِكَ مَوْجُوْدَةٌ

wal-ighathata liman istaghatha bika mawjudatun
the aid of him who seeks Your aid is available,

وَ الْاِعَانَةَ لِمَنِ اسْتَعَانَ بِكَ مَبْذُوْلَةٌ

wal-i`anata liman ista`ana bika mabdhulatun
the help of him who seeks Your help is obtainable,

وَ عِدَاتِكَ لِعِبَادِكَ مُنْجَزَةٌ

wa `idatika li`ibadika munjazatun

Your promises to Your servants are fulfilled,

وَ زَلَلَ مَنِ اسْتَقَالَكَ مُقَالَةٌ

wa zalala man istaqalaka muqalatun

the slips of him who implore You to excuse him are forgivable,

وَ اَعْمَالَ الْعَامِلِيْنَ لَدَيْكَ مَحْفُوْظَةٌ

wa a`mala al`amilina ladayka mahfuzatun

the deeds of those who act for You are preserved,

وَ اَرْزَاقَكَ اِلَى الْخَلَآئِقِ مِنْ لَّدُنْكَ نَازِلَةٌ

wa arzaqaka ila alkhala'iqi min ladunka nazilatun

Your sustenance to the creatures are descending from You,

وَ عَوَآئِدَ الْمَزِيْدِ اِلَيْهِمْ وَاصِلَةٌ

wa `awa'ida almazidi ilayhim wasilatun

Your gifts for further conferrals are reaching them,

وَ ذُنُوْبَ الْمُسْتَغْفِرِيْنَ مَغْفُوْرَةٌ

wa dhunuba almustaghfirina maghfuratun

the sins of those imploring Your forgiveness are forgiven,

وَ حَوَآئِجَ خَلْقِكَ عِنْدَكَ مَقْضِيَّةٌ

wa hawa'ija khalqika `indaka maqdiyyatun

the requests of Your creatures are granted by You,

وَ جَوَآئِزَ السَّآئِلِيْنَ عِنْدَكَ مُوَفَّرَةٌ

wa jawa'iza alssa'ilina `indaka muwaffaratun

the prizes of those begging You are offered,

وَ عَوَآئِدَ الْمَزِيْدِ مُتَوَاتِرَةٌ

wa `awa'ida almazidi mutawatiratun

Your gifts for further conferrals are uninterrupted,

وَ مَوَآئِدَ الْمُسْتَطْعِمِيْنَ مُعَدَّةٌ

wa mawa'ida almustat`imina mu`addatun
the dining tables for those seeking Your feeding are prepared,

وَ مَنَاهِلَ الظِّمَآءِ مُتْرَعَةٌ

wa manahila alzzama'i mutra`atun
and the springs of quenching their thirst are brimful.

اَللّٰهُمَّ فَاسْتَجِبْ دُعَآئِىْ

allahumma fastajib du`a'i
O Allah, (so) respond to my prayer,

وَ اقْبَلْ ثَنَآئِىْ

waqbal thana'i
accept my thanksgiving for You,

وَ اجْمَعْ بَيْنِىْ وَ بَيْنَ اَوْلِيَآئِىْ

wajma` bayni wa bayna awliya'i
and join me to my masters,

بِحَقِّ مُحَمَّدٍ وَّ عَلِيٍّ

bihaqqi muhammadin wa `aliyyin
[I beseech You] in the name of Muhammad, `Ali,

وَ فَاطِمَةَوَٱلْحَسَنِ وَٱلْحُسَيْنِ

wa fatimata walhasani walhusayni
Fatimah, al-Hasan, and al-Husayn.

اِنَّكَ وَلِىُّ نَعْمَآئِىْ

innaka waliyyu na`ma'i
You are verily the only source of my boons,

وَ مُنْتَهٰى مُنَاىَ

wa muntaha munaya
the ultimate goal of my wishes,

وَ غَايَةُ رَجَآئِيْ فِيْ مُنْقَلَبِيْ وَ مَثْوَايَ۔

wa ghayatu raja'i fi munqalabi wa mathwaya
and the target of my hope in my recourses and settlement.

Pause for a minute and then continue with the following:

اَنْتَ اِلٰهِيْ وَ سَيِّدِيْ وَ مَوْلَايَ

anta ilahi wa sayyidi wa mawlaya
You are verily my God, Master, and Lord.

اغْفِرْ لِاَوْلِيَآئِنَا

ighfir li-awliya'ina
(Please) forgive our friend,

وَ كُفَّ عَنَّا اَعْدَآئَنَا

wa kuffa `anna a`da'ana
prevent our enemies against us,

وَ اشْغَلْهُمْ عَنْ اَذَانَا

wa ashghilhum `an adhana
distract them from harming us,

وَ اَظْهِرْ كَلِمَةَ الْحَقِّ

wa azhir kalimata alhaqqi
give prevalence to the Word of Truth

وَ اجْعَلْهَا الْعُلْيَا

waj`alha al`ulya
and make it the supreme,

وَ اَدْحِضْ كَلِمَةَ الْبَاطِلِ

wa adhid kalimata albatili
and frustrate the word of falsehood

وَ اجْعَلْهَا السُّفْلٰى

waj`alha alssufla
and make it the lowliest.

إِنَّكَ عَلَىٰ كُلِّ شَيْءٍ قَدِيرٌ۔

innaka `ala kulli shay'in qadirun

Verily, You have power over all things.

The Prayers

You may offer prayers after which you recite the following:

اَللَّهُمَّ إِنِّي صَلَّيْتُ هَاتَيْنِ ٱلرَّكْعَتَيْنِ

allahumma inni sallattu hatayni alrrak`atayni

O Allah, I have offered these two units of prayer,

هَدِيَّةً مِنِّي إِلَىٰ سَيِّدِي وَمَوْلاَيَ

hadiyyatan minni ila sayyidi wa mawlaya

as present from me to my master and chief:

وَلِيِّكَ وَأَخِي رَسُولِكَ

waliyyika wa akhi rasulika

Your intimate servant, the brother of Your Messenger,

أَمِيرِ ٱلْمُؤْمِنِينَ

amiri almu'minina

the Commander of the Faithful

وَسَيِّدِ ٱلْوَصِيِّينَ

wa sayyidi alwasiyyina

and the chief of the Prophets' successors;

عَلِيِّ بْنِ أَبِي طَالِبٍ

`aliyyi bni abi talibin

namely, `Ali the son of Abu-Talib,

صَلَوَاتُ ٱللَّهِ عَلَيْهِ وَعَلَىٰ آلِهِ

salawatu allahi `alayhi wa `ala alihi

may Allah's blessings be upon him and his household.

اَللَّهُمَّ فَصَلِّ عَلَىٰ مُحَمَّدٍ وَآلِ مُحَمَّدٍ

allahumma fasalli `ala muhammadin wa ali muhammadin

So, O Allah, (please do) send blessings upon Muhammad and the Household of Muhammad,

وَتَقَبَّلْهَا مِنِّي

wa taqabbalha minni

accept that prayer from me,

وَٱجْزِنِي عَلَىٰ ذٰلِكَ جَزَاءَ ٱلْمُحْسِنِينَ

wajzini `ala dhalika jaza'a almuhsinina

and confer upon me with the reward that You give to the good-doers.

اَللَّهُمَّ لَكَ صَلَّيْتُ

allahumma laka sallaytu

O Allah, to You have I offered prayer,

وَلَكَ رَكَعْتُ

wa laka raka`tu

genuflected,

وَلَكَ سَجَدْتُ

wa laka sajadtu

and prostrated myself;

وَحْدَكَ لاَ شَرِيكَ لَكَ

wahdaka la sharika laka

to You alone without associating anyone with You,

لأَنَّهُ لاَ تَكُونُ ٱلصَّلاَةُ

li'annahu la takunu alssalatu

because prayers,

وَٱلرُّكُوعُ وَٱلسُّجُودُ إلاَّ لَكَ

walrruku`u walssujudu illa laka

genuflections, and prostrations are submitted to none save You,

لأَنَّكَ أَنْتَ ٱللَّهُ لاَ إِلٰهَ إِلاَّ أَنْتَ

li'annaka anta allahu la ilaha illa anta
because You are Allah; there is no god save You.

اَللَّهُمَّ صَلِّ عَلَىٰ مُحَمَّدٍ وَآلِ مُحَمَّدٍ

allahumma salli `ala muhammadin wa ali muhammadin
O Allah, (please do) bless Muhammad and the Household of Muhammad,

وَتَقَبَّلْ مِنِّي زِيَارَتِي

wa taqabbal minni ziyarati
admit my visit,

وَأَعْطِنِي سُؤْلِي

wa a`tini su'li
and respond to my requests

بِمُحَمَّدٍ وَآلِهِ ٱلطَّاهِرِينَ

bimuhammadin wa alihi alttahirina
in the name of Muhammad and his Household—the immaculate ones.

The Farewell

One who intends to leave the holy shrine of Imam `Ali ('a) may say the following form of bidding farewell:

اَلسَّلاَمُ عَلَيْكَ وَرَحْمَةُ ٱللَّهِ وَبَرَكَاتُهُ

alssalamu `alayka wa rahmatu allahi wa barakatuhu
Peace and Allah's mercy and blessings be upon you.

أَسْتَوْدِعُكَ ٱللَّهَ وَأَسْتَرْعِيكَ وَأَقْرَأُ عَلَيْكَ ٱلسَّلاَمَ

astawdi`uka allaha wa astar`ika wa aqra'u `alayka alssalama
I entrust you with Allah and ask Him to keep you under His custody and to send blessings upon you.

آمَنَّا بِٱللَّهِ وَبِٱلرُّسُلِ وَبِمَا جَاءَتْ بِهِ

amanna billahi wa bilrrusuli wa bima ja'at bihi
We believe in Allah, in the Messengers, and in what they have conveyed to us,

وَدَعَتْ إِلَيْهِ وَدَلَّتْ عَلَيْهِ

wa da`at ilayhi wa dallat `alayhi
in that to which they have called, and in that to which they have guided.

فَاكْتُبْنَا مَعَ الشَّاهِدِينَ

faktubna ma`a alshshahidina
So, (please, our Lord,) include us with the witnesses.

اَللَّهُمَّ لاَ تَجْعَلْهُ آخِرَ الْعَهْدِ مِنْ زِيَارَتِي إِيَّاهُ

allahumma la taj`alhu akhira al`ahdi min ziyarati iyyahu
O Allah, (please) do not decide this visit of mine to him (i.e. the Imam) to be the last,

فَإِنْ تَوَفَّيْتَنِي قَبْلَ ذٰلِكَ

fa'in tawaffaytani qabla dhalika
and if you cause me to die before that,

فَإِنّي أَشْهَدُ فِي مَمَاتِي

fa'inni ashhadu fi mamati
then I bear witness in my death

عَلَىٰ مَا شَهِدْتُ عَلَيْهِ فِي حَيَاتِي

`ala ma shahidtu `alayhi fi hayati
to the same things to which I have born witness in my lifetime:

أَشْهَدُ أَنَّ أَمِيرَ ٱلْمُؤْمِنِينَ عَلِيّاً

ashhadu anna amira almu'minina `aliyyan
I bear witness that `Ali the Commander of the Faithful,

وَٱلْحَسَنَ وَٱلْحُسَيْنَ

walhasana walhusayna
and al-Hasan, al-Husayn,

وَعَلِيَّ بْنَ ٱلْحُسَيْنِ

wa `aliyya bna alhusayni
`Ali ibn al-Husayn,

وَمُحَمَّدَ بْنَ عَلِيٍّ

wa muhammada bna `aliyyin

Muhammad ibn `Ali,

وَجَعْفَرَ بْنَ مُحَمَّدٍ

wa ja`fara bna muhammadin

Ja`far ibn Muhammad,

وَمُوسَىٰ بْنَ جَعْفَرٍ

wa musa bna ja`farin

Musa ibn Ja`far,

وَعَلِيَّ بْنَ مُوسَىٰ

wa `aliyya bna musa

`Ali ibn Musa,

وَمُحَمَّدَ بْنَ عَلِيٍّ

wa muhammada bna `aliyyin

Muhammad ibn `Ali,

وَعَلِيَّ بْنَ مُحَمَّدٍ

wa `aliyya bna muhammadin

`Ali ibn Muhammad,

وَٱلْحَسَنَ بْنَ عَلِيٍّ

walhasana bna `aliyyin

al-Hasan ibn `Ali,

وَٱلْحُجَّةَ بنَ الْحَسَنِ

walhujjata bna alhasani

and al-Hujjah (the Argument of Allah) ibn al-Hasan—

صَلَوَاتُكَ عَلَيْهِمْ أَجْمَعِينَ أَئِمَّتِي

salawatuka `alayhim ajma`ina a'immati

may Your blessings be upon all of them—are my Imams.

وَأَشْهَدُ أَنَّ مَنْ قَتَلَهُمْ وَحَارَبَهُمْ مُشْرِكُونَ

wa ashhadu anna man qatalahum wa harabahum mushrikuna

I also bear witness that all of those who have slain and fought against them are polytheists

وَمَنْ رَدَّ عَلَيْهِمْ فِي أَسْفَلِ دَرَكٍ مِنَ ٱلْجَحِيمِ

wa man radda `alayhim fi asfali darakin min aljahimi

and that all of those who reject them shall be in the lowest class of Hellfire.

وَأَشْهَدُ أَنَّ مَنْ حَارَبَهُمْ لَنَا أَعْدَاءٌ

wa ashhadu anna man harabahum lana a`da'un

I also bear witness that those who have fought against the Imams are our enemies

وَنَحْنُ مِنْهُمْ بُرَاءُ

wa nahnu minhum bura'u

and we disavow them,

وَأَنَّهُمْ حِزْبُ ٱلشَّيْطَانِ

wa annahum hizbu alshshaytani

because they are indeed the party of Satan.

وَعَلَىٰ مَنْ قَتَلَهُمْ لَعْنَةُ ٱللَّهِ وَٱلْمَلاَئِكَةِ وَٱلنَّاسِ أَجْمَعِينَ

wa `ala man qatalahum la`natu allahi walmala'ikati walnnasi ajma`ina

The curse of Allah, His angels and all the peoples be upon those who killed the Imams,

وَمَنْ شَرِكَ فِيهِمْ وَمَنْ سَرَّهُ قَتْلُهُمْ

wa man sharika fihim wa man sarrahu qatluhum

and upon those who had any role in killing them and those who were pleased for their having been killed.

ٱللَّهُمَّ إِنِّي أَسْأَلُكَ بَعْدَ ٱلصَّلاَةِ وَٱلتَّسْلِيمِ

allahumma inni as'aluka ba`da alssalati walttaslimi

O Allah, as I begin with invoking Your peace and blessings upon them,

أَنْ تُصَلِّيَ عَلَىٰ مُحَمَّدٍ وَعَلِيٍّ

an tusalliya `ala muhammadin wa `aliyyin
I pray you to bless Muhammad, `Ali,

وَفَاطِمَةَ وَٱلْحَسَنِ وَٱلْحُسَيْنِ

wa fatimata walhasani walhusayni
Fatimah, al-Hasan, al-Husayn,

وَعَلِيٍّ وَمُحَمَّدٍ وَجَعْفَرٍ وَمُوسَىٰ

wa `aliyyin wa muhammadin wa ja`farin wa musa
`Ali, Muhammad, Ja`far, Musa,

وَعَلِيٍّ وَمُحَمَّدٍ وَعَلِيٍّ وَٱلْحَسَنِ وَٱلْحُجَّةِ

wa `aliyyin wa muhammadin wa `aliyyin walhasani walhujjati
`Ali, Muhammad, `Ali, al-Hasan, and al-Hujjah,

وَلاَ تَجْعَلْهُ آخِرَ ٱلْعَهْدِ مِنْ زِيَارَتِهِ

wa la taj`alhu akhira al`ahdi min ziyaratihi
and not to decide this visit of me to his tomb to be the last,

فَإِنْ جَعَلْتَهُ فَٱحْشُرْنِي مَعَ هٰؤُلاَءِ ٱلْمُسَمَّيْنَ ٱلأَئِمَّةِ

fa'in ja`altahu fahshurni ma`a ha'ula'i almusammayna al-a'immati
and if you decide so, then (please) include me with these Imams to whom I have referred.

ٱللَّهُمَّ وَذَلِّلْ قُلُوبَنَا لَهُمْ بِٱلطَّاعَةِ وَٱلْمُنَاصَحَةِ

allahumma wa dhallil qulubana lahum biltta`ati walmunasahati
O Allah, (please) cause our hearts to be subservient to them by showing obedience to them, well-wishing,

وَٱلْمَحَبَّةِ وَٱلْمُؤَازَرَةِ وَٱلتَّسْلِيمِ

walmahabbati walmu'azarati walttaslimi
love for them, support, and submission.

IMAM HUSAYN (A)

The Visitation

اَلسَّلاَمُ عَلَيْكَ يَا وَارِثَ آدَمَ صَفْوَةِ ٱللَّهِ

alssalamu `alayka ya waritha adama safwati allahi
Peace be upon you, O inheritor of Adam the choice of Allah.

اَلسَّلاَمُ عَلَيْكَ يَا وَارِثَ نُوحٍ نَبِيِّ ٱللَّهِ

alssalamu `alayka ya waritha nuhin nabiyyi allahi
Peace be upon you, O inheritor of Noah the prophet of Allah.

اَلسَّلاَمُ عَلَيْكَ يَا وَارِثَ إِبْرَاهِيمَ خَلِيلِ ٱللَّهِ

alssalamu `alayka ya waritha ibrahima khalili allahi
Peace be upon you, O inheritor of Abraham the intimate friend of Allah.

اَلسَّلاَمُ عَلَيْكَ يَا وَارِثَ مُوسَىٰ كَلِيمِ ٱللَّهِ

alssalamu `alayka ya waritha musa kalimi allahi
Peace be upon you, O inheritor of Moses the spoken by Allah.

اَلسَّلاَمُ عَلَيْكَ يَا وَارِثَ عِيسَىٰ رُوحِ ٱللَّهِ

alssalamu `alayka ya waritha `isa ruhi allahi
Peace be upon you, O inheritor of Jesus the spirit of Allah.

اَلسَّلاَمُ عَلَيْكَ يَا وَارِثَ مُحَمَّدٍ حَبِيبِ ٱللَّهِ

alssalamu `alayka ya waritha muhammadin habibi allahi
Peace be upon you, O inheritor of Muhammad the most beloved by Allah.

اَلسَّلاَمُ عَلَيْكَ يَا وَارِثَ أَمِيرِ ٱلْمُؤْمِنِينَ عَلَيْهِ ٱلسَّلاَمُ

alssalamu `alayka ya waritha amiri almu'minina
Peace be upon you, O inheritor of the Commander of the Faithful, peace be upon him.

اَلسَّلاَمُ عَلَيْكَ يَا بْنَ مُحَمَّدٍ ٱلْمُصْطَفَىٰ

alssalamu `alayka yabna muhammadin almustafa
Peace be upon you, O son of Muhammad the well-chosen Prophet.

ٱلسَّلاَمُ عَلَيْكَ يَا بْنَ عَلِيٍّ ٱلْمُرْتَضَىٰ

alssalamu `alayka yabna `aliyyin almurtada
Peace be upon you, O son of `Ali the well-pleased.

ٱلسَّلاَمُ عَلَيْكَ يَا بْنَ فَاطِمَةَ ٱلزَّهْرَاءِ

alssalamu `alayka yabna fatimata alzzahra'i
Peace be upon you, O son of Fatimah the luminous lady.

ٱلسَّلاَمُ عَلَيْكَ يَا بْنَ خَدِيجَةَ ٱلْكُبْرَىٰ

alssalamu `alayka yabna khadijata alkubra
Peace be upon you, O son of Khadijah the grand lady.

ٱلسَّلاَمُ عَلَيْكَ يَا ثَارَ ٱللَّهِ وَٱبْنَ ثَارِهِ

alssalamu `alayka ya thara allahi wabna tharihi
Peace be upon you, O vengeance of Allah, son of His vengeance,

وَٱلْوِتْرَ ٱلْمَوْتُورَ

walwitra almawtura
and the unavenged so far.

أَشْهَدُ أَنَّكَ قَدْ أَقَمْتَ ٱلصَّلاَةَ

ashhadu annaka qad aqamta alssalata
I bear witness that you performed the prayers,

وَآتَيْتَ ٱلزَّكَاةَ

wa atayta alzzakata
defrayed the poor-rate,

وَأَمَرْتَ بِٱلْمَعْرُوفِ

wa amarta bilma`rufi
enjoined the right,

وَنَهَيْتَ عَنِ ٱلْمُنْكَرِ

wa nahayta `an almunkari
forbade the wrong,

وَأَطَعْتَ ٱللَّهَ وَرَسُولَهُ حَتَّىٰ أَتَاكَ ٱلْيَقِينُ

wa ata`ta allaha wa rasulahu hatta ataka alyaqinu
and obeyed Allah and His Messenger until death came upon you.

فَلَعَنَ ٱللَّهُ أُمَّةً قَتَلَتْكَ

fala`ana allahu ummatan qatalatka
So, may Allah curse the people who slew you.

وَلَعَنَ ٱللَّهُ أُمَّةً ظَلَمَتْكَ

wa la`ana allahu ummatan zalamatka
May Allah curse the people who persecuted you.

وَلَعَنَ ٱللَّهُ أُمَّةً سَمِعَتْ بِذٰلِكَ فَرَضِيَتْ بِهِ

wa la`ana allahu ummatan sami`at bidhalika faradiyat bihi
May Allah curse the people who were pleased when they had heard of that.

يَا مَوْلاَيَ يَا أَبَا عَبْدِ ٱللَّهِ

ya mawlaya ya aba `abdillahi
O my Master, O Abu-`Abdullah!

أَشْهَدُ أَنَّكَ كُنْتَ نُوراً فِي ٱلأَصْلاَبِ ٱلشَّامِخَةِ

ashhadu annaka kunta nuran fi al-aslabi alshshamikhati
I bear witness that you were light in the sublime loins

وَٱلأَرْحَامِ ٱلْمُطَهَّرَةِ

wal-arhami almutahharati
and purified wombs;

لَمْ تُنَجِّسْكَ ٱلْجَاهِلِيَّةُ بِأَنْجَاسِهَا

lam tunajjiska aljahiliyyatu bi'anjasiha
the impurities of the Ignorance Era could not object you to filth

وَلَمْ تُلْبِسْكَ مِنْ مُدْلَهِمَّاتِ ثِيَابِهَا

wa lam tulbiska min mudlahimmati thiyabiha
nor could it dress you its murky clothes.

وَأَشْهَدُ أَنَّكَ مِنْ دَعَائِمِ ٱلدِّينِ

wa ashhadu annaka min da`a'imi alddini

I also bear witness that you are one of the mainstays of the religion

وَأَرْكَانِ ٱلْمُؤْمِنِينَ

wa arkani almu'minina

and the supports of the faithful believers.

وَأَشْهَدُ أَنَّكَ ٱلإِمَامُ ٱلْبَرُّ ٱلتَّقِيُّ

wa ashhadu annaka al-imamu albarru alttaqiyyu

I also bear witness that you are the God-fearing, pious,

ٱلرَّضِيُّ ٱلزَّكِيُّ

alrradiyyu alzzakiyyu

pleased, immaculate,

ٱلْهَادِي ٱلْمَهْدِيُّ

alhadi almahdiyyu

guide, and well-guided Imam.

وَأَشْهَدُ أَنَّ ٱلأَئِمَّةَ مِنْ وُلْدِكَ كَلِمَةُ ٱلتَّقْوَىٰ

wa ashhadu anna al-a'immata min wuldika kalimatu alttaqwa

And (I bear witness) that the Imams from your progeny are the spokesmen of piety,

وَأَعْلاَمُ ٱلْهُدَىٰ

wa a`lamu alhuda

the signs of guidance,

وَٱلْعُرْوَةُ ٱلْوُثْقَىٰ

wal`urwatu alwuthqa

the firmest handle (of Islam),

وَٱلْحُجَّةُ عَلَىٰ أَهْلِ ٱلدُّنْيَا

walhujjatu `ala ahli alddunya

and the decisive Argument against the inhabitants of the world.

وَأُشْهِدُ ٱللَّهَ وَمَلاَئِكَتَهُ

wa ushhidu allaha wa mala'ikatahu
And I call Allah, His angels,

وَأَنْبِيَاءَهُ وَرُسُلَهُ

wa anbiya'ahu wa rusulahu
His Prophets, and His Messenger

أَنِّي بِكُمْ مُؤْمِنٌ وَبِإِيَابِكُمْ

anni bikum mu'minun wa bi'yabikum
to witness for me that I believe in you all and in your Return,

مُوقِنٌ بِشَرَائِعِ دِينِي وَخَوَاتِيمِ عَمَلِي

muqinun bishara'i`i dini wa khawatimi `amali
I have full confidence in the laws of my religion and in the seals of my deeds,

وَقَلْبِي لِقَلْبِكُمْ سِلْمٌ

wa qalbi liqalbikum silmun
my heart is at peace with you all,

وَأَمْرِي لأَمْرِكُمْ مُتَّبِعٌ

wa amri li'amrikum muttbi`un
and all my affairs are based on your commands.

صَلَوَاتُ اللهِ عَلَيْكُمْ وَعَلَىٰ أَرْوَاحِكُمْ

salawatu allahi `alaykum wa `ala arwahikum
May Allah's benedictions be on your souls,

وَعَلَىٰ أَجْسَادِكُمْ وَعَلَىٰ أَجْسَامِكُمْ

wa `ala ajsadikum wa `ala ajsamikum
your bodies, your forms,

وَعَلَىٰ شَاهِدِكُمْ وَعَلَىٰ غَائِبِكُمْ

wa `ala shahidikum wa `ala gha'ibkum
the present and the absent from you,

وَعَلَىٰ ظَاهِرِكُمْ وَعَلَىٰ بَاطِنِكُمْ

wa `ala zahirikum wa `ala batinikum
and the apparent and the invisible from you.

Then, you may continue and say these words:

بِأَبِي أَنْتَ وَأُمِّي يَا بْنَ رَسُولِ ٱللَّهِ

bi'abi anta wa ummi yabna rasuli allahi
My father and mother be sacrificed for you, O son of the Messenger of Allah!

بِأَبِي أَنْتَ وَأُمِّي يَا أَبَا عَبْدِ ٱللَّهِ

bi'abi anta wa ummi ya aba `abdillahi
My father and mother be sacrificed for you, O Abu `Abdullah!

لَقَدْ عَظُمَتِ ٱلرَّزِيَّةُ

laqad `azumat alrraziyyatu
Extremely terrible was the calamity

وَجَلَّتِ ٱلْمُصِيبَةُ بِكَ عَلَيْنَا

wa jallat almusibatu bika `alayna
and astounding is the misfortune that you suffered upon us

وَعَلَىٰ جَمِيعِ أَهْلِ ٱلسَّمَاوَاتِ وَٱلأَرْضِ

wa `ala jami`i ahli alssamawati wal-ardi
and upon all the inhabitants of the heavens and the earth.

فَلَعَنَ ٱللَّهُ أُمَّةً أَسْرَجَتْ وَأَلْجَمَتْ

fala`ana allahu ummatan asrajat wa aljamat
Therefore, Allah may curse the people who saddled up, gave rein to their horses,

وَتَهَيَّأَتْ لِقِتَالِكَ

wa tahayya'at liqitalika
and prepared themselves to kill you.

يَا مَوْلاَيَ يَا أَبَا عَبْدِ ٱللَّهِ

ya mawlaya ya aba `abdillahi
O my Master, O Abu `Abdullah!

قَصَدْتُ حَرَمَكَ

qasadtu haramaka
I moved towards your sanctuary

وَأَتَيْتُ إِلَىٰ مَشْهَدِكَ

wa ataytu ila mashhadika
and came to your shrine

أَسْأَلُ ٱللَّهَ بِٱلشَّأْنِ ٱلَّذِي لَكَ عِنْدَهُ

as'alu allaha bilshsha'ni alladhi laka `indahu
beseeching Allah in the name of the standing that you enjoy with Him

وَبِٱلْمَحَلِّ ٱلَّذِي لَكَ لَدَيْهِ

wa bilmahalli alladhi laka ladayhi
and the position that you occupy with Him

أَنْ يُصَلِّيَ عَلَىٰ مُحَمَّدٍ وَآلِ مُحَمَّدٍ

an yusalliya `ala muhammadin wa ali muhammadin
to send blessings on Muhammad and on the Household of Muhammad

وَأَنْ يَجْعَلَنِي مَعَكُمْ فِي ٱلدُّنْيَا وَٱلآخِرَةِ

wa an yaj`alani ma`akum fi alddunya wal-akhirati
and to keep me with you in this world and in the Hereafter.

The Prayers

Then, you should stand up for offering a two-unit prayer next to the side of the Imam's head. In this prayer, you can recite any Surah you like. When you finish, you should say these words:

اَللَّهُمَّ إِنِّي صَلَّيْتُ وَرَكَعْتُ وَسَجَدْتُ

allahumma inni sallaytu wa raka`tu wa sajadtu
O Allah, I have offered a prayer, genuflected, and prostrated myself

لَكَ وَحْدَكَ لاَ شَرِيكَ لَكَ

laka wahdaka la sharika laka
for Your sake purely without setting any partner with You

لأَنَّ ٱلصَّلاَةَ وَٱلرُّكُوعَ وَٱلسُّجُودَ

li'anna alssalata walrruku`a walssujuda

since all prayers, genuflection, and prostration

لاَ تَكُونُ إِلاَّ لَكَ

la takunu illa laka

suit none except You.

لإِنَّكَ أَنْتَ ٱللَّهُ لاَ إِلٰهَ إِلاَّ أَنْتَ

li'annaka anta allahu la ilaha illa anta

Because You are Allah, there in n0 god save You.

اَللَّهُمَّ صَلِّ عَلَىٰ مُحَمَّدٍ وَآلِ مُحَمَّدٍ

allahumma salli `ala muhammadin wa ali muhammadin

O Allah, (please) send blessings on Muhammad and the Household of Muhammad,

وَأَبْلِغْهُمْ عَنِّي أَفْضَلَ ٱلسَّلاَمِ وَٱلتَّحِيَّةِ

wa ablighhum `anni afdala alssalami walttahiyyati

and convey to them my best greetings and compliments

وَٱرْدُدْ عَلَيَّ مِنْهُمُ ٱلسَّلاَمَ

wardud `alayya minhum alssalama

and convey to me their replies.

اَللَّهُمَّ وَهَاتَانِ ٱلرَّكْعَتَانِ

allahumma wa hatani alrrak`atani

O Allah, these two units of prayer

هَدِيَّةٌ مِنِّي إِلَىٰ مَوْلاَيَ

hadiyyatun minni ila mawlaya

are present from me to my master

ٱلْحُسَيْنِ بْنِ عَلِيٍّ عَلَيْهِمَا ٱلسَّلاَمُ

alhusayni bni `aliyyin `alayhima alssalamu

al-Husayn the son of `Ali, peace be upon both of them.

اَللَّهُمَّ صَلِّ عَلَىٰ مُحَمَّدٍ وَعَلَيْهِ

allahumma salli `ala muhammadin wa `alayhi

O Allah, send blessings on Muhammad and on him,

وَتَقَبَّلْ مِنِّي وَأْجُرْنِي عَلَىٰ ذٰلِكَ

wa taqabbal minni wa'jurni `ala dhalika

accept my effort, and reward me for it

بِأَفْضَلِ أَمَلِي وَرَجَائِي فِيكَ

bi'afdali amali wa raja'i fika

in the best rewarding that I anticipate and hope from You

وَفِي وَلِيِّكَ يَا وَلِيَّ ٱلْمُؤْمِنِينَ

wa fi waliyyika ya waliyya almu'minina

and from Your saint, O Guardian of the faithful!

Visitation of Ali Akber (a)

Then, move to the side of the Imam's feet, stop at the place of the head of `Ali ibn al-Husayn ('a) and say the following words:

اَلسَّلاَمُ عَلَيْكَ يَا بْنَ رَسُولِ ٱللَّهِ

alssalamu `alayka yabna rasuli allahi

Peace be upon you, O son of the Messenger of Allah.

اَلسَّلاَمُ عَلَيْكَ يَا بْنَ نَبِيِّ ٱللَّهِ

alssalamu `alayka yabna nabiyyi allahi

Peace be upon you, O son of the Prophet of Allah.

اَلسَّلاَمُ عَلَيْكَ يَا بْنَ أَمِيرِ ٱلْمُؤْمِنِينَ

alssalamu `alayka yabna amiri almu'minina

Peace be upon you, O son of the commander of the faithful.

اَلسَّلاَمُ عَلَيْكَ يَا بْنَ ٱلْحُسَيْنِ ٱلشَّهِيدِ

alssalamu `alayka yabna alhusayni alshshahidi

Peace be upon you, O son of al-Husayn the martyr.

ٱلسَّلاَمُ عَلَيْكَ أَيُّهَا ٱلشَّهِيدُ

alssalamu `alayka ayyuha alshshahidu
Peace be upon you, O martyr.

ٱلسَّلاَمُ عَلَيْكَ أَيُّهَا ٱلْمَظْلُومُ وَٱبْنُ ٱلْمَظْلُومِ

alssalamu `alayka ayyuha almazlumu wabnu almazlumi
Peace be upon you, O wronged and harassed and the son of the wrong and harassed.

لَعَنَ ٱللَّهُ أُمَّةً قَتَلَتْكَ

la`ana allahu ummatan qatalatka
Curse of Allah be on those who killed you.

وَلَعَنَ ٱللَّهُ أُمَّةً ظَلَمَتْكَ

wa la`ana allahu ummatan zalamatka
Curse of Allah be on those who persecuted you.

وَلَعَنَ ٱللَّهُ أُمَّةً سَمِعَتْ بِذٰلِكَ فَرَضِيتْ بِهِ

wa la`ana allahu ummatan sami`at bidhalika faradiyat bihi
Curse of Allah be on those who heard this even but rested satisfied.

You should then say the following words:

ٱلسَّلاَمُ عَلَيْكَ يَا وَلِيَّ ٱللَّهِ وَٱبْنَ وَلِيِّهِ

alssalamu `alayka ya waliyya allahi wabna waliyyihi
Peace be upon you, O intimate servant of Allah and the son of His intimate servant.

لَقَدْ عَظُمَتِ ٱلْمُصِيبَةُ

laqad `azumat almusibatu
Extremely terrible was the calamity

وَجَلَّتِ ٱلرَّزِيَّةُ بِكَ عَلَيْنَا

wa jallat alrraziyyatu bika `alayna
and astounding is the misfortune that you suffered, upon us

وَعَلَىٰ جَمِيعِ ٱلْمُسْلِمِينَ

wa `ala jami`i almuslimina
and upon all Muslims.

فَلَعَنَ ٱللَّهُ أُمَّةً قَتَلَتْكَ

fala`ana allahu ummatan qatalatka
So, curse of Allah be on those who killed you

وَأَبْرَأُ إِلَىٰ ٱللَّهِ وَإِلَيْكَ مِنْهُمْ

wa abra'u ila allahi wa ilayka minhum
and I disavow them in the presence of Allah and You.

Visitation of the Martyrs

You should then leave from the door that is at the side of `Ali ibn al-Husayn's feet, direct towards the martyrs, and say the following words:

اَلسَّلاَمُ عَلَيْكُمْ يَا أَوْلِيَاءَ ٱللَّهِ وَأَحِبَّائَهُ

alssalamu `alaykum ya awliya'a allahi wa ahibba'ahu
Peace be upon all of you, O friends and dears of Allah.

اَلسَّلاَمُ عَلَيْكُمْ يَا أَصْفِيَاءَ ٱللَّهِ وَأَوِدَّاءَهُ

alssalamu `alaykum ya asfiya'a allahi wa awidda'ahu
Peace be upon all of you, O choice of Allah and sincerely attached to Him.

اَلسَّلاَمُ عَلَيْكُمْ يَا أَنْصَارَ دِينِ ٱللَّهِ

alssalamu `alaykum ya ansara dini allahi
Peace be upon all of you, O supporters of Allah's religion.

اَلسَّلاَمُ عَلَيْكُمْ يَا أَنْصَارَ رَسُولِ ٱللَّهِ

alssalamu `alaykum ya ansara rasuli allahi
Peace be upon all of you, O supporters of the Messenger of Allah.

اَلسَّلاَمُ عَلَيْكُمْ يَا أَنْصَارَ أَمِيرِ ٱلْمُؤْمِنِينَ

alssalamu `alaykum ya ansara amiri almu'minina
Peace be upon all of you, O supporters of the Commander of the Faithful.

اَلسَّلاَمُ عَلَيْكُمْ يَا أَنْصَارَ فَاطِمَةَ سَيِّدَةِ نِسَاءِ ٱلْعَالَمِينَ

alssalamu `alaykum ya ansara fatimata sayyidati nisa'i al`alamina

Peace be upon all of you, O supporters of Fatimah the doyenne of the women of this world.

اَلسَّلاَمُ عَلَيْكُمْ يَا أَنْصَارَ أَبِي مُحَمَّدٍ

alssalamu `alaykum ya ansara abi muhammadin

Peace be upon all of you, O supporters of Abu Muhammad,

ٱلْحَسَنِ بْنِ عَلِيٍّ ٱلْوَلِيِّ ٱلنَّاصِحِ

alhasani ibni `aliyyin alwaliyyi alnnasihi

al-Hasan the son of `Ali, the saintly and sincere.

اَلسَّلاَمُ عَلَيْكُمْ يَا أَنْصَارَ أَبِي عَبْدِ ٱللَّهِ

alssalamu `alaykum ya ansara abi `abdillahi

Peace be upon all of you, O supporters of Abu-`Abdullah.

بِأَبِي أَنْتُمْ وَأُمِّي

bi'abi antum wa ummi

My father and mother be sacrificed for you.

طِبْتُمْ وَطَابَتِ ٱلأَرْضُ ٱلَّتِي فِيهَا دُفِنْتُمْ

tibtum wa tabat al-ardu allati fiha dufintum

Verily, pure be you and pure be the soil in which you were buried.

وَفُزْتُمْ فَوْزاً عَظِيماً

wa fuztum fawzan `aziman

You attained great success.

فَيَا لَيْتَنِي كُنْتُ مَعَكُمْ فَأَفُوزَ مَعَكُمْ

fayalaytani kuntu ma`akum fa'afuza ma`akum

Would that I were with you so that I could also share the accomplishment with you.

AL-ABBAS IBN 'ALI (A)

Abbas was the son of Imam Ali (a), the first Imam and successor of the Prophet (peace be upon him and his progeny). He was the brother of Imam Husayn (a). By his supreme sacrifice, Abbas became a universal soul that transcends time and space.

The Visitation

Start with reciting the following at the entrance of the shrine.

سَلاَمُ ٱللَّهِ وَسَلاَمُ مَلاَئِكَتِهِ ٱلْمُقَرَّبِينَ

salamu allahi wa salamu mala'ikatihi almuqarrabina
Peace of Allah and peace of His favorite angels,

وَأَنْبِيَائِهِ ٱلْمُرْسَلِينَ

wa anbiya'ihi almursalina
His commissioned prophets,

وَعِبَادِهِ ٱلصَّالِحِينَ

wa `ibadihi alssalihina
His righteous servants,

وَجَمِيعِ ٱلشُّهَدَاءِ وَٱلصِّدِّيقِينَ

wa jami`i alshshuhada'i walssiddiqina
all the martyrs, and all the veracious (ones),

وَٱلزَّاكِيَاتُ ٱلطَّيِّبَاتُ فِيمَا تَغْتَدِي وَتَرُوحُ

walzzakiyatu alttayyibatu fima taghtadi wa taruhu
and also pure, true blessings that come and go,

عَلَيْكَ يَا بْنَ أَمِيرِ ٱلْمُؤْمِنِينَ

`alayka yabna amiri almu'minina
be upon you, O son of the Commander of the Faithful.

أَشْهَدُ لَكَ بِٱلتَّسْلِيمِ وَٱلتَّصْدِيقِ

ashhadu laka bilttaslimi walttasdiqi

I testify to you of submission (to the will of God), honest acceptance as true,

وَٱلْوَفَاءِ وَٱلنَّصِيحَةِ

walwafa'i walnnasihati

loyalty, and sincerity

لِخَلَفِ ٱلنَّبِيِّ صَلَّىٰ ٱللَّهُ عَلَيْهِ وَآلِهِ ٱلْمُرْسَلِ

likhalafi alnnabiyyi salla allahu `alayhi wa alihi almursali

to the descendant of the commissioned Prophet, Allah's blessings be upon him and his Household,

وَٱلسِّبْطِ ٱلْمُنْتَجَبِ

walssibti almuntajabi

the chosen grandson (of the Prophet),

وَٱلدَّلِيلِ ٱلْعَالِمِ

walddalili al`alimi

the well knowledgeable guide (to the true religion),

وَٱلْوَصِيِّ ٱلْمُبَلِّغِ

walwasiyyi almuballighi

the conveying successor,

وَٱلْمَظْلُومِ ٱلْمُهْتَضَمِ

walmazlumi almuhtadami

and the wrongfully oppressed one.

فَجَزَاكَ ٱللَّهُ عَنْ رَسُولِهِ

fajazaka allahu `an rasulihi

So, Allah may reward you on behalf of His Messenger,

وَعَنْ أَمِيرِ ٱلْمُؤْمِنِينَ

wa `an amiri almu'minina

the Commander of the Faithful,

وَعَنِ ٱلْحَسَنِ وَٱلْحُسَيْنِ

wa `an alhasani walhusayni

al-Hasan, and al-Husayn,

صَلَوَاتُ ٱللَّهِ عَلَيْهِمْ

salawatu allahi `alayhim

peace of Allah be upon them,

أَفْضَلَ ٱلْجَزَاءِ

afdala aljaza'i

with the best reward

بِمَا صَبَرْتَ وَٱحْتَسَبْتَ وَأَعَنْتَ

bima sabarta wahtasabta wa a`anta

for your steadfastness, dedication (to the sake of God), and support (for the right party).

فَنِعْمَ عُقْبَىٰ ٱلدَّارِ

fani`ma `uqba alddari

Very excellent be the reward of the eternal life.

لَعَنَ ٱللَّهُ مَنْ قَتَلَكَ

la`ana allahu man qatalaka

Allah's curse be on him who killed you.

وَلَعَنَ ٱللَّهُ مَنْ جَهِلَ حَقَّكَ

wa la`ana allahu man jahila haqqaka

Allah's curse be on him who ignored your position

وَٱسْتَخَفَّ بِحُرْمَتِكَ

wastakhaffa bihurmatika

and belittled your sanctity.

وَلَعَنَ ٱللَّهُ مَنْ حَالَ بَيْنَكَ وَبَيْنَ مَاءِ ٱلْفُرَاتِ

wa la`ana allahu man hala baynaka wa bayna ma'i alfurati

Allah's curse be on him who precluded you from the water of the Euphrates.

أَشْهَدُ أَنَّكَ قُتِلْتَ مَظْلُوما

ashhadu annaka qutilta mazluman
I testify that you were killed wrongfully

وَأَنَّ ٱللَّهَ مُنْجِزٌ لَكُمْ مَا وَعَدَكُمْ

wa anna allaha munjizun lakum ma wa`adakum
and that Allah will verily fulfill His promise that He made with you.

جِئْتُكَ يَا بْنَ أَمِيرِ ٱلْمُؤْمِنِينَ وَافِداً إِلَيْكُمْ

ji'tuka yabna amiri almu'minina wafidan ilaykum
O son of the Commander of the Faithful, I have come to you to present myself before you.

وَقَلْبِي مُسَلِّمٌ لَكُمْ وَتَابِعٌ

wa qalbi musallimun lakum wa tabi`un
My heart is submissive to you and is following you.

وَأَنَا لَكُمْ تَابِعٌ

wa ana lakum tabi`un
And I am your follower.

وَنُصْرَتِي لَكُمْ مُعَدَّةٌ

wa nusrati lakum mu`addatun
I am ready to support you

حَتَّىٰ يَحْكُمَ ٱللَّهُ

hatta yahkuma Allahu
until Allah decides.

وَهُوَ خَيْرُ ٱلْحَاكِمِينَ

wa huwa khayru alhakimina
He is surely the best of all those who decide.

فَمَعَكُمْ مَعَكُمْ

fama`akum ma`akum
I am verily with you,

لاَ مَعَ عَدُوِّكُمْ

la ma`a `aduwwikum

not with your enemy.

إِنِّي بِكُمْ وَبِإِيَابِكُمْ مِنَ ٱلْمُؤْمِنِينَ

inni bikum wa bi'iyabikum min almu'minina

I am one of those who believe in you and believe in your Return.

وَبِمَنْ خَالَفَكُمْ وَقَتَلَكُمْ مِنَ ٱلْكَافِرِينَ

wa biman khalafakum wa qatalakum min alkafirina

I also one of those who deny your opposites and killers.

قَتَلَ ٱللَّهُ أُمَّةً قَتَلَتْكُمْ بِٱلأَيْدِي وَٱلأَلْسُنِ

qatala allahu ummatan qatalatkum bil-aidi wal-alsuni

Allah may kill the group who killed you with hands and tongues (by giving orders of killing you.)

Inside the Shrine

You should then enter, and say the following words:

السَّلاَمُ عَلَيْكَ أَيُّهَا ٱلعَبْدُ ٱلصَّالِحُ

alssalamu `alayka ayyuha al`abdu alssalihu

Peace be upon you, O righteous servant (of Allah)

ٱلْمُطِيعُ لِلَّهِ وَلِرَسُولِهِ وَلأَمِيرِ ٱلْمُؤْمِنِينَ

almuti`u lillahi wa lirasulihi wa li'amiri almu'minina

and obedient to Allah, to His Messenger, to the Commander of the Faithful,

وَٱلْحَسَنِ وَٱلْحُسَيْنِ صَلَّىٰ ٱللَّهُ عَلَيْهِمْ وَسَلَّمَ

walhasani walhusayni salla allahu `alayhim wa sallama

to al-Hasan, and to al-Husayn, peace and greetings of Allah be upon them.

السَّلاَمُ عَلَيْكَ وَرَحْمَةُ ٱللَّهِ وَبَرَكَاتُهُ

alssalamu `alayka wa rahmatu allahi wa barakatuhu

Peace, Allah's mercy, blessings,

وَمَغْفِرَتُهُ وَرِضْوَانُهُ وَعَلَىٰ رُوحِكَ وَبَدَنِكَ

wa maghfiratuhu wa ridwanuhu wa `ala ruhika wa badanika
forgiveness, and gratifications be upon you, your soul, and your body.

أَشْهَدُ وَأُشْهِدُ ٱللَّهَ

ashhadu wa ushhidu allaha
I testify, and call Allah to witness,

أَنَّكَ مَضَيْتَ عَلَىٰ مَا مَضَىٰ بِهِ ٱلْبَدْرِيُّونَ

annaka madayta `ala ma mada bihi albadriyyuna
that you abided by the same course that was taken by the warriors of Badr

وَٱلْمُجَاهِدُونَ فِي سَبِيلِ ٱللَّهِ

walmujahiduna fi sabili allahi
and the strivers for Allah's sake

ٱلْمُنَاصِحُونَ لَهُ فِي جِهَادِ أَعْدَائِهِ

almunasihuna lahu fi jihadi a`da'ihi
who sincerely served Him in the battlefields against His enemies,

ٱلْمُبَالِغُونَ فِي نُصْرَةِ أَوْلِيَائِهِ

almubalighuna fi nusrati awliya'ihi
did their bests for supporting His disciples,

ٱلذَّابُّونَ عَنْ أَحِبَّائِهِ

aldhdhabbuna `an ahibba'ihi
and defended His intimate ones.

فَجَزَاكَ ٱللَّهُ أَفْضَلَ ٱلْجَزَاءِ

fajazaka allahu afdala aljaza'i
So, Allah may reward you the best,

وَأَكْثَرَ ٱلْجَزَاءِ

wa akthara aljaza'i
the maximum,

وَأَوْفَرَ ٱلْجَزَاءِ

wa awfara aljaza'i
the most abundant,

وَأَوْفَىٰ جَزَاءِ أَحَدٍ مِمَّنْ وَفَىٰ بِبَيْعَتِهِ

wa awfa jaza'i ahadin mimman wa fa bibay`atihi
and the most conclusive reward that He may give to anyone who fulfills his homage,

وَٱسْتَجَابَ لَهُ دَعْوَتَهُ

wastajaba lahu da`watahu
answers the call (of the religion),

وَأَطَاعَ وُلاةَ أَمْرِهِ

wa ata`a wulata amrihi
and obeys his (divinely elected) leaders.

أَشْهَدُ أَنَّكَ قَدْ بَالَغْتَ فِي ٱلنَّصِيحَةِ

ashhadu annaka qad balaghta fi alnnasihati
I testify that you acted extremely sincerely

وَأَعْطَيْتَ غَايَةَ ٱلْمَجْهُودِ

wa a`tayta ghayata almajhudi
and exerted all your efforts (in this regard).

فَبَعَثَكَ ٱللَّهُ فِي ٱلشُّهَدَاءِ

faba`athaka allahu fi alshshuhada'i
Allah may attach you to the martyrs,

وَجَعَلَ رُوحَكَ مَعَ أَرْوَاحِ ٱلسُّعَدَاءِ

wa ja`ala ruhaka ma`a arwahi alssu`ada'i
add your soul to the souls of the happy ones,

وَأَعْطَاكَ مِنْ جِنَانِهِ أَفْسَحَهَا مَنْزِلاً

wa a`taka min jinanihi afsahaha manzilan
give you the largest abode in His Paradise

وَأَفْضَلَهَا غُرَفاً

wa afdalaha ghurafan
and the most handsome room,

وَرَفَعَ ذِكْرَكَ فِي عِلِّيِّينَ

wa rafa`a dhikraka fi `illiyyina
exalt your mention in `Illiyyin (the most elevated position),

وَحَشَرَكَ مَعَ ٱلنَّبِيِّينَ وَٱلصِّدِّيقِينَ

wa hasharaka ma`a alnnabiyyina walssiddiqina
and join you to the Prophets, the veracious ones,

وَٱلشُّهَدَاءِ وَٱلصَّالِحِينَ

walshshuhada'i walssalihina
the martyrs, and the righteous ones.

وَحَسُنَ أُوْلٰئِكَ رَفِيقاً

wa hasuna ula'ika rafiqan
Very excellent is the companionship of such ones.

أَشْهَدُ أَنَّكَ لَمْ تَهِنْ وَلَمْ تَنْكُلْ

ashhadu annaka lam tahin wa lam tankul
I testify that you did not lag behind and did not turn away the face,

وَأَنَّكَ مَضَيْتَ عَلَىٰ بَصِيرَةٍ مِنْ أَمْرِكَ

wa annaka madayta `ala basiratin min amrika
and that you left this life with full awareness of the truth,

مُقْتَدِياً بِٱلصَّالِحِينَ

muqtadiyan bilssalihina
following the examples of the righteous ones

وَمُتَّبِعاً لِلنَّبِيِّينَ

wa muttabi`an lilnnabiyyina
and sticking to the Prophets.

فَجَمَعَ ٱللَّهُ بَيْنَنَا وَبَيْنَكَ

fajama`a allahu baynana wa baynaka
So, Allah may gather us with you,

وَبَيْنَ رَسُولِهِ وَأَوْلِيَائِهِ

wa bayna rasulihi wa awliya'ihi
with His Messenger, and with His disciples

فِي مَنَازِلِ ٱلْمُخْبِتِينَ

fi manazili almukhbitina
in the abodes of those who practiced humbly (with their Lord).

فَإِنَّهُ أَرْحَمُ ٱلرَّاحِمِينَ

fa'innahu arhamu alrrahimina
He is certainly the most merciful of all the merciful ones.

The Prayers

You may then turn to the side of the head and offer a two-unit prayer. Afterwards, you may offer prayers as many as you wish. You may also supplicate Almighty Allah earnestly.

Additional Supplications

After these prayers, you may say the following supplicatory prayer:

اَللَّهُمَّ صَلِّ عَلَىٰ مُحَمَّدٍ وَآلِ مُحَمَّدٍ

allahumma salli `ala muhammadin wa ali muhammadin
O Allah, (please) send blessings upon Muhammad and the Household of Muhammad

وَلا تَدَعْ لِي فِي هٰذَا ٱلْمَكَانِ ٱلْمُكَرَّمِ وَٱلْمَشْهَدِ ٱلْمُعَظَّمِ ذَنْباً إِلاَّ غَفَرْتَهُ

wa la tada` li fi hadha almakani almukarrami walmashhadi almu`azzami dhanban illa ghafartahu
and do not leave for me, in this honored place and glorified shrine, any sin that I did but that You forgive it,

وَلا هَمّاً إِلاَّ فَرَّجْتَهُ

wa la hamman illa farrjtahu
any care but that You relieve it,

وَلا مَرَضاً إِلاَّ شَفَيْتَهُ

wa la maradan illa shafaytahu
any illness but that You cure it,

وَلا عَيْباً إِلاَّ سَتَرْتَهُ

wa la `ayban illa satartahu
any defect buth that You cover up,

وَلا رِزْقاً إِلاَّ بَسَطْتَهُ

wa la rizqan illa basattahu
any source of sustenance but that You expand it,

وَلا خَوْفاً إِلاَّ آمَنْتَهُ

wa la khawfan illa amantahu
any item of terror but that You pacify it,

وَلا شَمْلاً إِلاَّ جَمَعْتَهُ

wa la shamlan illa jama`tahu
any disunity but that You reunify it,

وَلا غَائِباً إِلاَّ حَفِظْتَهُ وَأَدْنَيْتَهُ

wa la gha'iban illa hafiztahu wa adnaytahu
any absent one but that You guard it and approach (him to me),

وَلا حَاجَةً مِنْ حَوَائِجِ ٱلدُّنْيَا وَٱلآخِرَةِ

wa la hajatan min hawa'iji alddunya wal-akhirati
and any single need, among the many needs for this life as well as the life to come

لَكَ فِيهَا رِضَىً وَلِيَ فِيهَا صَلاحٌ

laka fiha ridan wa liya fiha salahun
whose settlement achieves your gratification and my good,

إِلاَّ قَضَيْتَهَا يَا أَرْحَمَ ٱلرَّاحِمِينَ

illa qadaytaha ya arhama alrrahimina
but that You grant it. O He Who is the most merciful of all the merciful ones!

You may then return to the tomb, stop at the side of the legs, and say the following words:

السَّلاَمُ عَلَيْكَ يَا أَبَا ٱلْفَضْلِ ٱلعَبَّاسَ بْنَ أَمِيرِ ٱلْمُؤْمِنِينَ

alssalamu `alayka ya aba alfadli al`abbasa ibna amiri almu'minina
Peace be upon you, O Abu'l-Fadl al-`Abbas the son of the Commander of the Faithful.

السَّلاَمُ عَلَيْكَ يَا بْنَ سَيِّدِ ٱلْوَصِيِّينَ

alssalamu `alayka yabna sayyidi alwasiyyina
Peace be upon you, O son of the chief of the successors (of the Prophets).

السَّلاَمُ عَلَيْكَ يَا بْنَ أَوَّلِ ٱلْقَوْمِ إِسْلاَماً

alssalamu `alayka yabna awwali alqawmi islaman
Peace be upon you, O son of the foremost to Islam,

وَأَقْدَمِهِمْ إِيمَاناً

wa aqdamihim imanan
the first to believe,

وَأَقْوَمِهِمْ بِدِينِ ٱللَّهِ

wa aqwamihim bidini allahi
the best to have served the religion of Allah,

وَأَحْوَطِهِمْ عَلَىٰ ٱلإِسْلاَمِ

wa ahwatihim `ala al-islami
and the most careful for Islam.

أَشْهَدُ لَقَدْ نَصَحْتَ لِلَّهِ وَلِرَسُولِهِ وَلأَخِيكَ

ashhadu laqad nasahta lillahi wa lirasulihi wa li'akhika
I bear witness that you served Allah, His Messenger, and your brother sincerely.

فَنِعْمَ ٱلأَخُ ٱلْمُوَاسِي

fani`ma al-akhu almuwasi

You were the most excellent self-sacrificing brother.

فَلَعَنَ ٱللَّهُ أُمَّةً قَتَلَتْكَ

fala`ana allahu ummatan qatalatka

So, Allah's curse be on the group who killed you.

وَلَعَنَ ٱللَّهُ أُمَّةً ظَلَمَتْكَ

wa la`ana allahu ummatan zalamatka

Allah's curse be on the group who wronged you.

وَلَعَنَ ٱللَّهُ أُمَّةً ٱسْتَحَلَّتْ مِنْكَ ٱلْمَحَارِمَ

wa la`ana allahu ummatan istahallat minka almaharima

Allah's curse be on the group who violated your sanctities

وَٱنْتَهَكَتْ حُرْمَةَ ٱلإِسْلاَمِ

wantahakat hurmata al-islami

and infringed the sanctity of Islam.

فَنِعْمَ ٱلصَّابِرُ ٱلْمُجَاهِدُ

fani`ma alssabiru almujahidu

You were the most excellent steadfast fighter,

ٱلْمُحَامِي ٱلنَّاصِرُ

almuhami alnnasiru

protector, supporter,

وَٱلأَخُ ٱلدَّافِعُ عَنْ أَخِيهِ

wal-akhu alddafi`u `an akhihi

and brother who defended his brother,

ٱلْمُجِيبُ إِلَىٰ طَاعَةِ رَبِّهِ

almujibu ila ta`ati rabbihi

responded to the obedience to his Lord,

ٱلرَّاغِبُ فِيمَا زَهِدَ فِيهِ غَيْرُهُ مِنَ ٱلثَّوَابِ ٱلْجَزِيلِ

alrraghibu fima zahida fihi ghayruhu min alththwabi aljazili
and worked desirably for gaining the abundant reward, which others refused,

وَٱلثَّنَاءِ ٱلْجَمِيلِ

walththna'i aljamili
and the nice tribute.

وَأَلْحَقَكَ ٱللَّهُ بِدَرَجَةِ آبَائِكَ فِي جَنَّاتِ ٱلنَّعِيمِ

wa alhaqaka allahu bidarajati aba'ika fi jannati alnna`imi
So, Allah may attach you to the rank of your fathers in the gardens of bliss.

اَللَّهُمَّ إِنِّي تَعَرَّضْتُ لِزِيَارَةِ أَوْلِيَائِكَ رَغْبَةً فِي ثَوَابِكَ

allahumma inni ta`arradtu liziyarati awliya'ika raghbatan fi thawabika
O Allah, I have done the pilgrimage to Your disciples out of my desire for (winning) your reward

وَرَجَاءً لِمَغْفِرَتِكَ وَجَزِيلِ إِحْسَانِكَ

wa raja'an limaghfiratika wa jazili ihsanika
and my wish for Your forgiveness and Your abundant benevolence.

فَأَسْأَلُكَ أَنْ تُصَلِّيَ عَلَىٰ مُحَمَّدٍ وَآلِهِ ٱلطَّاهِرِينَ

fa's'aluka an tusalliya `ala muhammadin wa alihi alttahirina
So, I implore You to send Your blessings upon Muhammad and his immaculate Household

وَأَنْ تَجْعَلَ رِزْقِي بِهِمْ دَارّاً

wa an taj`ala rizqi bihim darran
and to make my sustenance flow copiously in their names,

وَعَيْشِي بِهِمْ قَارّاً

wa `ayshi bihim qarran
my living delightful in their names,

وَزِيَارَتِي بِهِمْ مَقْبُولَةً

wa ziyarati bihim maqbulatan
my pilgrimage rewardable in their names,

وَحَيَاتِي بِهِمْ طَيِّبَةً

wa hayati bihim tayyibatan
and my life pleasant in their names,

وَأَدْرِجْنِي إِدْرَاجَ ٱلْمُكْرَمِينَ

wa adrijni idraja almukramina
to make me take to the conduct of the honored ones,

وَٱجْعَلْنِي مِمَّنْ يَنْقَلِبُ مِنْ زِيَارَةِ مَشَاهِدِ أَحِبَّائِكَ

waj`alni mimman yanqalibu min ziyarati mashahidi ahibba'ika
to make me one of those who, as returning from the pilgrimage to the tombs of Your beloved ones,

مُفْلِحاً مُنْجِحاً

muflihan munjihan
win success and prosperity

قَدِ ٱسْتَوْجَبَ غُفْرَانَ ٱلذُّنُوبِ

qad istawjaba ghufrana aldhdhunubi
and deserve forgiveness of sins,

وَسَتْرَ ٱلْعُيُوبِ

wa satra al`uyubi
covering up of defects,

وَكَشْفَ ٱلْكُرُوبِ

wa kashfa alkurubi
and relief of disasters.

إِنَّكَ أَهْلُ ٱلتَّقْوَىٰ وَأَهْلُ ٱلْمَغْفِرَةِ

innaka ahlu alttaqwa wa ahlu almaghfirati
You are surely worthy of being feared and worthy of forgiving.

Once Ready to Leave

If you intend to take leave, you may approach the holy tomb and say the following words, which has been reported from Abu-Hamzah al-Thumali and have been mentioned by other scholars:

أَسْتَوْدِعُكَ ٱللَّهَ وَأَسْتَرْعِيكَ

astawdi`uka allaha wa astar`ika

I entrust you with Allah, beseech Him to keep you under His guard,

وَأَقْرَأُ عَلَيْكَ ٱلسَّلاَمَ

wa aqra'u `alayka alssalama

and invoke peace upon you.

آمَنَّا بِٱللَّهِ وَبِرَسُولِهِ وَبِكِتَابِهِ

amanna billahi wa birasulihi wa bikitabihi

We have believed in Allah, in His Messenger, in His Book,

وَبِمَا جَاءَ بِهِ مِنْ عِنْدِ ٱللَّهِ

wa bima ja'a bihi min `indi allahi

and in that which he conveyed from Allah.

ٱللَّهُمَّ فَٱكْتُبْنَا مَعَ ٱلشَّاهِدِينَ

allahumma faktubna ma`a alshshahidina

O Allah, record our names with the witnesses.

ٱللَّهُمَّ لا تَجْعَلْهُ آخِرَ ٱلعَهْدِ مِنْ زِيَارَتِي قَبْرَ ٱبْنِ أَخِي رَسُولِكَ

allahumma la taj`alhu akhira al`ahdi min ziyarati qabra ibni akhi rasulika

O Allah do not decide this pilgrimage to the tomb of the son of Your Messenger's brother to be the last one of mine.

صَلَّى ٱللَّهُ عَلَيْهِ وَآلِهِ

salla allahu `alayhi wa alihi

Peace be upon him (i.e. the Messenger) and upon his Household.

وَٱرْزُقْنِي زِيَارَتَهُ أَبَداً مَا أَبْقَيْتَنِي

warzuqni ziyaratahu abadan ma abqaytani

Grant me opportunities to visit him so long as You keep me alive,

وَٱحْشُرْنِي مَعَهُ وَمَعَ آبَائِهِ فِي ٱلْجِنَانِ

wahshurni ma`ahu wa ma`a aba'ihi fi aljinani

join me to him and to his fathers in the gardens of Paradise,

وَعَرِّفْ بَيْنِي وَبَيْنَهُ وَبَيْنَ رَسُولِكَ وَأَوْلِيَائِكَ

wa `arrif bayni wa baynahu wa bayna rasulika wa awliya'ika

and introduce me to him, to Your Messenger, and to Your disciples.

اَللَّهُمَّ صَلِّ عَلَىٰ مُحَمَّدٍ وَآلِ مُحَمَّدٍ

allahumma salli `ala muhammadin wa ali muhammadin

O Allah, send Your blessings to Muhammad and the Household of Muhammad

وَتَوَفَّنِي عَلَىٰ ٱلإِيمَانِ بِكَ

wa tawaffani `ala al'imani bika

and take me to You while I am abiding by the believing in You,

وَٱلتَّصْدِيقِ بِرَسُولِكَ

walttasdiqi birasulika

giving credence to Your Messenger,

وَٱلوِلاَيَةِ لِعَلِيِّ بْنِ أَبِي طَالِبٍ وَٱلأَئِمَّةِ مِنْ وُلْدِهِ

walwilayati li`aliyyi bni abi talibin wal-a'immati min wuldihi

being faithful to `Ali the son of Abu-Talib and the Imams from his progeny,

وَٱلْبَرَاءَةِ مِنْ عَدُوِّهِمْ

walbara'ati min `aduwwihim

and disavowing their enemy.

فَإِنِّي قَدْ رَضِيتُ يَا رَبِّي بِذٰلِكَ

fa'inni qad raditu ya rabbi bidhalika

My Lord, I have accepted such.

وَصَلَّىٰ ٱللَّهُ عَلَىٰ مُحَمَّدٍ وَآلِ مُحَمَّدٍ

wa salla allahu `ala muhammadin wa ali muhammadin

Allah may send blessings upon Muhammad and the Household of Muhammad.

THE GREAT MOSQUE OF KUFAH

The Virtues

Kūfah is one of the four towns chosen by God Almighty. The expression "Mount Sīnā" (Ṭūri Sīnīn) mentioned in Sūrat al-Tīn has been interpreted as referring to it. It is mentioned in a report that it is Allah's sanctuary (ḥaram) and that of the Apostle of Allah (ṣ) and the Commander of the Faithful ('a). It also says that a penny given in charity here equals a hundred offered elsewhere, and that two rak'ahs offered here equal a hundred offered elsewhere.

It is one of the spots where a Muslim traveler has the option to offer his obligatory prayers with or without qaṣr. It has been said that the reward of a prayer offered in this mosque equals that of a ḥajj pilgrimage approved and accepted by Allah, or that of a thousand prayers offered elsewhere.

It is mentioned in some reports that it has been a place of worship for many prophets, and that it will as well be the venue of prayer for Imam Mahdī, may Allah bless him. According to one report, one thousand prophets and one thousand legatees of prophets have prayed in it. Some reports suggest that the Mosque of Kūfah is greater in merit than Al-Aqṣā Mosque in Bayt al-Maqdis.

Ibn Qūlawayh cites a report that Imam Muḥammad al-Bāqir ('a) said that if people knew the virtues of the Mosque of Kūfah they would arrange the means of journey to visit this mosque from distant towns. He also said that the reward of performing an obligatory prayer in it equals that of an accepted ḥajj pilgrimage, and a supererogatory prayer therein equals in reward that of an accepted 'umrah.

According to another report, the merit of performing obligatory and supererogatory prayers in it is like that of a ḥajj and 'umrah performed in the company of the Apostle of Allah (ṣ).

Shaykh Kulaynī and other major compilers of ḥadith have cited a report on the authority of Hārūn b. Khārijah wherein he says, "Imam Ja'far al-Ṣādiq ('a) said to me, 'O Hārūn, how far is the Mosque of Kūfah from your place? Is it at a mile's distance?' 'No,' I said. 'Do you offer all your prayers there?' he asked me. 'No,' I replied. He said, 'Had I lived near that mosque, I would not miss performing a single prayer in it. Do you have any idea about the merit of that place? There has not been any righteous servant of God, nor any prophet, who has not prayed in the Mosque of Kūfah. When the Apostle of Allah (ṣ) was being taken on his nocturnal journey to the heavens, Gabriel asked him, "O Apostle of Allah, do you know where we are now? We are right in front of the Mosque of Kūfah."

The Prophet (ṣ) said, "Ask the Lord to permit me to come down in it and offer two rak'ahs of prayer." Gabriel sought God Almighty's permission and He granted it, whereat the Prophet (ṣ) alighted in the mosque and offered two rak'ahs of prayer. Indeed, there is a garden from among the gardens of paradise on its right side, another in its middle and a third at its rear. The reward of a single obligatory prayer offered therein equals that of a thousand prayers performed elsewhere, and the reward of one supererogatory prayer there equals that of five hundred prayers. Even just sitting there just sitting there without reciting the Qur'ān or performing any dhikr has the reward of worship. If the people knew the merits of this place they would visit it, even if one could move only by crawling on the ground like an infant.'"

An account of the virtues of this mosque was given earlier under the seventh ziyārah of the Commander of the Faithful ('a) (p. 136). From some reports it appears that the right side of the mosque has a greater merit than its left side.

The Observances

While entering the town of Kūfah one should say,

بِسْمِ اللهِ وَ بِاللهِ، وَ فِي سَبِيلِ اللهِ، وَ عَلىٰ مِلَّةِ رَسُولِ اللهِ صَلَّى اللهُ عَلَيْهِ وَ آلِهِ، اَللّٰهُمَّ أَنْزِلْنِي مُنْزَلًا مُبَارَكًا وَ أَنْتَ خَيْرُ الْمُنْزِلِينَ

In the Name of Allah, by Allah, on the path of Allah and in keeping with the creed of the Apostle of Allah, may Allah bless him and his Family. O Allah, conduct me to a blessed destination and You are the best of those who bring the voyagers to their destinations.

While on the way to the Mosque of Kūfah and till reaching its gate, keep saying,

اَللهُ أَكْبَرُ وَ لاَ إِلٰهَ إِلَّا اللهُ وَ الْحَمْدُ لِلهِ وَ سُبْحَانَ اللهِ

Allah is greater. There is no god besides Allah. All praise belongs to Allah, and may Allah be glorified!

At the Entrance of the Mosque On reaching the mosque, stop at the gate, say the following and enter, preferably through the gate at the rear of the mosque, commonly known as "Bāb al-Fīl."

اَلسَّلاَمُ عَلىٰ سَيِّدِنَا رَسُولِ اللهِ مُحَمَّدِ بْنِ عَبْدِ اللهِ وَ آلِهِ الطَّاهِرِينَ، اَلسَّلاَمُ عَلىٰ أَمِيرِ الْمُؤْمِنِينَ عَلِيِّ بْنِ أَبِي طَالِبٍ وَ رَحْمَةُ اللهِ وَ بَرَكَاتُهُ وَ عَلىٰ مَجَالِسِهِ وَ مَشَاهِدِهِ، وَ مَقَامِ حِكْمَتِهِ، وَ آثَارِ آبَائِهِ آدَمَ وَ نُوحٍ وَ إِبْرَاهِيمَ وَ إِسْمَاعِيلَ، وَ تِبْيَانِ بَيِّنَاتِهِ

Peace be to our master, Muḥammad ibn 'Abdillah, the Apostle of Allah, and his immaculate Family. Peace be to 'Alī ibn Abī Ṭālib, the Commander of the Faithful, and may Allah's mercy and His blessings be upon him and upon the venues of his sessions and audiences, the seats of his judgement and the relics of his forebears, Adam, Noah, Abraham and Ishmael, and the memorabilia of his proofs.

اَلسَّلاَمُ عَلَى الْإِمَامِ الْحَكِيمِ الْعَدْلِ، الصِّدِّيقِ الْأَكْبَرِ، اَلْفَارُوقِ بِالْقِسْطِ، اَلَّذِي فَرَّقَ اللهُ بِهِ بَيْنَ الْحَقِّ وَ الْبَاطِلِ، وَ الْكُفْرِ وَ الْإِيمَانِ، وَ الشِّرْكِ وَ التَّوْحِيدِ، لِيَهْلِكَ مَنْ هَلَكَ عَنْ بَيِّنَةٍ، وَ يَحْيَا مَنْ حَيَّ عَنْ بَيِّنَةٍ

Peace be to the wise and just Imam, the most veracious one, who set apart (truth from falsehood) on the basis of justice, through whom Allah separated the truth from falsehood, faith from unfaith, and monotheism from polytheism, so that he who perishes might perish by a manifest proof, and he who lives may live on by a manifest proof.

أَشْهَدُ أَنَّكَ أَمِيرُ الْمُؤْمِنِينَ وَ خَاصَّةُ نَفْسِ الْمُنْتَجَبِينَ، وَ زَيْنُ الصِّدِّيقِينَ، وَ صَابِرُ الْمُمْتَحَنِينَ، وَ أَنَّكَ حَكَمُ اللهِ فِي أَرْضِهِ، وَ قَاضِي أَمْرِهِ،وَ بَابُ حِكْمَتِهِ،

I bear witness that you are the Commander of the Faithful, the choicest of the elect, the ornament of the truthful, the most steadfast of the tested ones, and that you are God's arbiter on His earth, adjudicator by His command, the gateway of His wisdom,

وَ عَاقِدُ عَهْدِهِ، وَ النَّاطِقُ بِوَعْدِهِ، وَ الْحَبْلُ الْمَوْصُولُ بَيْنَهُ وَ بَيْنَ عِبَادِهِ، وَ كَهْفُ النَّجَاةِ، وَ مِنْهَاجُ التُّقَىٰ، وَ الدَّرَجَةُ الْعُلْيَا، وَ مُهَيْمِنُ الْقَاضِي الْأَعْلَىٰ

the concluder of His covenant, the declarer of His promise, and the connecting cord between Him and His servants, the haven of deliverance, the path of Godfearing, the highest degree and custodian of the Supreme Judge.

يَا أَمِيرَ الْمُؤْمِنِينَ بِكَ أَتَقَرَّبُ إِلَى اللهِ زُلْفَى، أَنْتَ وَلِيِّي وَ سَيِّدِي وَ وَسِيلَتِي فِي الدُّنْيَا وَ الْآخِرَةِ

O Commander of the Faithful, through you do I seek nearness to Allah and you are my guardian, my master and my recourse in this world and the Hereafter! On entering the mosque say,

اَللهُ أَكْبَرُ، اَللهُ أَكْبَرُ، اَللهُ أَكْبَرُ، هٰذَا مَقَامُ الْعَائِذِ بِاللهِ، وَ بِمُحَمَّدٍ حَبِيبِ اللهِ صَلَّى اللهُ عَلَيْهِ وَ آلِهِ، وَ بِوِلَايَةِ أَمِيرِ الْمُؤْمِنِينَ، وَ الْأَئِمَّةِ الْمَهْدِيِّينَ الصَّادِقِينَ النَّاطِقِينَ الرَّاشِدِينَ، اَلَّذِينَ أَذْهَبَ اللهُ عَنْهُمُ الرِّجْسَ وَ طَهَّرَهُمْ تَطْهِيرًا،

Allah is greater. Allah is greater. Allah is greater. I, who stand here, take refuge with Allah, with Muḥammad, Allah's beloved, may Allah bless him and his Family, and in the wilāyah of the Commander of the Faithful and the Imams, the veracious guides and the rightly guided ones, from whom Allah has repelled all impurity and purified them with a thorough purification.

رَضِيتُ بِهِمْ أَئِمَّةً وَ هُدَاةً وَ مَوَالِيَّ، سَلَّمْتُ لِأَمْرِ اللهِ لَا أُشْرِكُ بِهِ شَيْئًا، وَ لَا أَتَّخِذُ مَعَ اللهِ وَلِيًّا، كَذَبَ الْعَادِلُونَ بِاللهِ وَ ضَلُّوا ضَلَالًا بَعِيدًا، حَسْبِيَ اللهُ وَ أَوْلِيَاءُ اللهِ،

I am well-pleased with them as my Imams, guides and masters. I comply with Allah's commands, and I do not ascribe any partner to Him, nor do I take anyone as guardian besides Allah. Those who equate others with Allah have lied and strayed into far error. Sufficient are for me Allah and His awliyā.

أَشْهَدُ أَنْ لَا إِلٰهَ إِلَّا اللهُ وَحْدَهُ لَا شَرِيكَ لَهُ، وَ أَشْهَدُ أَنَّ مُحَمَّدًا عَبْدُهُ وَ رَسُولُهُ صَلَّى اللهُ عَلَيْهِ وَ آلِهِ، وَ أَنَّ عَلِيًّا وَ الْأَئِمَّةَ الْمَهْدِيِّينَ مِنْ ذُرِّيَّتِهِ عَلَيْهِمُ السَّلَامُ أَوْلِيَائِي وَ حُجَّةُ اللهِ عَلَىٰ خَلْقِهِ

I testify that there is no god besides Allah, that He is One and has no partner. I testify that Muḥammad is His servant and apostle—may Allah bless him and his Family—and that cAlī and the rightly-guided Imams of his descent, peace be to them, are my masters and Allah's testament to His creation.

The Fourth Pillar (Maqām-o Ibrāhīm)

Then proceed to the fourth pillar, associated with the Prophet Abraham ('a), which is near the "Bāb al-Anmāṭ" and besides the fifth pillar. There, offer four

rak'ahs, two rak'ahs with al-Fātiḥah and Sūrat al-Tawḥīd and the remaining two with al-Fātiḥah and Sūrat al-Qadr.

After prayers, say the tasbīḥ of Ḥaḍrat Fāṭimah ('a) and then say,

اَلسَّلاَمُ عَلىٰ عِبَادِ اللهِ الصَّالِحِينَ الرَّاشِدِينَ، اَلَّذِينَ أَذْهَبَ اللهُ عَنْهُمُ الرِّجْسَ وَ طَهَّرَهُمْ تَطْهِيرًا، وَ جَعَلَهُمْ أَنْبِيَاءَ مُرْسَلِينَ، وَ حُجَّةً عَلَى الْخَلْقِ أَجْمَعِينَ، وَ سَلاَمٌ عَلَى الْمُرْسَلِينَ، وَ الْحَمْدُ لِلهِ رَبِّ الْعَالَمِينَ، ذٰلِكَ تَقْدِيرُ الْعَزِيزِ الْعَلِيمِ

Peace be to Allah's righteous and rightly guided servants, from whom He has repelled all impurity and purified them with a thorough purification. He has made them prophetic envoys and appointed them to be testament to all His creation. Peace be to the apostles and all praise belongs to Allah, the Lord of all the world. That is the ordaining of the All-mighty, the All-knowing. (36:38.)

Then say seven times, "Salāmun 'alā Nūḥin fil 'ālamīn" ('Peace be to Noah, throughout the nations!)(37:79)
Then say,

نَحْنُ عَلىٰ وَصِيَّتِكَ يَا وَلِيَّ الْمُؤْمِنِينَ، اَلَّتِي أَوْصَيْتَ بِهَا ذُرِّيَّتَكَ مِنَ الْمُرْسَلِينَ وَ الصِّدِّيقِينَ، وَ نَحْنُ مِنْ شِيعَتِكَ وَ شِيعَةِ نَبِيِّنَا مُحَمَّدٍ صَلَّى اللهُ عَلَيْهِ وَ آلِهِ وَ عَلَيْكَ وَ عَلىٰ جَمِيعِ الْمُرْسَلِينَ وَ الْأَنْبِيَاءِ وَ الصَّادِقِينَ،

O friend of the faithful, we remain loyal to the exhortation you made to the apostles and the truthful ones of your descent, and we are your followers and followers of our Prophet, Muḥammad, may Allah bless him and his Family, and bless you and all the apostles, prophets, and the truthful ones.

وَ نَحْنُ عَلىٰ مِلَّةِ إِبْرَاهِيمَ، وَ دِينِ مُحَمَّدٍ النَّبِيِّ الْأُمِّيِّ، وَ الْأَئِمَّةِ الْمَهْدِيِّينَ، وَ وِلاَيَةِ مَوْلاَنَا عَلِيٍّ أَمِيرِ الْمُؤْمِنِينَ

We stand fast by the creed of Abraham and the religion of Muḥammad, the untaught prophet, the rightly guided Imams, and by the wilāyah of our master, Ali, the Commander of the Faithful.

اَلسَّلاٰمُ عَلَى الْبَشِيرِ النَّذِيرِ، صَلَوَاتُ اللهِ عَلَيْهِ وَ رَحْمَتُهُ وَ رِضْوَانُهُ وَ بَرَكَاتُهُ، وَ عَلىٰ وَصِيِّهِ وَ خَلِيفَتِهِ، اَلشَّاهِدِ لِلهِ مِنْ بَعْدِهِ عَلىٰ خَلْقِهِ، عَلِيٍّ أَمِيرِ الْمُؤْمِنِينَ، اَلصِّدِّيقِ الْأَكْبَرِ، وَ الْفَارُوقِ الْمُبِينِ، اَلَّذِي أَخَذْتَ بَيْعَتَهُ عَلَى الْعَالَمِينَ،

Peace be to the bearer of good news and the warner—may Allah's blessings, His mercy, pleasure, and bounties be upon him and upon his legatee and successor, who was after him Allah's witness to His creation: 'Alī, the Commander of the Faithful, the greatest of the truthful, the manifest separator (between truth and falsehood), for whom was taken the oath of allegiance from all the people.

رَضِيتُ بِهِمْ أَوْلِيَاءَ وَ مَوَالِيَّ وَ حُكَّامًا فِي نَفْسِي وَ وُلْدِي [وَلَدِي] وَ أَهْلِي، وَ مَالِي وَ قِسْمِي، وَ حِلِّي وَ إِحْرَامِي، وَ إِسْلاٰمِي وَ دِينِي، وَ دُنْيَايَ وَ آخِرَتِي، وَ مَحْيَايَ وَ مَمَاتِي،

I accept them as my guardians, masters and arbiters in relation to my own self, my children, family, property and share, in all my circumstances without and within the state of pilgrim sanctity, in my compliance and faith, my world and Hereafter, and my life and death.

أَنْتُمُ الْأَئِمَّةُ فِي الْكِتَابِ، وَ فَصْلُ الْمَقَامِ، وَ فَصْلُ الْخِطَابِ، وَ أَعْيُنُ الْحَيِّ الَّذِي لاٰ يَنَامُ،

You are the Imams in the Scripture, the conclusive and final word, the sentinels of the Living One who does not sleep.

وَ أَنْتُمْ حُكَمَاءُ اللهِ، وَ بِكُمْ حَكَمَ اللهُ، وَ بِكُمْ عُرِفَ حَقُّ اللهِ، لاٰ إِلٰهَ إِلَّا اللهُ، مُحَمَّدٌ رَسُولُ اللهِ، أَنْتُمْ نُورُ اللهِ مِنْ بَيْنِ أَيْدِينَا وَ مِنْ خَلْفِنَا، أَنْتُمْ سُنَّةُ اللهِ الَّتِي بِهَا سَبَقَ الْقَضَاءُ

You are Allah's sages: through you He judges, and through you Allah's rights are known. There is no god besides Allah, Muḥammad is the Apostle of Allah, and you are the light of Allah, in our own time and the future. You are Allah's precedent in whose favour the divine decree has already gone forth.

يَا أَمِيرَ الْمُؤْمِنِينَ، أَنَا لَكُمْ مُسَلِّمٌ تَسْلِيمًا، لاٰ أُشْرِكُ بِاللهِ شَيْئًا، وَ لاٰ أَتَّخِذُ مِنْ دُونِهِ وَلِيًّا، اَلْحَمْدُ لِلهِ الَّذِي هَدَانِي بِكُمْ، وَ مَا كُنْتُ لِأَهْتَدِيَ لَوْ لاٰ أَنْ هَدَانِيَ اللهُ، اَللهُ أَكْبَرُ، اَللهُ أَكْبَرُ، اَللهُ أَكْبَرُ، اَلْحَمْدُ لِلهِ عَلىٰ مَا هَدَانَا

O Commander of the Faithful, I am totally compliant to you. I do not ascribe any partner to Allah, nor seek any guardian besides Him. All praise belongs to Allah who guided me to you, and I would not have been guided had Allah not guided me. Allah is greater. Allah is greater. Allah is greater. Allah is greater. Thanks to Allah for guiding us!

Dikkat al-Qaḍā' & Bayt al-Ṭasht

The Dikkat al-Qaḍā' ('the Bench of Judgement') is a location in the mosque where the Commander of the Faithful ('a) used to sit in judgement. There was a short pillar in that place on which was inscribed the Qur'ānic verse,

إِنَّ اللهَ يَأْمُرُ بِالْعَدْلِ وَ الْإِحْسَانِ

Indeed, Allah enjoins justice and kindness. (16:90)

The Bayt al-Ṭasht is the spot where a wonderful episode occurred involving an unmarried girl. She had gone into a pond where a leech-like parasite had entered her womb and gradually grown in bulk by sucking blood. Her bulging belly had led her brothers to conclude that she was pregnant. They wanted to kill her for bringing shame on the family. The case was brought before the Commander of the Faithful ('a). He had a curtain set up at one side of the mosque and sat the girl down behind it. Then he had her examined by a midwife, who after examining her declared that she was indeed carrying a child in her belly. Then at the Imam's order they brought a basin full of slime and mud and the girl was told to sit in it. The parasite came out of the girl's body at the smell of the slime. According to some accounts, the Imam miraculously stretched out his hand and fetched a handful of snow from the mountains of Syria and placed it by the basin, whereupon the parasite came out of the girl's belly. A point to be noted here is concerning the sequence of the observances of this mosque.

According to the customary order, after the above observance pertaining to the Fourth Pillar, one proceeds to perform the observance relating to the spot at the middle of the mosque. The observances pertaining to the Dikkat al-Qaḍā' and Bayt al-Ṭasht are performed at the end, after finishing the observance relating to the station of Imam Ja'far al-Ṣādiq ('a).

The observance of Dikkat al-Qaḍā consists of offering two rak'ahs of prayer in that place, with Sūrat al-Fātiḥah and any sūrah.

After the prayer and tasbīḥ of Ḥaḍrat Fātimah ('a) say,

يَا مَالِكِي وَ مُمَلِّكِي وَ مُتَغَمِّدِي بِالنِّعَمِ الْجِسَامِ مِنْ غَيْرِ اسْتِحْقَاقٍ، وَجْهِي خَاضِعٌ لِمَا تَعْلُوهُ الْأَقْدَامُ لِجَلَالِ وَجْهِكَ الْكَرِيمِ

O my Owner and Bestower of my possessions, who have enveloped me with Your immense blessings without my having deserved them! I lower and humble my face to the ground, which is trodden under feet, for the sake of the majesty of Your noble Face!

لَا تَجْعَلْ هٰذِهِ الشِّدَّةَ وَ لَا هٰذِهِ الْمِحْنَةَ مُتَّصِلَةً بِاسْتِيصَالِ الشَّأْفَةِ، وَ امْنَحْنِي مِنْ فَضْلِكَ مَا لَمْ تَمْنَحْ بِهِ أَحَدًا مِنْ غَيْرِ مَسْأَلَةٍ، أَنْتَ الْقَدِيمُ الْأَوَّلُ الَّذِي لَمْ تَزَلْ وَ لَا تَزَالُ، صَلِّ عَلَىٰ مُحَمَّدٍ وَ آلِ مُحَمَّدٍ وَ اغْفِرْ لِي وَ ارْحَمْنِي،

Do not let this hardship and ordeal lead up to utter destruction. Grant me, out of Your grace, that which You do not grant to anybody without his asking. You are the First and the Pre-eternal One who have always existed and will continue to exist. Bless Muhammad and the Family of Muhammad and forgive me and have mercy on me.

وَ زَكِّ عَمَلِي، وَ بَارِكْ لِي فِي أَجَلِي، وَ اجْعَلْنِي مِنْ عُتَقَائِكَ وَ طُلَقَائِكَ مِنَ النَّارِ، بِرَحْمَتِكَ يَا أَرْحَمَ الرَّاحِمِينَ

Purify my conduct and bless the span of my life and make me one of those whom You have spared and delivered from the Fire, O Most Merciful of the merciful!

Bayt al-Tasht

At the Bayt al-Ṭasht, which is next to the Dikkat al-Qaḍā, offer two rak'ahs, as Imam al-Ṣādiq ('a) is reported to have offered two rak'ahs at this place.

Then, after salām and tasbīḥ, say,

اَللّٰهُمَّ إِنِّي ذَخَرْتُ تَوْحِيدِي إِيَّاكَ، وَ مَعْرِفَتِي بِكَ، وَ إِخْلَاصِي لَكَ، وَ إِقْرَارِي بِرُبُوبِيَّتِكَ، وَ ذَخَرْتُ وِلَايَةَ مَنْ أَنْعَمْتَ عَلَيَّ بِمَعْرِفَتِهِمْ مِنْ بَرِيَّتِكَ، مُحَمَّدٍ وَ عِتْرَتِهِ صَلَّى اللهُ عَلَيْهِمْ، لِيَوْمِ فَزَعِي إِلَيْكَ عَاجِلًا وَ آجِلًا

O Allah, I treasure my faith in Your Oneness, my knowledge of You, my dedication to You, my admission of Your Lordship, and I treasure as well my allegiance to Muḥammad and his Family—Your creatures with whose fellowship You have blessed me—for the day that I seek refuge in You, in life and after death.

،وَ قَدْ فَزِعْتُ إِلَيْكَ وَ إِلَيْهِمْ يَا مَوْلَايَ فِي هٰذَا الْيَوْمِ وَ فِي مَوْقِفِي هٰذَا، وَ سَأَلْتُكَ مَادَّتِي مِنْ نِعْمَتِكَ
وَ إِزَاحَةَ مَا أَخْشَاهُ مِنْ نِقْمَتِكَ، وَ الْبَرَكَةَ فِيمَا رَزَقْتَنِيهِ، وَتَحْصِينَ صَدْرِي مِنْ كُلِّ هَمٍّ وَ جَائِحَةٍ
وَمَعْصِيَةٍ فِي دِينِي وَ دُنْيَايَ وَ آخِرَتِي، يَا أَرْحَمَ الرَّاحِمِينَ

O my Master, I seek refuge with You and them, today and in this place where I stand, and beseech You to expand Your blessing, to spare me from Your vengeance, which I fear, to bless what You provide me with, and to protect my heart from every worry, affliction and sin, with regard to my faith, my conduct in this life and my condition in the Hereafter, O Most Merciful of the merciful!

The Mosque's Center

This spot is called Dikkat al-Mi'rāj, apparently because the Apostle of Allah (ṣ) came down here with the permission of God Almighty and offered two rak'ahs at this place.

The tradition pertaining to this episode was mentioned at the beginning of this chapter.

Two rak'ahs are to be offered at the middle of the mosque, with al-Fātiḥah and Sūrat al-Tawḥīd in the first and al-Fātiḥah and Sūrat al-Kāfirūn in the second. After salām and tasbīḥ of Fāṭimah Zahrā ('a), say,

اَللّٰهُمَّ أَنْتَ السَّلَامُ، وَ مِنْكَ السَّلَامُ، وَ إِلَيْكَ يَعُودُ السَّلَامُ، وَ دَارُكَ دَارُ السَّلَامِ، حَيِّنَا رَبَّنَا مِنْكَ
بِالسَّلَامِ

O Allah, You are Peace, from You proceeds all peace, and to You returns all peace, and Your abode is the abode of peace. Our Lord, greet us with Your greeting of 'Peace.'

اَللّٰهُمَّ إِنِّي صَلَّيْتُ هٰذِهِ الصَّلَاةَ ابْتِغَاءَ رَحْمَتِكَ وَ رِضْوَانِكَ وَ مَغْفِرَتِكَ، وَ تَعْظِيمًا لِمَسْجِدِكَ، اَللّٰهُمَّ
فَصَلِّ عَلىٰ مُحَمَّدٍ وَ آلِ مُحَمَّدٍ، وَ ارْفَعْهَا فِي عِلِّيِّينَ، وَ تَقَبَّلْهَا مِنِّي يَا أَرْحَمَ الرَّاحِمِينَ

O Allah, I have offered this prayer, seeking Your mercy, Your pleasure and Your pardon, and to honour Your mosque. O Allah, bless Muḥammad and the Family of Muḥammad and raise my prayer to the 'Illīyūn and accept it from me, O Most Merciful of the merciful!

The Seventh Pillar

The seventh pillar is the place where God Almighty inspired Adam ('a) to pray for repentance.

Proceed towards this place and, standing near the pillar, say while facing the qiblah,

بِسْمِ اللهِ وَ بِاللهِ، وَ عَلىٰ مِلَّةِ رَسُولِ اللهِ صَلَّى اللهُ عَلَيْهِ وَ آلِهِ، وَ لاٰ إِلٰهَ إِلَّا اللهُ مُحَمَّدٌ رَسُولُ اللهِ

In Allah's Name, by Allah and following the creed of Allah's Apostle, may Allah bless him and his Family. There is no god besides Allah and Muḥammad is the Apostle of Allah.

اَلسَّلاٰمُ عَلىٰ أَبِينَا آدَمَ، وَ أُمِّنَا حَوَّاءَ، اَلسَّلاٰمُ عَلىٰ هَابِيلَ الْمَقْتُولِ ظُلْمًا وَ عُدْوَانًا عَلىٰ مَوَاهِبِ اللهِ وَ رِضْوَانِهِ، اَلسَّلاٰمُ عَلىٰ شَيْثٍ صَفْوَةِ اللهِ الْمُخْتَارِ الْأَمِينِ، وَ عَلَى الصَّفْوَةِ الصَّادِقِينَ مِنْ ذُرِّيَّتِهِ الطَّيِّبِينَ، أَوَّلِهِمْ وَ آخِرِهِمْ

Peace be to Adam, our father, and Eve, our mother. Peace be to Abel, who was slain wrongfully and unjustly, out of envy for Allah's gifts and His approval. Peace be to Shayth, Allah's elect and His chosen trustee, and peace be to the paragons of veracity from his pure progeny, from the first of them to the last.

اَلسَّلاٰمُ عَلىٰ إِبْرَاهِيمَ وَ إِسْمَاعِيلَ وَ إِسْحَاقَ وَ يَعْقُوبَ، وَ عَلىٰ ذُرِّيَّتِهِمُ الْمُخْتَارِينَ، اَلسَّلاٰمُ عَلىٰ مُوسَىٰ كَلِيمِ اللهِ، اَلسَّلاٰمُ عَلىٰ عِيسَىٰ رُوحِ اللهِ

Peace be to Abraham, Ishmael, Isaac, and Jacob and to their chosen descendants! Peace be to Moses, Allah's interlocutor! Peace be to Jesus, Allah's spirit!

اَلسَّلاٰمُ عَلىٰ مُحَمَّدِ بْنِ عَبْدِ اللهِ خَاتَمِ النَّبِيِّينَ، اَلسَّلاٰمُ عَلىٰ أَمِيرِ الْمُؤْمِنِينَ وَ ذُرِّيَّتِهِ الطَّيِّبِينَ، وَ رَحْمَةُ اللهِ وَ بَرَكَاتُهُ، اَلسَّلاٰمُ عَلَيْكُمْ فِي الْأَوَّلِينَ، اَلسَّلاٰمُ عَلَيْكُمْ فِي الْآخِرِينَ

Peace be to Muḥammad ibn 'Abd Allāh, the Seal of the Prophets. Peace be to the Commander of the Faithful and his immaculate descendants and may Allah's mercy and blessings be upon them! Peace be to you, among the former generations! Peace be to you, among the latter generations!

اَلسَّلاٰمُ عَلىٰ فَاطِمَةَ الزَّهْرَاءِ، اَلسَّلاٰمُ عَلَى الْأَئِمَّةِ الْهَادِينَ، شُهَدَاءِ اللهِ عَلىٰ خَلْقِهِ، اَلسَّلاٰمُ عَلَى الرَّقِيبِ الشَّاهِدِ عَلَى الْأُمَمِ لِلّٰهِ رَبِّ الْعَالَمِينَ

Peace be to Fāṭimah Zahrā! Peace be to the Imams, the guides and Allah's witnesses to His creation! Peace be to him who is the sentinel and witness over the nations on behalf of Allah, the Lord of all the worlds!

Then offer four rak'ahs, with al-Fātiḥah and Sūrat al-Qadr in the first and al-Fātiḥah and Sūrat al-Tawḥīd in the second rak'ah. The third and fourth rak'ahs are to be offered in a similar manner. After the tasbīḥ of Ḥaḍrat Fāṭimah ('a), say,

اَللّٰهُمَّ إِنْ كُنْتُ قَدْ عَصَيْتُكَ فَإِنِّي قَدْ أَطَعْتُكَ فِي الْإِيمَانِ مِنِّي بِكَ، مَنًّا مِنْكَ عَلَيَّ، لاٰ مَنًّا مِنِّي عَلَيْكَ،
وَ أَطَعْتُكَ فِي أَحَبِّ الْأَشْيَاءِ لَكَ، لَمْ أَتَّخِذْ لَكَ وَلَدًا، وَ لَمْ أَدْعُ لَكَ شَرِيكًا،

O Allah, though I have disobeyed You, yet I have been obedient to You with regard to my faith in You—a favour You have done me, not a favour I may have done—and I have obeyed You with regard to something which is dearest of all things in Your eyes: I did not ascribe any child to You nor any partner.

وَ قَدْ عَصَيْتُكَ فِي أَشْيَاءَ كَثِيرَةٍ عَلىٰ غَيْرِ وَجْهِ الْمُكَابَرَةِ لَكَ، وَ لَا الْخُرُوجِ عَنْ عُبُودِيَّتِكَ، وَ لَا
الْجُحُودِ لِرُبُوبِيَّتِكَ، وَ لٰكِنِ اتَّبَعْتُ هَوَايَ وَ أَزَلَّنِي الشَّيْطَانُ بَعْدَ الْحُجَّةِ عَلَيَّ وَ الْبَيَانِ،

Although I have sinned against You with regard to many things, that was not due to insolence on my behalf, nor due to a denial of my servanthood, nor a negation of Your lordship. Rather, I followed my desire and Satan made me stumble, after Your teaching had left me no room for any excuse!

فَإِنْ تُعَذِّبْنِي فَبِذُنُوبِي غَيْرَ ظَالِمٍ لِي، وَ إِنْ تَعْفُ عَنِّي وَ تَرْحَمْنِي فَبِجُودِكَ وَ كَرَمِكَ يَا كَرِيمُ

If You punish me it will be because of my sins, and that will not be unjust, and if You pardon me and have mercy on me, that would be on account of Your generosity and magnanimity, O Munificent One!

اَللّٰهُمَّ إِنَّ ذُنُوبِي لَمْ يَبْقَ لَهَا إِلَّا رَجَاءُ عَفْوِكَ، وَ قَدْ قَدَّمْتُ آلَةَ الْحِرْمَانِ، فَأَنَا أَسْأَلُكَ اللهُمَّ مَا لاٰ
أَسْتَوْجِبُهُ، وَ أَطْلُبُ مِنْكَ مَا لاٰ أَسْتَحِقُّهُ

O Allah, my sins have left me with no option but to pin hopes on Your pardon, though I have already made myself deserve its denial. O Allah, I seek what I do not deserve and desire what I do not merit.

اَللّٰهُمَّ إِنْ تُعَذِّبْنِي فَبِذُنُوبِي، وَ لَمْ تَظْلِمْنِي شَيْئًا، وَ إِنْ تَغْفِرْ لِي فَخَيْرُ رَاحِمٍ أَنْتَ يَا سَيِّدِي، اَللّٰهُمَّ
أَنْتَ أَنْتَ وَ أَنَا أَنَا، أَنْتَ الْعَوَّادُ بِالْمَغْفِرَةِ، وَ أَنَا الْعَوَّادُ بِالذُّنُوبِ، وَ أَنْتَ الْمُتَفَضِّلُ بِالْحِلْمِ، وَ أَنَا الْعَوَّادُ
بِالْجَهْلِ

O Allah, if You punish me for my sins, that will not be unjust of You, and if You forgive me, You are indeed the best of the merciful, O my Master! O Allah, You are You, and I am I! You keep on turning to me with clemency and I keep on reverting into sin! You go on being gracious to me out of Your forbearance, and I keep on regressing out of my ignorance!

اَللّٰهُمَّ فَإِنِّي أَسْأَلُكَ يا كَنْزَ الضُّعَفاءِ، يا عَظِيمَ الرَّجاءِ، يا مُنْقِذَ الْغَرْقَىٰ، يا مُنْجِيَ الْهَلْكَىٰ، يا مُمِيتَ الْأَحْياءِ، يا مُحْيِيَ الْمَوْتَىٰ

O Allah, I beseech You, O treasure of the weak, O worthy of great hopes, O saviour of the drowning, O deliverer of the perishing, O bringer of death to the living and quickener of the dead!

أَنْتَ اللهُ لا إِلٰهَ إِلَّا أَنْتَ، أَنْتَ الَّذِي سَجَدَ لَكَ شُعاعُ الشَّمْسِ، وَ دَوِيُّ الْماءِ، وَ حَفِيفُ الشَّجَرِ، وَ نُورُ الْقَمَرِ، وَ ظُلْمَةُ اللَّيْلِ، وَ ضَوْءُ النَّهارِ، وَ خَفَقانُ الطَّيْرِ

You are Allah, there is no god besides You! To You pay reverence the rays of the Sun, the roar of the waters, the rustling of the trees, the light of the moon, the darkness of the night, the radiance of the day and the fluttering of the birds.

فَأَسْأَلُكَ اللهُمَّ يا عَظِيمُ بِحَقِّكَ عَلىٰ مُحَمَّدٍ وَ آلِهِ الصَّادِقِينَ، وَ بِحَقِّ مُحَمَّدٍ وَ آلِهِ الصَّادِقِينَ عَلَيْكَ، وَ بِحَقِّكَ عَلىٰ عَلِيٍّ، وَ بِحَقِّ عَلِيٍّ عَلَيْكَ، وَ بِحَقِّكَ عَلىٰ فاطِمَةَ، وَ بِحَقِّ فاطِمَةَ عَلَيْكَ، وَ بِحَقِّكَ عَلَى الْحَسَنِ، وَ بِحَقِّ الْحَسَنِ عَلَيْكَ، وَ بِحَقِّكَ عَلَى الْحُسَيْنِ، وَ بِحَقِّ الْحُسَيْنِ عَلَيْكَ

O Allah, I beseech You, O Supreme One, by Your right on Muḥammad and the truthful Imams of his Family, and by the right that Muḥammad and the truthful ones of his Family have on You, by Your right on cAlī and by cAlī's right on You, by Your right on Fāṭimah and Fāṭimah's right on You, by Your right on al-Ḥasan and by al-Ḥasan's right on You, by Your right on al-Ḥusayn and by al-Ḥusayn's right on You,

فَإِنَّ حُقُوقَهُمْ عَلَيْكَ مِنْ أَفْضَلِ إِنْعامِكَ عَلَيْهِمْ، وَ بِالشَّأْنِ الَّذِي لَكَ عِنْدَهُمْ، وَ بِالشَّأْنِ الَّذِي لَهُمْ عِنْدَكَ، صَلِّ عَلَيْهِمْ يا رَبِّ صَلاةً دائِمَةً مُنْتَهَىٰ رِضاكَ

for indeed their rights on You are the best of Your blessings You have granted them! And by the station You have with them, and by the station they have with You, I beseech You to bless them, O Lord, with an everlasting blessing to an extent that will please You.

وَ اغْفِرْ لِي بِهِمُ الذُّنُوبَ الَّتِي بَيْنِي وَ بَيْنَكَ، وَ أَرْضِ عَنِّي خَلْقَكَ، وَ أَتْمِمْ عَلَيَّ نِعْمَتَكَ كَمَا أَتْمَمْتَهَا عَلَىٰ آبَائِي مِنْ قَبْلُ، وَ لاَ تَجْعَلْ لِأَحَدٍ مِنَ الْمَخْلُوقِينَ عَلَيَّ فِيهَا امْتِنَانًا، وَ امْنُنْ عَلَيَّ كَمَا مَنَنْتَ عَلَىٰ آبَائِي مِنْ قَبْلُ، يَا كهيعص

For their sake, forgive me the sins that intervene between me and You! Reconcile Your creatures with me and complete Your blessing upon me, inasmuch as You completed for my ancestors before, and do not allow these blessings to be marred by favours from any of the creatures. Favour me as You have favoured my ancestors before,

اَللّٰهُمَّ كَمَا صَلَّيْتَ عَلَىٰ مُحَمَّدٍ وَ آلِهِ، فَاسْتَجِبْ لِي دُعَائِي فِيمَا سَأَلْتُ يَا كَرِيمُ يَا كَرِيمُ يَا كَرِيمُ

O Allah, inasmuch as You have blessed Muḥammad and his Family, answer my petition about what I have asked You, O Munificent One, O Munificent One, O Munificent One! Then make prostration, and say while prostrating,

يَا مَنْ يَقْدِرُ عَلَىٰ حَوَائِجِ السَّائِلِينَ، وَ يَعْلَمُ مَا فِي ضَمِيرِ الصَّامِتِينَ، يَا مَنْ لاَ يَحْتَاجُ إِلَى التَّفْسِيرِ، يَا مَنْ يَعْلَمُ خَائِنَةَ الْأَعْيُنِ وَ مَا تُخْفِي الصُّدُورُ

O You who are able to grant the requests of all petitioners and know what is in the hearts of those who are mute! O You, who need no explanation! O You who know treacherous glances of the eyes and secrets concealed in the breasts!

يَا مَنْ أَنْزَلَ الْعَذَابَ عَلَىٰ قَوْمِ يُونُسَ، وَ هُوَ يُرِيدُ أَنْ يُعَذِّبَهُمْ فَدَعَوْهُ وَ تَضَرَّعُوا إِلَيْهِ فَكَشَفَ عَنْهُمُ الْعَذَابَ، وَ مَتَّعَهُمْ إِلَىٰ حِينٍ، قَدْ تَرَىٰ مَكَانِي، وَ تَسْمَعُ دُعَائِي، وَ تَعْلَمُ سِرِّي وَ عَلاَنِيَتِي وَ حَالِي

O You who sent down punishment on the people of Jonah, desiring to punish them, whereat they called You and entreated You, whereupon You removed their punishment and provided them for a while! You see my place and hear my call, knowing my private and public matters and my state!

صَلِّ عَلَىٰ مُحَمَّدٍ وَ آلِ مُحَمَّدٍ، وَ اكْفِنِي مَا أَهَمَّنِي مِنْ أَمْرِ دِينِي وَ دُنْيَايَ وَ آخِرَتِي يَا سَيِّدِي

Bless Muḥammad and the Family of Muḥammad and suffice me with regard to all that is of concern to me in relation to my faith, my life in the world and the Hereafter, O my Master! Repeat the phrase "Yā sayyidī" seventy times.

Then, rising from prostration, say,

يَا رَبِّ أَسْأَلُكَ بَرَكَةَ هٰذَا الْمَوْضِعِ، وَ بَرَكَةَ أَهْلِهِ، وَ أَسْأَلُكَ أَنْ تَرْزُقَنِي مِنْ رِزْقِكَ رِزْقًا حَلاَلًا طَيِّبًا
تَسُوقُهُ إِلَيَّ بِحَوْلِكَ وَ قُوَّتِكَ، وَ أَنَا خَائِضٌ فِي عَافِيَةٍ، يَا أَرْحَمَ الرَّاحِمِينَ

O Lord! I beseech You to grant me the barakah of this place and the barakah of its worthies. I beseech You to provide me with Your lawful and pure provision that You cater to me with Your power and might, while I continue to dwell in well-being, O Most Merciful of the merciful!

After this supplication and before saying the above-mentioned supplication "Yā man yaqdiru 'alā ḥawā'ij..." in the state of prostration, one should say the following supplication.

اَللّٰهُمَّ إِنَّكَ تَعْلَمُ وَ لاَ أَعْلَمُ، وَ تَقْدِرُ وَ لاَ أَقْدِرُ، وَ أَنْتَ عَلاَّمُ الْغُيُوبِ، صَلِّ اللّٰهُمَّ عَلَىٰ مُحَمَّدٍ وَ آلِ
مُحَمَّدٍ، وَ اغْفِرْ لِي وَ ارْحَمْنِي وَ تَجَاوَزْ عَنِّي وَ تَصَدَّقْ عَلَيَّ مَا أَنْتَ أَهْلُهُ، يَا أَرْحَمَ الرَّاحِمِينَ

O Allah, You know and I do not know. You ordain and I do not. You are the knower of all the Unseen. Bless Muḥammad and the Family of Muḥammad and forgive me, have mercy on me, and overlook my faults, and grant me that which is worthy of You, O Most Merciful of the merciful!

It is to be noted that there are many reports concerning the virtues of this pillar. Shaykh Kulaynī reports with a reliable chain of authorities that the Commander of the Faithful ('a) used to offer prayers facing this pillar, standing close to it. It is mentioned in a reliable report that every night 60,000 angels descend from the heaven to offer prayers at the seventh pillar. This happens every night and will go on till the day of judgement, without any of the angels ever returning. According to another reliable tradition, Imam Ja'far al-Ṣādiq ('a) is reported to have held that the seventh pillar is the station of Abraham ('a).

Shaykh Kulaynī in Kāfī has cited a report with a ṣāḥīḥ chain of authorities from Abū Ismā'īl al-Sarrāj, from Mu'āwiyah b. Wahb, from Abū Ḥamzah al-Thumālī, from Aṣbagh b. Nubātah that Aṣbagh took Abū Ḥamzah's hand and while pointing to the seventh pillar said, "This pillar is the station of the Commander of the Faithful ('a), where he used to pray. Imam al-Ḥasan ('a) used to pray by the fifth pillar. At times, when the Commander of the Faithful was not present, he would offer prayers in the latter's place, and it is near Bāb Kindah."

The Fifth Pillar

Among the distinguished spots in the Mosque of Kūfah is the fifth pillar, where the pilgrim should offer prayer and supplicate God Almighty to grant his petitions. It is mentioned in reliable reports that this was the place where the Prophet Abraham, the Friend of the All-beneficent, used to pray, and this is not contrary to the other reports, for it is possible that he used to offer prayers in all these spots. In a reliable report Imam Ja'far al-Ṣādiq ('a) is quoted as having said that the fifth pillar is the station of Gabriel ('a), while according to the above-mentioned report it is also the station of Imam al-Ḥasan ('a). That which can be inferred from the reports is that the spots near the fifth and the seventh pillar are the more meritorious locations of this mosque.

One should offer near the fifth pillar two rak'ahs, with al-Fātiḥah and any other sūrah, and after salām and tasbīḥ say,

اَللّٰهُمَّ إِنِّي أَسْأَلُكَ بِجَمِيعِ أَسْمَائِكَ كُلِّهَا، مَا عَلِمْنَا مِنْهَا وَ مَا لاٰ نَعْلَمُ، وَ أَسْأَلُكَ بِاسْمِكَ الْعَظِيمِ الْأَعْظَمِ الْكَبِيرِ الْأَكْبَرِ الَّذِي مَنْ دَعَاكَ بِهِ أَجَبْتَهُ، وَ مَنْ سَأَلَكَ بِهِ أَعْطَيْتَهُ

O Allah, I beseech You by all Your Names—those that we know and those we do not—and I beseech You by Your great and supreme Name, the greatest and the supreme most, when someone invokes You by it You answer him, when someone requests You by it You grant him,

وَ مَنِ اسْتَنْصَرَكَ بِهِ نَصَرْتَهُ، وَ مَنِ اسْتَغْفَرَكَ بِهِ غَفَرْتَ لَهُ، وَ مَنِ اسْتَعَانَكَ بِهِ أَعَنْتَهُ، وَ مَنِ اسْتَرْزَقَكَ بِهِ رَزَقْتَهُ، وَ مَنِ اسْتَغَاثَكَ بِهِ أَغَثْتَهُ، وَ مَنِ اسْتَرْحَمَكَ بِهِ رَحِمْتَهُ

when someone seeks Your help by it You help him, when someone pleads for Your pardon by it You forgive him, when someone seeks Your aid by it You assist him, when someone appeals to You by it for Your provision You provide him, when someone implores You by it for succour You succour him, and when someone beseeches Your mercy by it You have mercy on him,

وَ مَنِ اسْتَجَارَكَ بِهِ أَجَرْتَهُ، وَ مَنْ تَوَكَّلَ عَلَيْكَ بِهِ كَفَيْتَهُ، وَ مَنِ اسْتَعْصَمَكَ بِهِ عَصَمْتَهُ، وَ مَنِ اسْتَنْقَذَكَ بِهِ مِنَ النَّارِ أَنْقَذْتَهُ

when someone seeks refuge with You by it You shelter him, when someone relies upon You by it You suffice him, when someone seeks

Your protection by it You protect him, when someone entreats You by it to be saved from the Fire You deliver him,

،وَ مَنِ اسْتَعْطَفَكَ بِهِ تَعَطَّفْتَ لَهُ، وَ مَنْ أَمَّلَكَ بِهِ أَعْطَيْتَهُ، اَلَّذِي اتَّخَذْتَ بِهِ آدَمَ صَفِيًّا، وَ نُوحًا نَجِيًّا وَ إِبْرَاهِيمَ خَلِيلًا، وَ مُوسَىٰ كَلِيمًا وَ عِيسَىٰ رُوحًا، وَ مُحَمَّدًا حَبِيبًا، وَ عَلِيًّا وَصِيًّ صَلَّى اللهُ عَلَيْهِمْ أَجْمَعِينَ، أَنْ تَقْضِيَ لِي حَوَائِجِي

when someone pleads for Your kindness by it You are gentle to him, when someone pins his hope on You by it You grant him—Your Name by virtue of which You made Adam Your chosen one, Noah Your confidant, Abraham Your dedicated friend, Moses Your interlocutor, Jesus Your spirit, and Muḥammad Your beloved, cAlī his legatee, may Allah bless them all, to fulfil my needs,

وَ تَعْفُوَ عَمَّا سَلَفَ مِنْ ذُنُوبِي، وَ تَتَفَضَّلَ عَلَيَّ بِمَا أَنْتَ أَهْلُهُ، وَ لِجَمِيعِ الْمُؤْمِنِينَ وَ الْمُؤْمِنَاتِ لِلدُّنْيَا وَ الْآخِرَةِ، يَا مُفَرِّجَ هَمِّ الْمَهْمُومِينَ، وَ يَا غِيَاثَ الْمَلْهُوفِينَ، لَا إِلٰهَ إِلَّا أَنْتَ، سُبْحَانَكَ يَا رَبَّ الْعَالَمِينَ

to forgive my past sins, to grant me that which is worthy of You and to do the same for all the faithful, men and women, in the life of the world and the Hereafter, O Reliever of the worries of the anguished, O Succourer of the aggrieved, there is no god besides You, glory be to You, O Lord of all the worlds!

The Third Pillar at the Station of Imam Zayn al-'Ābidīn ('a)

Two rak'ahs are to be offered here with al-Fātiḥah and some other sūrah, and after salām and tasbīḥ one should say,

بِسْمِ اللهِ الرَّحْمٰنِ الرَّحِيمِ، اَللّٰهُمَّ إِنَّ ذُنُوبِي قَدْ كَثُرَتْ وَ لَمْ يَبْقَ لَهَا إِلَّا رَجَاءُ عَفْوِكَ، وَ قَدْ قَدَّمْتُ آلَةَ الْحِرْمَانِ إِلَيْكَ، فَأَنَا أَسْأَلُكَ اللّٰهُمَّ مَا لَا أَسْتَوْجِبُهُ، وَ أَطْلُبُ مِنْكَ مَا لَا أَسْتَحِقُّهُ

In the Name of Allah, the All-beneficent, the all-Merciful. O Allah, my sins are indeed numerous, and they have left me with no option except to pin hopes on Your pardon, though I have already made myself deserve its denial. O Allah, I ask of You what I deserve not and seek from You what I merit not.

اَللّٰهُمَّ إِنْ تُعَذِّبْنِي فَبِذُنُوبِي وَ لَمْ تَظْلِمْنِي شَيْئًا، وَ إِنْ تَغْفِرْ لِي فَخَيْرُ رَاحِمٍ أَنْتَ يَا سَيِّدِي

O Allah, if You punish me for my sins, it will not be unjust of You, and if You forgive me, You are indeed the best of the merciful, O my Master!

اَللّٰهُمَّ أَنْتَ أَنْتَ وَ أَنَا أَنَا، أَنْتَ الْعَوَّادُ بِالْمَغْفِرَةِ، وَ أَنَا الْعَوَّادُ بِالذُّنُوبِ، وَ أَنْتَ الْمُتَفَضِّلُ بِالْحِلْمِ، وَ أَنَا الْعَوَّادُ بِالْجَهْلِ

O Allah, You are You and I am I! You keep on turning to me with pardon, and I keep on reverting to sin! You go one being gracious out of Your forbearance and I keep on regressing out of my ignorance!

اَللّٰهُمَّ فَإِنِّي أَسْأَلُكَ يَا كَنْزَ الضُّعَفَاءِ، يَا عَظِيمَ الرَّجَاءِ، يَا مُنْقِذَ الْغَرْقَىٰ، يَا مُنْجِيَ الْهَلْكَىٰ، يَا مُمِيتَ الْأَحْيَاءِ؛ يَا مُحْيِيَ الْمَوْتَىٰ، أَنْتَ اللهُ الَّذِي لَا إِلٰهَ إِلَّا أَنْتَ، أَنْتَ الَّذِي سَجَدَ لَكَ شُعَاعُ الشَّمْسِ، وَ نُورُ الْقَمَرِ، وَ ظُلْمَةُ اللَّيْلِ، وَ ضَوْءُ النَّهَارِ، وَ خَفَقَانُ الطَّيْرِ

O Allah, I beseech You, O treasure of the weak, O worthy of great hopes, O rescuer of the drowning, O deliverer of the doomed, O bringer of death to the living and quickener of the dead! You are Allah, there is no god besides You, to You pay reverence the rays of the sun, the roar of the waters, the rustling of the trees, the light of the moon, the darkness of the night, the radiance of the day and the fluttering of the birds.

فَأَسْأَلُكَ اللهُمَّ يَا عَظِيمُ بِحَقِّكَ يَا كَرِيمُ عَلَىٰ مُحَمَّدٍ وَ آلِهِ الصَّادِقِينَ، وَ بِحَقِّ مُحَمَّدٍ وَ آلِهِ الصَّادِقِينَ عَلَيْكَ

O Allah, I beseech You, O Supreme One, O Munificent One, by Your right on Muḥammad and the truthful ones of his Family, and by the right of Muḥammad and the truthful ones of his Family on You,

وَ بِحَقِّكَ عَلَىٰ عَلِيٍّ، وَ بِحَقِّ عَلِيٍّ عَلَيْكَ، وَ بِحَقِّكَ عَلَىٰ فَاطِمَةَ، وَ بِحَقِّ فَاطِمَةَ عَلَيْكَ، وَ بِحَقِّكَ عَلَى الْحَسَنِ، وَ بِحَقِّ الْحَسَنِ عَلَيْكَ، وَ بِحَقِّكَ عَلَى الْحُسَيْنِ، وَ بِحَقِّ الْحُسَيْنِ عَلَيْكَ، فَإِنَّ حُقُوقَهُمْ مِنْ أَفْضَلِ إِنْعَامِكَ عَلَيْهِمْ، وَ بِالشَّأْنِ الَّذِي لَكَ عِنْدَهُمْ

by Your right on cAlī and by the right of cAlī on You, by Your right on Fāṭimah and the right of Fāṭimah on You, by Your right on al-Ḥasan and by the right of al-Ḥasan on You, by Your right on al-Ḥusayn and by the right of al-Ḥusayn on You, for indeed their rights on You are the best of blessings You have granted them.

وَ بِالشَّأْنِ الَّذِي لَهُمْ عِنْدَكَ، صَلِّ يَا رَبِّ عَلَيْهِمْ صَلَاةً دَائِمَةً مُنْتَهَى رِضَاكَ، وَ اغْفِرْ لِي بِهِمُ الذُّنُوبَ الَّتِي بَيْنِي وَ بَيْنَكَ، وَ أَتْمِمْ نِعْمَتَكَ عَلَيَّ كَمَا أَتْمَمْتَهَا عَلَىٰ آبَائِي مِنْ قَبْلُ، يَا كٓهٰيٰعٓصٓ

And I beseech You by the station You have with them, and by the station they have with You, to bless them, O Lord, with an everlasting blessing, to the extent that will please You, and forgive, for their sake, my sins that intervene between me and You, and complete Your blessing on me, inasmuch as You completed for my ancestors before, O Kāf-Hā-Yā-cAyn-Ṣād!

اَللّٰهُمَّ كَمَا صَلَّيْتَ عَلٰى مُحَمَّدٍ وَ آلِ مُحَمَّدٍ، فَاسْتَجِبْ لِي دُعَائِي فِيمَا سَأَلْتُكَ

O Allah, inasmuch as You have blessed Muḥammad and his Family, answer my petition with regard to what I have asked You.

Then make prostration and, laying the right cheek on the ground, say,

يَا سَيِّدِي يَا سَيِّدِي يَا سَيِّدِي، صَلِّ عَلٰى مُحَمَّدٍ وَ آلِ مُحَمَّدٍ، وَ اغْفِرْ لِي وَ اغْفِرْ لِي وَ اغْفِرْ لِي

O my Master! O my Master! O my Master! Bless Muḥammad and the Family of Muḥammad, and forgive me! Forgive me! Forgive me! Repeat these words several times in a state of tearful humility. Then laying the left cheek on the ground, say these words again repeatedly \and make any petition you want.

The Mosque's Visitors

Some popular and unreliable compilations mention an observance to be performed here. However, that observance, taught by Imam Ja'far al-Ṣādiq ('a) to one of his companions, is not limited to this spot.

The manner of its performance, as taught by the Imam to a companion, is mentioned in a report. The Imam is reported to have asked him, "Don't you pass by the great mosque of Kūfah while going out for work in the mornings?" "I do," he replied. The Imam said, "Offer four rak'ahs in that mosque and after the prayer say,

إِلَهِي إِنْ كُنْتُ قَدْ عَصَيْتُكَ فَإِنِّي قَدْ أَطَعْتُكَ فِي أَحَبِّ الْأَشْيَاءِ إِلَيْكَ، لَمْ أَتَّخِذْ لَكَ وَلَدًا، وَ لَمْ أَدْعُ لَكَ شَرِيكًا، وَ قَدْ عَصَيْتُكَ فِي أَشْيَاءَ كَثِيرَةٍ عَلٰى غَيْرِ وَجْهِ الْمُكَابَرَةِ لَكَ، وَ لَا الْإِسْتِكْبَارِ عَنْ عِبَادَتِكَ، وَ لَا الْجُحُودِ لِرُبُوبِيَّتِكَ، وَ لَا الْخُرُوجِ عَنِ الْعُبُودِيَّةِ لَكَ

My God, even if I have disobeyed You, I have obeyed You with regard to something which is dearest of things in Your eyes: I did not ascribe any child to You nor any partner. Although I have sinned against You with regard to many things, that was not due to insolence on my behalf, nor caused by an arrogant attitude towards Your worship, nor meant as a denial of Your Lordship, nor due to renunciation of my servanthood.

وَ لٰكِنِ اتَّبَعْتُ هَوَايَ، وَ أَزَلَّنِيَ الشَّيْطَانُ بَعْدَ الْحُجَّةِ وَ الْبَيَانِ، فَإِنْ تُعَذِّبْنِي فَبِذُنُوبِي غَيْرَ ظَالِمٍ أَنْتَ لِي، وَ إِنْ تَعْفُ عَنِّي وَ تَرْحَمْنِي فَبِجُودِكَ وَ كَرَمِكَ يَا كَرِيمُ

Rather, I followed my desire and Satan made me stumble, after Your teaching had left me no room for any excuse! Hence if You punish me for my sins, that will not be unjust, and if You pardon me and have mercy on me, that will be on account of Your generosity and magnanimity, O Munificent One! Also say,

غَدَوْتُ بِحَوْلِ اللهِ وَ قُوَّتِهِ، غَدَوْتُ بِغَيْرِ حَوْلٍ مِنِّي وَ لاَ قُوَّةٍ وَ لٰكِنْ بِحَوْلِ اللهِ وَ قُوَّتِهِ، يَا رَبِّ أَسْأَلُكَ بَرَكَةَ هٰذَا الْبَيْتِ وَ بَرَكَةَ أَهْلِهِ، وَ أَسْأَلُكَ أَنْ تَرْزُقَنِي رِزْقًا حَلاَلاً طَيِّبًا تَسُوقُهُ إِلَيَّ بِحَوْلِكَ وَ قُوَّتِكَ، وَ أَنَا خَائِضٌ فِي عَافِيَتِكَ

I rise in the morning with Allah's power and His might. I rise in the morning, not by my own power and strength, but by the power and might of Allah. O Lord, I beseech You to grant me the barakah of this house and the barakah of its worthies. I beseech You to provide me with Your lawful and pure provision that You cater to me with Your power and might while I continue to dwell in Your gift of well-being!

In a reliable report, Abū Ḥamzah al-Thumālī says, "One day, as I sat in the Mosque of Kūfah, I saw a man enter through the Bāb Kindah. He was the handsomest of men and well-dressed. A most pleasant fragrance hung around him. He had a turban on his head and wore a shirt and a gown. There were Arab shoes in his feet, which he removed as he approached the seventh pillar. While standing, he raised his hands to the ears and said the takbīr in a manner which made my hair stand and filled me with a feeling of awe. Then he offered four rak'ahs of prayer, performing the kneelings and prostrations in the worthiest manner. Then he recited the supplication Ilāhî in kuntu qad 'aṣaytuk... until he reached the words Yā karīm. Then he prostrated as he repeated the words Yā karīm as many times as he could in a single breath. Then, while still prostrating, he said the supplication Yā man yaqdiru ḥawâ'ijis sâ'ilīn... followed by Yā sayyidī! seventy times."

These supplications were cited above in the observance of the seventh pillar. Abū Ḥamzah says, "When he raised his head, I recognized him. It was 'Alī ibn al-Ḥusayn. I kissed his hands and asked him, 'What has brought you here?' The Imam replied, 'I came for what you saw me doing.' " That is, for prayer in the Mosque of Kūfah.

Bāb al-Faraj, or the Station of Noah

After finishing the observance of the third pillar, proceed towards the bench at Bāb Amīr al-Mu'minīn ('a), which is a platform next to the door of the mosque that used to open toward the house of the Commander of the Faithful ('a).

Offer four rak'ahs there with al-Fātiḥah and any other sūrah, and after the tasbīḥ say,

اَللّٰهُمَّ صَلِّ عَلىٰ مُحَمَّدٍ وَ آلِ مُحَمَّدٍ، وَ اقْضِ حَاجَتِي يَا اللهُ، يَا مَنْ لاٰ يَخِيبُ سَائِلُهُ، وَ لاٰ يَنْفَدُ
نَائِلُهُ، يَا قَاضِيَ الْحَاجَاتِ، يَا مُجِيبَ الدَّعَوَاتِ، يَا رَبَّ الْأَرَضِينَ وَ السَّمَاوَاتِ، يَا كَاشِفَ الْكُرُبَاتِ،
يَا وَاسِعَ الْعَطِيَّاتِ

O Allah, bless Muḥammad and the Family of Muḥammad, and fulfil my need! O Allah, You don't disappoint those who ask You, nor are Your gifts ever exhausted. O fulfiller of needs, O answerer of supplications, O Lord of the heavens and the earths, O remover of distress, O bounteous giver of gifts,

يَا دَافِعَ النَّقِمَاتِ، يَا مُبَدِّلَ السَّيِّئَاتِ حَسَنَاتٍ، عُدْ عَلَيَّ بِطَوْلِكَ وَ فَضْلِكَ وَ إِحْسَانِكَ، وَ اسْتَجِبْ
دُعَائِي فِيمَا سَأَلْتُكَ وَ طَلَبْتُ مِنْكَ، بِحَقِّ نَبِيِّكَ وَ وَصِيِّكَ وَ أَوْلِيَائِكَ الصَّالِحِينَ

O repeller of adversities, O changer of vices into virtues, turn to me with Your bounteousness, grace and beneficence, and grant my petition concerning things that I ask You and beseech You for, by the right of Your Prophet, Your vicegerent and Your righteous awliyā!

Another Prayer at this Place Another observance for this station is a two-rak'ah prayer. After the prayer and tasbīḥ, say,

اَللّٰهُمَّ إِنِّي حَلَلْتُ بِسَاحَتِكَ لِعِلْمِي بِوَحْدَانِيَّتِكَ وَ صَمَدَانِيَّتِكَ، وَ أَنَّهُ لاٰ قَادِرَ عَلىٰ قَضَاءِ حَاجَتِي غَيْرُكَ،
وَ قَدْ عَلِمْتُ يَا رَبِّ أَنَّهُ كُلَّمَا شَاهَدْتُ نِعْمَتَكَ عَلَيَّ اشْتَدَّتْ فَاقَتِي إِلَيْكَ

O Allah, I have alighted in Your courtyard because of my knowledge that You are One and All-embracing, and that no one except You has the ability to fulfil my need. I know, my Lord, that whenever I have watched Your blessings on me, my need for You has become more intense!

وَ قَدْ طَرَقَنِي يَا رَبِّ مِنْ مُهِمِّ أَمْرِي مَا قَدْ عَرَفْتَهُ، لِأَنَّكَ عَالِمٌ غَيْرُ مُعَلَّمٍ

My Lord, a crucial matter has befallen me, as You know, for You know without anyone informing You!

وَ أَسْأَلُكَ بِالْإِسْمِ الَّذِي وَضَعْتَهُ عَلَى السَّمَاوَاتِ فَانْشَقَّتْ، وَ عَلَى الْأَرَضِينَ فَانْبَسَطَتْ، وَ عَلَى النُّجُومِ فَانْتَشَرَتْ، وَ عَلَى الْجِبَالِ فَاسْتَقَرَّتْ

I beseech You by Your Name which made the heavens split when set on them, and spread out the earths, dispersed the stars and stabilized the mountains when set on them.

وَ أَسْأَلُكَ بِالْإِسْمِ الَّذِي جَعَلْتَهُ عِنْدَ مُحَمَّدٍ وَ عِنْدَ عَلِيٍّ وَ عِنْدَ الْحَسَنِ وَ عِنْدَ الْحُسَيْنِ وَ عِنْدَ الْأَئِمَّةِ كُلِّهِمْ صَلَوَاتُ اللهِ عَلَيْهِمْ أَجْمَعِينَ، أَنْ تُصَلِّيَ عَلَىٰ مُحَمَّدٍ وَ آلِ مُحَمَّدٍ، وَ أَنْ تَقْضِيَ لِي يَا رَبِّ حَاجَتِي، وَ تُيَسِّرَ عَسِيرَهَا، وَ تَكْفِيَنِي مُهِمَّهَا

I beseech You by the Name which You committed to Muḥammad, to cAlī, to al-Ḥasan, al-Ḥusayn and all the Imams, may Your blessings be upon them all, to bless Muḥammad and the Family of Muḥammad and to fulfil, my Lord, my need, remove its difficulty, and suffice me in getting through its ponderous part.

،وَ تَفْتَحَ لِي قُفْلَهَا، فَإِنْ فَعَلْتَ ذٰلِكَ فَلَكَ الْحَمْدُ، وَ إِنْ لَمْ تَفْعَلْ فَلَكَ الْحَمْدُ، غَيْرَ جَائِرٍ فِي حُكْمِكَ وَ لَا حَائِفٍ فِي عَدْلِكَ

Open for me its lock, for if You do, You are worthy of gratitude and praise, and if You do not, You are still worthy of gratitude and praise, for You are neither unjust in Your judgements nor unfair in dispensing justice!

Then laying the right side of your face on the ground say,

اَللّٰهُمَّ إِنَّ يُونُسَ بْنَ مَتّٰى عَبْدَكَ وَ نَبِيَّكَ دَعَاكَ فِي بَطْنِ الْحُوتِ فَاسْتَجَبْتَ لَهُ، وَ أَنَا أَدْعُوكَ فَاسْتَجِبْ لِي بِحَقِّ مُحَمَّدٍ وَ آلِ مُحَمَّدٍ

O Allah, Jonah son of Matthew, Your servant and prophet, supplicated You in the fish's belly, whereupon You answered him, and I supplicate You so answer me by the right of Muḥammad and the Family of Muḥammad!

Then supplicate for whatever need you may have. Then laying the left side of the face on the ground say,

اَللّٰهُمَّ إِنَّكَ أَمَرْتَ بِالدُّعَاءِ، وَ تَكَفَّلْتَ بِالْإِجَابَةِ، وَ أَنَا أَدْعُوكَ كَمَا أَمَرْتَنِي، فَصَلِّ عَلىٰ مُحَمَّدٍ وَ آلِ مُحَمَّدٍ، وَ اسْتَجِبْ لِي كَمَا وَعَدْتَنِي يَا كَرِيمُ

O Allah, You have commanded Your servants to supplicate and promised to answer them. I supplicate to You as You have commanded me, so bless Muḥammad and the Family of Muḥammad and answer me as You have promised, O Munificent One! Then laying your forehead on the ground, say,

يَا مُعِزَّ كُلِّ ذَلِيلٍ، وَ يَا مُذِلَّ كُلِّ عَزِيزٍ، تَعْلَمُ كُرْبَتِي، فَصَلِّ عَلىٰ مُحَمَّدٍ وَ آلِهِ، وَ فَرِّجْ عَنِّي يَا كَرِيمُ

O giver of might and honour to the weak and the abased! O humbler of the mighty, You know my distress. So bless Muḥammad and his Family and grant me relief, O Munificent One! A Prayer for Need at this Place This prayer consists of four rak'ahs. After the prayer and tasbīḥ, say,

اَللّٰهُمَّ إِنِّي أَسْأَلُكَ يَا مَنْ لاٰ تَرَاهُ الْعُيُونُ، وَ لاٰ تُحِيطُ بِهِ الظُّنُونُ، وَ لاٰ يَصِفُهُ الْوَاصِفُونَوَ لاٰ تُغَيِّرُهُ الْحَوَادِثُ، وَ لاٰ تُفْنِيهِ الدُّهُورُ

O Allah, I beseech You! O You who are neither seen by the eyes, nor comprehended by the minds, whom describers cannot describe, whom events cannot change, and ages cannot annihilate!

تَعْلَمُ مَثَاقِيلَ الْجِبَالِ، وَ مَكَائِيلَ الْبِحَارِ، وَ وَرَقَ الْأَشْجَارِ، وَ رَمْلَ الْقِفَارِ، وَ مَا أَضَاءَتْ بِهِ الشَّمْسُ وَ الْقَمَرُ، وَ أَظْلَمَ عَلَيْهِ اللَّيْلُ، وَ وَضَحَ عَلَيْهِ النَّهَارُ، وَ لاٰ تُوَارِي مِنْكَ سَمَاءٌ سَمَاءً، وَ لاٰ أَرْضٌ أَرْضًا، وَ لاٰ جَبَلٌ مَا فِي أَصْلِهِ، وَ لاٰ بَحْرٌ مَا فِي قَعْرِهِ

You know the weights of the mountains, the measures of the seas, the leaves of the trees and the sands of the deserts, and all that over which the sun and the moon shine, all that the night covers in darkness and the day illuminates! One heaven does not conceal another heaven from You, nor one earth another, nor does the mountains hide what lies at their roots, nor the oceans what lies in their depths!

أَسْأَلُكَ أَنْ تُصَلِّيَ عَلىٰ مُحَمَّدٍ وَ آلِ مُحَمَّدٍ، وَ أَنْ تَجْعَلَ خَيْرَ أَمْرِي آخِرَهُ، وَ خَيْرَ أَعْمَالِي خَوَاتِيمَهَا وَ خَيْرَ أَيَّامِي يَوْمَ أَلْقَاكَ، إِنَّكَ عَلىٰ كُلِّ شَيْءٍ قَدِيرٌ

I beseech You to bless Muḥammad and the Family of Muḥammad and to make the final part of my life its best part, the best part of my conduct their motives, and the best of my days the day that I shall meet You! Indeed You have power over all things!

اَللّٰهُمَّ مَنْ أَرَادَنِي بِسُوءٍ فَأَرِدْهُ، وَ مَنْ كَادَنِي فَكِدْهُ، وَ مَنْ بَغَانِي بِهَلَكَةٍ فَأَهْلِكْهُ، وَ اكْفِنِي مَا أَهَمَّنِي مِمَّنْ دَخَلَ هَمُّهُ عَلَيَّ

O Allah, deter those who have evil intentions against me. Devise against those who plot against me. Destroy those who unjustly seek to destroy me. Take care of my concerns which cause me worry!

اَللّٰهُمَّ أَدْخِلْنِي فِي دِرْعِكَ الْحَصِينَةِ، وَ اسْتُرْنِي بِسِتْرِكَ الْوَاقِي، يَا مَنْ يَكْفِي مِنْ كُلِّ شَيْءٍ وَ لاَ يَكْفِي مِنْهُ شَيْءٌ، اِكْفِنِي مَا أَهَمَّنِي مِنْ أَمْرِ الدُّنْيَا وَ الْآخِرَةِ، وَ صَدِّقْ قَوْلِي وَ فِعْلِي، يَا شَفِيقُ يَا رَفِيقُ، فَرِّجْ عَنِّي الْمَضِيقَ، وَ لاَ تُحَمِّلْنِي مَا لاَ أُطِيقُ

O Allah, shelter me with Your secure shield and cover me with Your protective cover! O You who suffice against all things and against whom nothing can suffice! Suffice me with regard to my concerns pertaining to this world and the Hereafter and endorse my speech and conduct! O affectionate one, O gentle one, relieve me of the straits I am in and burden me not with what I cannot bear!

اَللّٰهُمَّ احْرُسْنِي بِعَيْنِكَ الَّتِي لاَ تَنَامُ، وَ ارْحَمْنِي بِقُدْرَتِكَ عَلَيَّ، يَا أَرْحَمَ الرَّاحِمِينَ، يَا عَلِيُّ يَا عَظِيمُ أَنْتَ عَالِمٌ بِحَاجَتِي، وَ عَلَىٰ قَضَائِهَا قَدِيرٌ، وَ هِيَ لَدَيْكَ يَسِيرٌ، وَ أَنَا إِلَيْكَ فَقِيرٌ، فَمُنَّ بِهَا عَلَيَّ يَا كَرِيمُ، إِنَّكَ عَلَىٰ كُلِّ شَيْءٍ قَدِيرٌ

O Allah, guard me with Your eye that does not sleep and have mercy on me with Your power over me, O Most Merciful of the merciful! O Exalted and Supreme One, You know my need and have the power to fulfil it, and it is simple for You, while I stand in need of You! So do me a favour by granting it, O Munificent One! Indeed You have power over all things!

Then make prostration and say,

إِلٰهِي قَدْ عَلِمْتَ حَوَائِجِي، فَصَلِّ عَلَىٰ مُحَمَّدٍ وَ آلِ مُحَمَّدٍ وَ اقْضِهَا، وَ قَدْ أَحْصَيْتَ ذُنُوبِي، فَصَلِّ عَلَىٰ مُحَمَّدٍ وَ آلِهِ وَ اغْفِرْهَا، يَا كَرِيمُ

My God, You know my needs, so bless Muḥammad and his Family and fulfil them! You know all my sins, so bless Muḥammad and his Family and forgive them, O Munificent One!

Then laying the right cheek on the ground say,

إِنْ كُنْتُ بِئْسَ الْعَبْدُ، فَأَنْتَ نِعْمَ الرَّبُّ، اِفْعَلْ بِي مَا أَنْتَ أَهْلُهُ، وَ لاَ تَفْعَلْ بِي مَا أَنَا أَهْلُهُ، يَا أَرْحَمَ الرَّاحِمِينَ

If I have been a bad servant, You have been an excellent Lord! Treat me as is worthy of You, not as I deserve, O Most Merciful of the merciful! Then laying the left cheek on the ground say,

اَللّٰهُمَّ إِنْ عَظُمَ الذَّنْبُ مِنْ عَبْدِكَ، فَلْيَحْسُنِ الْعَفْوُ مِنْ عِنْدِكَ يَا كَرِيمُ

O Allah, if the sins of this servant of Yours have been monstrous, Your forgiveness will indeed be gracious, O Munificent One!

Then laying your forehead on the ground say,

اِرْحَمْ مَنْ أَسَاءَ وَ اقْتَرَفَ، وَ اسْتَكَانَ وَ اعْتَرَفَ

Have mercy on me, who, having acted meanly and sinfully, entreats You and admits his sins!

This supplication, up to the words "Waghfirhā, yā karīm," is the same as the one prescribed in al-Mazār al-Qadīm for the observance pertaining to the station of Imam Zayn al-'Abidīn ('a) in the courtyard of the Sahlah Mosque.

The Niche of the Commander of the Faithful (a)

This is the place where the Commander of the Faithful ('a) was struck by the assassin's sword. The pilgrim performs a two-rak'ah prayer here with al-Fātiḥah and any sūrah. After salām and tasbīḥ say,

يَا مَنْ أَظْهَرَ الْجَمِيلَ وَ سَتَرَ الْقَبِيحَ، يَا مَنْ لَمْ يُؤَاخِذْ بِالْجَرِيرَةِ، وَ لَمْ يَهْتِكِ السِّتْرَ وَ السَّرِيرَةَ، يَا عَظِيمَ الْعَفْوِ، يَا حَسَنَ التَّجَاوُزِ، يَا وَاسِعَ الْمَغْفِرَةِ، يَا بَاسِطَ الْيَدَيْنِ بِالرَّحْمَةِ

O You who bring out all that is beautiful and cover up all that is ugly! O You who never take anyone to task for lapses of etiquette and do not expose hidden faults and secrets. O You whose clemency is great! O You who graciously overlook faults! O You whose forgiveness is immense! O You who have mercifully opened wide Your arms!

يٰا صَاحِبَ كُلِّ نَجْوَىٰ، يٰا مُنْتَهَىٰ كُلِّ شَكْوَىٰ، يٰا كَرِيمَ الصَّفْحِ، يٰا عَظِيمَ الرَّجَاءِ، يٰا سَيِّدِي صَلِّ عَلىٰ مُحَمَّدٍ وَ آلِ مُحَمَّدٍ، وَ افْعَلْ بِي مَا أَنْتَ أَهْلُهُ يٰا كَرِيمُ

O You who are companion to every secret discourse! O ultimate recourse of all complaints! O You who nobly overlook faults! O You in whom great hopes are placed! O my Master, bless Muḥammad and the Family of Muḥammad, and treat me as is worthy of You, O Munificent One! The Munajat of the Commander of the Faithful

اَللّٰهُمَّ إِنِّي أَسْأَلُكَ الْأَمَانَ يَوْمَ لاٰ يَنْفَعُ مَالٌ وَ لاٰ بَنُونَ إِلَّا مَنْ أَتَى اللهَ بِقَلْبٍ سَلِيمٍ

O Allah, I beseech You to spare me on the day when neither wealth nor children will avail, except him who comes to Allah with a sound heart. (26:88-89)

وَ أَسْأَلُكَ الْأَمَانَ يَوْمَ يَعَضُّ الظَّالِمُ عَلىٰ يَدَيْهِ يَقُولُ يٰا لَيْتَنِي اتَّخَذْتُ مَعَ الرَّسُولِ سَبِيلًا

I beseech You to spare me on the day when the wrongdoer will bite his hands, saying, 'I wish I had followed the Apostle's way!'(25:27)

وَ أَسْأَلُكَ الْأَمَانَ يَوْمَ يُعْرَفُ الْمُجْرِمُونَ بِسِيمَاهُمْ فَيُؤْخَذُ بِالنَّوَاصِي وَ الْأَقْدَامِ

I beseech You to spare me on the day when the guilty will be recognized by their mark; so they will be seized by the forelocks and the feet. (55:41)

وَ أَسْأَلُكَ الْأَمَانَ يَوْمَ لاٰ يَجْزِي وَالِدٌ عَنْ وَلَدِهِ، وَ لاٰ مَوْلُودٌ هُوَ جَازٍ عَنْ وَالِدِهِ شَيْئًا، إِنَّ وَعْدَ اللهِ حَقٌّ

I beseech You to spare me on the day— the day when a father shall not atone for his child, nor the child shall atone for its father in any wise. Indeed, Allah's promise is true. (31:33)

وَ أَسْأَلُكَ الْأَمَانَ يَوْمَ لاٰ يَنْفَعُ الظَّالِمِينَ مَعْذِرَتُهُمْ، وَ لَهُمُ اللَّعْنَةُ وَ لَهُمْ سُوءُ الدَّارِ

I beseech You to spare me on the day when the excuses of the wrongdoers will not benefit them, and the curse will lie on them, and for them will be the ills of the [ultimate] abode. (40:52)

وَ أَسْأَلُكَ الْأَمَانَ يَوْمَ لاٰ تَمْلِكُ نَفْسٌ لِنَفْسٍ شَيْئًا، وَ الْأَمْرُ يَوْمَئِذٍ لِلّٰهِ

I beseech You to spare me on the day when no soul will be of any avail to another soul and all command that day will belong to Allah.

وَ أَسْأَلُكَ الْأَمَانَ يَوْمَ يَفِرُّ الْمَرْءُ مِنْ أَخِيهِ، وَ أُمِّهِ وَ أَبِيهِ، وَ صَاحِبَتِهِ وَ بَنِيهِ، لِكُلِّ امْرِىءٍ مِنْهُمْ يَوْمَئِذٍ شَأْنٌ يُغْنِيهِ

I beseech You to spare me on the day when a man will evade his brother, his mother and father, his spouse and children—that day each of them will have a task to keep him preoccupied. (80:34-37)

وَ أَسْأَلُكَ الْأَمَانَ يَوْمَ يَوَدُّ الْمُجْرِمُ لَوْ يَفْتَدِي مِنْ عَذَابِ يَوْمِئِذٍ بِبَنِيهِ، وَ صَاحِبَتِهِ وَ أَخِيهِ، وَ فَصِيلَتِهِ الَّتِي تُؤْوِيهِ، وَ مَنْ فِي الْأَرْضِ جَمِيعًا ثُمَّ يُنْجِيهِ، كَلَّا إِنَّهَا لَظَى نَزَّاعَةً لِلشَّوَى

I beseech You to spare me on the day the guilty one will wish he could ransom himself from the punishment of that day at the price of his children, his spouse and his brother, his kin which had sheltered him and all those who are upon the earth, if that might deliver him. Never! Indeed it is a blazing fire, which strips away the scalp. (70:11-16)

مَوْلَايَ يَا مَوْلَايَ، أَنْتَ الْمَوْلَى وَ أَنَا الْعَبْدُ، وَ هَلْ يَرْحَمُ الْعَبْدَ إِلَّا الْمَوْلَى؟

My Master! O My Master! You are the Master and I am the servant. Will anyone but the Master have mercy on His servant?

مَوْلَايَ يَا مَوْلَايَ، أَنْتَ الْمَالِكُ وَ أَنَا الْمَمْلُوكُ، وَ هَلْ يَرْحَمُ الْمَمْلُوكَ إِلَّا الْمَالِكُ؟

My Master! O My Master! You are the Owner and I am Your slave. Will anyone have mercy on the slave except the Owner?

مَوْلَايَ يَا مَوْلَايَ، أَنْتَ الْعَزِيزُ وَ أَنَا الذَّلِيلُ، وَ هَلْ يَرْحَمُ الذَّلِيلَ إِلَّا الْعَزِيزُ؟

My Master! O My Master! You are the All-mighty and I am weak. Will anyone have mercy on someone who is weak except the All-mighty?

مَوْلَايَ يَا مَوْلَايَ، أَنْتَ الْخَالِقُ وَ أَنَا الْمَخْلُوقُ، وَ هَلْ يَرْحَمُ الْمَخْلُوقَ إِلَّا الْخَالِقُ؟

My Master! O My Master! You are the Creator and I am Your creature. Will anyone have mercy on the creature except the Creator?

مَوْلَايَ يَا مَوْلَايَ، أَنْتَ الْعَظِيمُ وَ أَنَا الْحَقِيرُ، وَ هَلْ يَرْحَمُ الْحَقِيرَ إِلَّا ا لْعَظِيمُ؟

My Master! O My Master! You are Supreme One and I am puny. Will anyone have mercy on the puny except the Supreme One?

مَوْلَايَ يَا مَوْلَايَ، أَنْتَ الْقَوِيُّ وَ أَنَا الضَّعِيفُ، وَ هَلْ يَرْحَمُ الضَّعِيفَ إِلَّا الْقَوِيُّ؟

My Master! O My Master! You are the All-strong and I am frail. Will anyone have mercy on the frail except the All-strong?

مَوْلَايَ يَا مَوْلَايَ، أَنْتَ الْغَنِيُّ وَ أَنَا الْفَقِيرُ، وَ هَلْ يَرْحَمُ الْفَقِيرَ إِلَّا الْغَنِيّ؟

My Master! O My Master! You are the All-sufficient and I am needy. Will anyone have mercy on the needy except the All-sufficient?

مَوْلَايَ يَا مَوْلَايَ، أَنْتَ الْمُعْطِي وَ أَنَا السَّائِلُ، وَ هَلْ يَرْحَمُ السَّائِلَ إِلَّا الْمُعْطِي؟

My Master! O My Master! You are the Giver and I am the beggar. Will anyone have mercy on the beggar except the Giver?

مَوْلَايَ يَا مَوْلَايَ، أَنْتَ الْحَيُّ وَ أَنَا الْمَيِّتُ، وَ هَلْ يَرْحَمُ الْمَيِّتَ إِلَّا الْحَيُّ؟

My Master! O My Master! You are the Living One and I am [essentially] devoid of life. Will anyone have mercy on the lifeless except the Living One?

مَوْلَايَ يَا مَوْلَايَ، أَنْتَ الْبَاقِي وَ أَنَا الْفَانِي، وَ هَلْ يَرْحَمُ الْفَانِيَ إِلَّا الْبَاقِي؟

My Master! O My Master! You are the Everlasting One and I am ephemeral. Will anyone have mercy on the ephemeral except the Everlasting One?

مَوْلَايَ يَا مَوْلَايَ، أَنْتَ الدَّائِمُ وَ أَنَا الزَّائِلُ، وَ هَلْ يَرْحَمُ الزَّائِلَ إِلَّا الدَّائِمُ؟

My Master! O My Master! You are the Eternal One and I am transitory. Will anyone except the Eternal One have mercy on one who is transitory?

مَوْلَايَ يَا مَوْلَايَ، أَنْتَ الرَّازِقُ وَ أَنَا الْمَرْزُوقُ، وَ هَلْ يَرْحَمُ الْمَرْزُوقَ إِلَّا الرَّازِقُ؟

My Master! O My Master! You are the All-provider and I am one who is provided. Will anyone except the All-provider have mercy on one who needs to be provided?

مَوْلَايَ يَا مَوْلَايَ، أَنْتَ الْجَوَادُ وَ أَنَا الْبَخِيلُ، وَ هَلْ يَرْحَمُ الْبَخِيلَ إِلَّا الْجَوَادُ؟

My Master! O My Master! You are the All-generous and I am the one who is stingy. Will anyone except the All-generous have mercy on one who is stingy?

مَوْلَايَ يَا مَوْلَايَ، أَنْتَ الْمُعَافِي وَ أَنَا الْمُبْتَلَىٰ، وَ هَلْ يَرْحَمُ الْمُبْتَلَىٰ إِلَّا الْمُعَافِي؟

My Master! O My Master! You are the All-healer and I am afflicted. Will anyone except the All-healer have mercy on one who is afflicted?

مَوْلَايَ يَا مَوْلَايَ، أَنْتَ الْكَبِيرُ وَ أَنَا الصَّغِيرُ، وَ هَلْ يَرْحَمُ الصَّغِيرَ إِلَّا الْكَبِيرُ؟

My Master! O My Master! You are the All-great and I am insignificant. Will anyone except the All-great have mercy on one who is small?

مَوْلَايَ يَا مَوْلَايَ، أَنْتَ الْهَادِي وَ أَنَا الضَّالُّ، وَ هَلْ يَرْحَمُ الضَّالَّ إِلَّا الْهَادِي ؟

My Master! O My Master! You are the Guide and I am the one who is astray. Will anyone except the Guide have mercy on the astray?

مَوْلَايَ يَا مَوْلَايَ، أَنْتَ الرَّحْمٰنُ وَ أَنَا الْمَرْحُومُ، وَ هَلْ يَرْحَمُ الْمَرْحُومَ إِلَّا الرَّحْمٰنُ ؟

My Master! O My Master! You are the All-beneficent and I am the one who stands in need of mercy. Will anyone except the All-beneficent have mercy on one who stands in need of mercy?

مَوْلَايَ يَا مَوْلَايَ، أَنْتَ السُّلْطَانُ وَ أَنَا الْمُمْتَحَنُ، وَ هَلْ يَرْحَمُ الْمُمْتَحَنَ إِلَّا السُّلْطَانُ ؟

My Master! O My Master! You are the Sovereign and I am the one in tribulation. Will anyone except the Sovereign have mercy on someone in tribulation?

مَوْلَايَ يَا مَوْلَايَ، أَنْتَ الدَّلِيلُ وَ أَنَا الْمُتَحَيِّرُ، وَ هَلْ يَرْحَمُ الْمُتَحَيِّرَ إِلَّا الدَّلِيلُ ؟

My Master! O My Master! You are the Guide and I am bewildered and lost. Will anyone except the Guide have mercy on the bewildered?

مَوْلَايَ يَا مَوْلَايَ، أَنْتَ الْغَفُورُ وَ أَنَا الْمُذْنِبُ، وَ هَلْ يَرْحَمُ الْمُذْنِبَ إِلَّا الْغَفُورُ ؟

My Master! O My Master! You are All-forgiving and I am the sinner. Will anyone except the All-forgiver have mercy on the sinner?

مَوْلَايَ يَا مَوْلَايَ، أَنْتَ الْغَالِبُ وَ أَنَا الْمَغْلُوبُ، وَ هَلْ يَرْحَمُ الْمَغْلُوبَ إِلَّا الْغَالِبُ ؟

My Master! O My Master! You are the All-prevailing and I am subdued. Will anyone except the All-prevailing have mercy on the subdued?

مَوْلَايَ يَا مَوْلَايَ، أَنْتَ الرَّبُّ وَ أَنَا الْمَرْبُوبُ، وَ هَلْ يَرْحَمُ الْمَرْبُوبَ إِلَّا الرَّبُّ ؟

My Master! O My Master! You are the Lord and I am the servant. Will anyone except the Lord have mercy on the servant?

مَوْلَايَ يَا مَوْلَايَ، أَنْتَ الْمُتَكَبِّرُ وَ أَنَا الْخَاشِعُ، وَ هَلْ يَرْحَمُ الْخَاشِعَ إِلَّا الْمُتَكَبِّرُ ؟

My Master! O My Master! You are the All-magnanimous Lord and I am Your submissive slave. Will anyone except the All-magnanimous Lord have mercy on His submissive slave?

مَوْلَايَ يَا مَوْلَايَ، اِرْحَمْنِي بِرَحْمَتِكَ، وَ ارْضَ عَنِّي بِجُودِكَ وَ كَرَمِكَ وَ فَضْلِكَ، يَا ذَا الْجُودِ وَ الْإِحْسَانِ، وَ الطَّوْلِ وَ الْإِمْتِنَانِ، بِرَحْمَتِكَ يَا أَرْحَمَ الرَّاحِمِينَ.

My Master! O My Master! Have mercy on me out of Your mercifulness, be pleased with me out of Your generosity, munificence and grace, O Munificent and Kind One, O All-bountiful dispenser of favours, by Your mercy, O Most Merciful of the merciful!

Sayyid Ibn Ṭāwūs has mentioned an elaborate supplication, known as Du'ā al-Amān, to be recited after this munājāt, not cited here for reasons of space. One may also recite here the sublime supplication that will be mentioned, God willing, in the observance pertaining to the Mosque of Zayd.

It should be noted that, as pointed out by us in Hadīyat al-Zā'irīn, there is a difference of opinion as to whether the niche where the Commander of the Faithful ('a) was struck by the assassin's sword is the same as the well-known niche, or the one which is not in use. Caution would suggest that one perform the observances of the niche at both the places, or in one of the two locations on alternate visits.

The Station of Imām al-Sādiq ('a)

The next observance to be performed is at the station of Imam al-Ṣādiq ('a) near the tomb of Muslim b. 'Aqīl, may God be pleased with him. One is to offer there two rak'ahs.

After salām and tasbīḥ say,

يٰا صَانِعَ كُلِّ مَصْنُوعٍ، وَ يٰا جَابِرَ كُلِّ كَسِيرٍ، وَ يٰا حَاضِرَ كُلِّ مَلَإٍ، وَ يٰا شَاهِدَ كُلِّ نَجْوَىٰ، وَ يٰا عَالِمَ كُلِّ خَفِيَّةٍ، وَ يٰا شَاهِدًا غَيْرَ غَائِبٍ، وَ يٰا غَالِبًا غَيْرَ مَغْلُوبٍ

O Maker of all things that are made, O Restorer of all broken beings to wholeness, O You who are present at every gathering, O Witness to all secret discourses, O Knower of all hidden things, O present one who is never absent, O Prevailer who is never subdued,

وَ يٰا قَرِيبًا غَيْرَ بَعِيدٍ، وَ يٰا مُونِسَ كُلِّ وَحِيدٍ، وَ يٰا حَيًّا حِينَ لاٰ حَيَّ غَيْرُهُ، يٰا مُحْيِيَ الْمَوْتَىٰ وَ مُمِيتَ الْأَحْيٰاءِ، اَلْقَائِمَ عَلىٰ كُلِّ نَفْسٍ بِمَا كَسَبَتْ، لاٰ إِلٰهَ إِلَّا أَنْتَ، صَلِّ عَلىٰ مُحَمَّدٍ وَ آلِ مُحَمَّدٍ

O Near One who is never far, O intimate friend of all who are lonely, O Living One who was living when there was no living being, O Giver of life to the lifeless and bringer of death to the living, O Sustainer of every soul despite what it earns, there is no god except You, bless Muḥammad and the Family of Muḥammad!

SAHLAH MOSQUE

The Virtues

After the Mosque of Kūfah there is no mosque in the region that equals the Sahlah Mosque in its merit. It is said to have been the home of the prophets Idrīs ('a) and Abraham ('a) and a place frequented by Khiḍr ('a). Imam Ja'far al-Ṣādiq ('a) is reported to have said to Abū Baṣīr, "O Abū Muḥammad, it is as if I already see the Master of the Era (i.e. the Twelfth Imam) taking up residence with his family in the Sahlah Mosque.

God Almighty has not sent any apostle without his having prayed in that mosque. Someone who stays in that mosque is like one who has tarried in the tent of the Apostle of Allah (ṣ). There is no faithful person, man or woman, whose heart does not long to visit that mosque. There is a rock in that mosque bearing portraits of the prophets. No one makes prayer in that mosque and supplicates with a genuine motive without going back with his petition answered. No one who prays for safety in that mosque is denied safety from what he fears." Describing further virtues of that mosque, the Imam said, "It is one of the holy spots where God loves to be called by His creatures. Every day and night angels arrive to visit that mosque and perform worship in it. Had I been living near where you live, I would have offered all my prayers in that mosque." He added, "O Abū Muḥammad, what I have not described of that mosque's virtues are more than what I have." Abū Baṣīr asked him if the Twelfth Imam will stay in it permanently. "Yes," he replied.

The Observances of the Sahlah Mosque A two-rak'ah prayer is to be offered here between maghrib and 'ishā. Imam Ja'far al-Ṣādiq ('a) is reported to have said that God Almighty shall relieve the distress of those who make this prayer here and supplicate Him. Ibn Ṭāwūs says that the best time for visiting the Sahlah Mosque is on Wednesday eve (i.e., Tuesday night) between the times of maghrib and 'ishā.

At the Entrance

It is mentioned in some works on ziyārah that when entering the mosque, one should first stand near the gate and say,

بِسْمِ اللهِ وَ بِاللهِ وَ مِنَ اللهِ وَ إِلَى اللهِ، وَ مَا شَاءَ اللهُ، وَ خَيْرُ الْأَسْمَاءِ لِلهِ، تَوَكَّلْتُ عَلَى اللهِ وَ لاَ حَوْلَ وَ لاَ قُوَّةَ إِلَّا بِاللهِ الْعَلِيِّ الْعَظِيمِ

In the Name of Allah, by Allah, from Allah, toward Allah, as Allah wishes, and the best of names belongs to Allah. I put my trust in Allah and there is no power or force except what derives from Allah, the All-exalted the All-supreme.

اَللّٰهُمَّ اجْعَلْنِي مِنْ عُمَّارِ مَسَاجِدِكَ وَ بُيُوتِكَ، اَللّٰهُمَّ إِنِّي أَتَوَجَّهُ إِلَيْكَ بِمُحَمَّدٍ وَ آلِ مُحَمَّدٍ، وَ أُقَدِّمُهُمْ بَيْنَ يَدَيْ حَوَائِجِي، فَاجْعَلْنِي اللهُمَّ بِهِمْ عِنْدَكَ وَجِيهًا فِي الدُّنْيَا وَ الْآخِرَةِ وَ مِنَ الْمُقَرَّبِينَ

O Allah, make me one of those who keep up Your mosques and houses of worship. O Allah, I turn to You through the mediation of Muḥammad and the Family of Muḥammad, setting them ahead of my petitions. O Allah, make me eminent with You through them in the world and the Hereafter and of those who are near to You.

اَللّٰهُمَّ اجْعَلْ صَلاَتِي بِهِمْ مَقْبُولَةً، وَ ذَنْبِي بِهِمْ مَغْفُورًا، وَ رِزْقِي بِهِمْ مَبْسُوطاً، وَ دُعَائِي بِهِمْ مُسْتَجَابًا، وَ حَوَائِجِي بِهِمْ مَقْضِيَّةً، وَ انْظُرْ إِلَيَّ بِوَجْهِكَ الْكَرِيمِ نَظْرَةً رَحِيمَةً أَسْتَوْجِبُ بِهَا الْكَرَامَةَ عِنْدَكَ، ثُمَّ لاَ تَصْرِفْهُ عَنِّي أَبَدًا، بِرَحْمَتِكَ يَا أَرْحَمَ الرَّاحِمِينَ

O Allah, for their sake accept my prayer, forgive my sins, expand my provision, answer my supplications, satisfy my needs and look at me mercifully with Your munificent Face, a look that will make me worthy of honour with You and which You will never turn away from me ever, with Your mercy, O Most Merciful of the merciful!

يَا مُقَلِّبَ الْقُلُوبِ وَ الْأَبْصَارِ، ثَبِّتْ قَلْبِي عَلَىٰ دِينِكَ وَ دِينِ نَبِيِّكَ وَ وَلِيِّكَ، وَ لاَ تُزِغْ قَلْبِي بَعْدَ إِذْ هَدَيْتَنِي، وَ هَبْ لِي مِنْ لَدُنْكَ رَحْمَةً، إِنَّكَ أَنْتَ الْوَهَّابُ

O Changer of the hearts and visions, keep me steady on Your religion, and do not let my heart swerve after that You have guided me, and grant me Your mercy; indeed You are the All-bestower.

اَللّٰهُمَّ إِلَيْكَ تَوَجَّهْتُ، وَ مَرْضَاتَكَ طَلَبْتُ، وَ ثَوَابَكَ ابْتَغَيْتُ، وَ بِكَ آمَنْتُ، وَ عَلَيْكَ تَوَكَّلْتُ. اَللّٰهُمَّ فَأَقْبِلْ بِوَجْهِكَ إِلَيَّ، وَ أَقْبِلْ بِوَجْهِي إِلَيْكَ

O Allah, I have turned to you, seeking Your pleasure and Your reward, placing faith in You and putting my trust in You! O Allah, turn to me by turning Your Face toward me and my face toward You!

Then one should recite the Throne Verse (2:255), Sūrat al-Falaq and Sūrat al-Nās, and after that say each of the following seven times: "Subḥānallāh, "Walḥamdu lillāh," "Wa lâ ilāha illallāh," "wallāhu akbar." Then say,

اَللّٰهُمَّ لَكَ الْحَمْدُ عَلىٰ مَا هَدَيْتَنِي، وَ لَكَ الْحَمْدُ عَلىٰ مَا فَضَّلْتَنِي، وَ لَكَ الْحَمْدُ عَلىٰ مَا شَرَّفْتَنِي، وَ لَكَ الْحَمْدُ عَلىٰ كُلِّ بَلاءٍ حَسَنٍ ابْتَلَيْتَنِي

O Allah, I have turned to you, seeking Your pleasure and Your reward, placing faith in You and putting my trust in You! O Allah, turn to me by turning Your Face toward me and my face toward You!

اَللّٰهُمَّ تَقَبَّلْ صَلاتِي وَ دُعَائِي، وَ طَهِّرْ قَلْبِي، وَ اشْرَحْ لِي صَدْرِي، وَ تُبْ عَلَيَّ، إِنَّكَ أَنْتَ التَّوَّابُ الرَّحِيمُ

O Allah, to You belongs all praise for guiding me! To You belongs all praise for the grace You have granted me! To You belongs all praise for the honour You have conferred on me! To You belongs all praise for every fair trial with which You have tested me!

After entering, one should offer the maghrib prayer and its nāfilah. Then offer the prayer of taḥiyyah of the mosque, seeking nearness to Allah. After the prayer of taḥiyyah, raise the hands towards the sky and say,

أَنْتَ اللهُ لاَ إِلٰهَ إِلَّا أَنْتَ مُبْدِئُ الْخَلْقِ وَ مُعِيدُهُمْ، وَ أَنْتَ اللهُ لاَ إِلٰهَ إِلَّا أَنْتَ خَالِقُ الْخَلْقِ وَ رَازِقُهُمْ

You are Allah, there being no god besides You, the Originator of the creatures and their Restorer. You are Allah, there being no god besides You, the Creator of the creatures and their Provider.

وَ أَنْتَ اللهُ لاَ إِلٰهَ إِلَّا أَنْتَ الْقَابِضُ الْبَاسِطُ، وَ أَنْتَ اللهُ لاَ إِلٰهَ إِلَّا أَنْتَ، مُدَبِّرُ الْأُمُورِ، وَ بَاعِثُ مَنْ فِي الْقُبُورِ، أَنْتَ وَارِثُ الْأَرْضِ وَ مَنْ عَلَيْهَا

You are Allah, there being no god besides You, the tightener and expander of provision. You are Allah, there being no god besides You, the director of all affairs, the Resurrector of those who are in the graves, the Inheritor of the earth and those who live upon it!

أَسْأَلُكَ بِاسْمِكَ الْمَخْزُونِ الْمَكْنُونِ الْحَيِّ الْقَيُّومِ، وَ أَنْتَ اللهُ لاَ إِلٰهَ إِلَّا أَنْتَ عَالِمُ السِّرِّ وَ أَخْفَى

I beseech You by Your hidden and treasured Name, the Living One and the All-sustainer! You are Allah, there being no god besides You, the Knower of all that is secret and that which is still more hidden!

أَسْأَلُكَ بِاسْمِكَ الَّذِي إِذَا دُعِيتَ بِهِ أَجَبْتَ، وَ إِذَا سُئِلْتَ بِهِ أَعْطَيْتَ

I beseech You by Your Name, when called by which You answer, and when invoked by it You grant!

وَ أَسْأَلُكَ بِحَقِّكَ عَلىٰ مُحَمَّدٍ وَ أَهْلِ بَيْتِهِ، وَ بِحَقِّهِمُ الَّذِي أَوْجَبْتَهُ عَلىٰ نَفْسِكَ، أَنْ تُصَلِّيَ عَلىٰ مُحَمَّدٍ وَ آلِ مُحَمَّدٍ، وَ أَنْ تَقْضِيَ لِي حَاجَتِي، اَلسَّاعَةَ، اَلسَّاعَةَ، يَا سَامِعَ الدُّعَاءِ، يَا سَيِّدَاهْ يَا مَوْلاَهْ يَا غِيَاثَاهْ

I beseech You by Your right over Muḥammad and his Family, and by their right which You have made incumbent on Yourself, to bless Muḥammad and the Family of Muḥammad, and to grant my need this very hour, O hearer of supplications! O Master! O my Guardian and Rescuer!

أَسْأَلُكَ بِكُلِّ اسْمٍ سَمَّيْتَ بِهِ نَفْسَكَ، أَوِ اسْتَأْثَرْتَ بِهِ فِي عِلْمِ الْغَيْبِ عِنْدَكَ، أَنْ تُصَلِّيَ عَلىٰ مُحَمَّدٍ وَ آلِ مُحَمَّدٍ، وَ أَنْ تُعَجِّلَ فَرَجَنَا السَّاعَةَ يَا مُقَلِّبَ الْقُلُوبِ وَ الْأَبْصَارِ، يَا سَمِيعَ الدُّعَاءِ

I beseech You by every Name wherewith You have named Yourself or held secret in Your knowledge of the Unseen, to bless Muḥammad and the Family of Muḥammad and to grant me immediate relief, this very hour, O Changer of hearts and visions! O Hearer of supplications!

Then make prostration and humbly implore God for whatever request you may have.

At the Station of Abraham ('a)

Then proceed towards the north-western corner of the mosque, the location of the house of the Prophet Abraham ('a) from where he is said to have gone forth to fight the Amalekites.

Offer two rak'ahs there. After the prayer and tasbīḥ say,

اَللّٰهُمَّ بِحَقِّ هٰذِهِ الْبُقْعَةِ الشَّرِيفَةِ، وَ بِحَقِّ مَنْ تَعَبَّدَ لَكَ فِيهَا، قَدْ عَلِمْتَ حَوَائِجِي فَصَلِّ عَلىٰ مُحَمَّدٍ وَ آلِ مُحَمَّدٍ وَ اقْضِهَا، وَ قَدْ أَحْصَيْتَ ذُنُوبِي، فَصَلِّ عَلىٰ مُحَمَّدٍ وَ آلِ مُحَمَّدٍ وَ اغْفِرْهَا

O Allah, for the sake of the right of this sacred shrine and the rights of those who have worshipped You in it, as You know my need, bless Muḥammad and the Family of Muḥammad and fulfil it! As You know my sins, bless Muḥammad and the Family of Muḥammad and forgive them.

اَللّٰهُمَّ أَحْيِنِي مَا كَانَتِ الْحَيَاةُ خَيْرًا لِي، وَ أَمِتْنِي إِذَا كَانَتِ الْوَفَاةُ خَيْرًا لِيعَلىٰ مُوَالاَةِ أَوْلِيَائِكَ وَ مُعَادَاةِ أَعْدَائِكَ، وَ افْعَلْ بِي مَا أَنْتَ أَهْلُهُ، يَا أَرْحَمَ الرَّاحِمِينَ

O Allah, keep me alive so long as life is good for me, and take me away when death is better for me and in a state of devotedness to Your awliyā and hostility toward Your enemies, and treat me as is worthy of You, O Most Merciful of the merciful!

At the Station of Idrīs (Enoch) (ʻa)

Then proceed towards another corner of the mosque towards the south-west and offer two rakʻahs. After the prayer, with raised hands say,

اَللّٰهُمَّ إِنِّي صَلَّيْتُ هٰذِهِ الصَّلاٰةَ ابْتِغَاءَ مَرْضَاتِكَ، وَ طَلَبَ نَائِلِكَ، وَ رَجَاءَ رِفْدِكَ وَ جَوَائِزِكَ، فَصَلِّ عَلىٰ مُحَمَّدٍ وَ آلِ مُحَمَّدٍ، وَ تَقَبَّلْهَا مِنِّي بِأَحْسَنِ قَبُولٍ، وَ بَلِّغْنِي بِرَحْمَتِكَ الْمَأْمُولَ، وَ افْعَلْ بِي مَا أَنْتَ أَهْلُهُ، يَا أَرْحَمَ الرَّاحِمِينَ

O Allah! I have offered this prayer seeking Your pleasure, desiring Your gift, expecting Your hospitality and awards! So, bless Muḥammad and the Family of Muḥammad and accept it from me with a most gracious acceptance, and enable me with Your mercy to attain what I aspire for, and treat me as is worthy of You, O Most Merciful of the merciful.

Then make prostration and lay each side of the face on the ground. At the Station of Khidr (Khadir) (ʻa) Then proceed towards the spot on the eastern side of the mosque and offer two rakʻahs. After the prayer, raising your hands, say,

اَللّٰهُمَّ إِنْ كَانَتِ الذُّنُوبُ وَ الْخَطَايَا قَدْ أَخْلَقَتْ وَجْهِي عِنْدَكَ، فَلَمْ تَرْفَعْ لِي إِلَيْكَ صَوْتًا، وَ لَمْ تَسْتَجِبْ لِي دَعْوَةً، فَإِنِّي أَسْأَلُكَ بِكَ يَا اللهُ فَإِنَّهُ لَيْسَ مِثْلَكَ أَحَدٌ، وَ أَتَوَسَّلُ إِلَيْكَ بِمُحَمَّدٍ وَ آلِهِ، وَ أَسْأَلُكَ أَنْ تُصَلِّيَ عَلىٰ مُحَمَّدٍ وَ آلِ مُحَمَّدٍ، وَ أَنْ تُقْبِلَ إِلَيَّ بِوَجْهِكَ الْكَرِيمِ، وَ تُقْبِلَ بِوَجْهِي إِلَيْكَ، وَ لاٰ تُخَيِّبَنِي حِينَ أَدْعُوكَ، وَ لاٰ تَحْرِمَنِي حِينَ أَرْجُوكَ، يَا أَرْحَمَ الرَّاحِمِينَ

O Allah, if my sins and offenses have impaired my visage with You, preventing my voice from rising to You and my prayers from being heard by You, I beseech You—by You, O Allah, who have no peer—taking recourse in the mediation of Muḥammad and his Family! I beseech You to bless Muḥammad and the Family of Muḥammad, and to turn to me with Your munificent Face and to turn my face toward You. Do not disappoint me when I supplicate You, and do not deprive me when I pin my hopes on You, O Most Merciful of the merciful!

At the Station of the the Righteous and the Prophets. In accordance with some lesser-known works on ziyārah, after this observance one is to offer two rak'ahs at another spot (known as "Maqām al-Ṣāliḥīn wal-Anbiyâ' wal-Mursalīn") on the eastern side of the mosque, and say, after the prayer,

اَللّٰهُمَّ إِنِّي أَسْأَلُكَ بِاسْمِكَ يَا اللهُ أَنْ تُصَلِّيَ عَلىٰ مُحَمَّدٍ وَ آلِ مُحَمَّدٍ، وَ أَنْ تَجْعَلَ خَيْرَ عُمْرِي آخِرَهُ، وَ خَيْرَ أَعْمَالِي خَوَاتِيمَهَا، وَ خَيْرَ أَيَّامِي يَوْمَ أَلْقَاكَ فِيهِ، إِنَّكَ عَلىٰ كُلِّ شَيْءٍ قَدِيرٌ

O Allah, I beseech You by Your Name, O Allah, to bless Muḥammad and the Family of Muḥammad and to make the final part of my life its best part, the best part of my works my last deeds, and the best of my days the day that I shall meet You! Indeed, You have power over all things!

اَللّٰهُمَّ تَقَبَّلْ دُعَائِي، وَ اسْمَعْ نَجْوَايَ، يَا عَلِيُّ يَا عَظِيمُ، يَا قَادِرُ يَا قَاهِرُ، يَا حَيًّا لاٰ يَمُوتُ، صَلِّ عَلىٰ مُحَمَّدٍ وَ آلِ مُحَمَّدٍ

O Allah, accept my supplication and hear my confidential petitions, O Most High, O All-supreme, O All-able, O All-dominant, O Living One who do not die, bless Muḥammad and the Family of Muḥammad

وَ اغْفِرْ لِيَ الذُّنُوبَ الَّتِي بَيْنِي وَ بَيْنَكَ، وَ لاٰ تَفْضَحْنِي عَلىٰ رُءُوسِ الْأَشْهَادِ، وَ احْرُسْنِي بِعَيْنِكَ الَّتِي لاٰ تَنَامُ، وَ ارْحَمْنِي بِقُدْرَتِكَ عَلَيَّ، يَا أَرْحَمَ الرَّاحِمِينَ، وَ صَلَّى اللهُ عَلىٰ سَيِّدِنَا مُحَمَّدٍ وَ آلِهِ الطَّاهِرِينَ، يَا رَبَّ الْعَالَمِينَ

and forgive my sins which stand between You and me, and do not humiliate me on the Day of Resurrection in front of all and sundry!

Guard me with Your eye which does not sleep and have mercy on me with Your power over me, O Most Merciful of the merciful! May Allah bless our master, Muḥammad, and his immaculate Family, O Lord of all the worlds!

At the Station of Imam Zayn al-'Ābidīn ('a) Thereafter offer two rak'ahs in the chamber built in the middle of the mosque, (nowadays known as the station of Imam Zayn al-'Abidīn ('a)), and after the prayer say,

يَا مَنْ هُوَ أَقْرَبُ إِلَيَّ مِنْ حَبْلِ الْوَرِيدِ، يَا فَعَّالًا لِمَا يُرِيدُ، يَا مَنْ يَحُولُ بَيْنَ الْمَرْءِ وَ قَلْبِهِ، صَلِّ عَلَىٰ مُحَمَّدٍ وَ آلِهِ، وَ حُلْ بَيْنَنَا وَ بَيْنَ مَنْ يُؤْذِينَا بِحَوْلِكَ وَ قُوَّتِكَ

O You who are nearer to me than my jugular vein! O You who accomplish whatever You desire! O You who intervene between a man and his heart! Bless Muḥammad and his Family and, with Your power and might, intervene between us and those who torment us!

يَا كَافِيَ مِنْ كُلِّ شَيْءٍ وَ لَا يَكْفِي مِنْهُ شَيْءٌ، اِكْفِنَا الْمُهِمَّ مِنْ أَمْرِ الدُّنْيَا وَ الْآخِرَةِ، يَا أَرْحَمَ الرَّاحِمِينَ

O You who suffice against all things and against whom nothing can suffice! Suffice us with regard to all our concerns pertaining to the world and the Hereafter, O Most Merciful of the merciful!

ZAYD'S MOSQUE

Prayer and Supplication

After the observances of the Sahlah Mosque, one should proceed towards Zayd's Mosque, which is in its vicinity, and offer there two rak'ahs.

After the prayer, with raised hands, say,

إِلٰهِي قَدْ مَدَّ إِلَيْكَ الْخَاطِئُ الْمُذْنِبُ يَدَيْهِ بِحُسْنِ ظَنِّهِ بِكَ، إِلٰهِي قَدْ جَلَسَ الْمُسِيءُ بَيْنَ يَدَيْكَ مُقِرًّا لَكَ بِسُوءِ عَمَلِهِ، وَ رَاجِيًا مِنْكَ الصَّفْحَ عَنْ زَلَلِهِ

My God, this sinner and offender stretches towards You his hands on account of his favourable opinion of You, warranting hope. My God, Your guilty servant sits before You having confessed to his evil conduct and expecting You to pardon his failings.

إِلٰهِي قَدْ رَفَعَ إِلَيْكَ الظَّالِمُ كَفَّيْهِ رَاجِيًا لِمَا لَدَيْكَ، فَلاَ تُخَيِّبْهُ بِرَحْمَتِكَ مِنْ فَضْلِكَ

My God, this wrongdoer has raised his hands hoping to receive that which is with You. Mercifully, do not disappoint him by denying him Your grace!

إِلٰهِي قَدْ جَثَا الْعَائِدُ إِلَى الْمَعَاصِي بَيْنَ يَدَيْكَ، خَائِفًا مِنْ يَوْمٍ تَجْثُو فِيهِ الْخَلاَئِقُ بَيْنَ يَدَيْكَ

My God, this one who keeps on relapsing into sin kneels before You, fearing the day when all creatures will be fallen on their knees before You!

إِلٰهِي جَاءَكَ الْعَبْدُ الْخَاطِئُ فَزِعًا مُشْفِقًا، وَ رَفَعَ إِلَيْكَ طَرْفَهُ حَذِرًا رَاجِيًا، وَ فَاضَتْ عَبْرَتُهُ مُسْتَغْفِرًا نَادِمًا

My God, Your errant servant comes to You, full of anxiety and panic, raising up to You his glance in fear and hope, his tears flowing, remorseful and imploring Your forgiveness!

وَ عِزَّتِكَ وَ جَلاَلِكَ مَا أَرَدْتُ بِمَعْصِيَتِي مُخَالَفَتَكَ، وَ مَا عَصَيْتُكَ إِذْ عَصَيْتُكَ وَ أَنَا بِكَ جَاهِلٌ، وَ لاَ لِعُقُوبَتِكَ مُتَعَرِّضٌ، وَ لاَ لِنَظَرِكَ مُسْتَخِفٌّ، وَ لٰكِنْ سَوَّلَتْ لِي نَفْسِي، وَ أَعَانَتْنِي عَلَىٰ ذٰلِكَ شِقْوَتِي وَ غَرَّنِي سِتْرُكَ الْمُرْخىٰ عَلَيَّ، فَمِنَ الآنَ مِنْ عَذَابِكَ مَنْ يَسْتَنْقِذُنِي؟

By Your might and glory, I did not wish to oppose You by my sinning. I did not disobey You when I sinned being ignorant of You, neither was it in order to expose myself to Your retribution, nor on account of disregard for You while You watched me! But my carnal soul tempted me and my wretchedness prompted me to commit it! The curtain You had drawn over my vices deluded me! Now who will save me from Your punishment?

وَ بِحَبْلِ مَنْ أَعْتَصِمُ إِنْ قَطَعْتَ حَبْلَكَ عَنِّي ؟ فَيَا سَوْأَتَاهُ غَدًا مِنَ الْوُقُوفِ بَيْنَ يَدَيْكَ إِذَا قِيلَ لِلْمُخِفِّينَ جُوزُوا، وَ لِلْمُثْقِلِينَ حُطُّوا، أَ فَمَعَ الْمُخِفِّينَ أَجُوزُ ؟ أَمْ مَعَ الْمُثْقِلِينَ أَحُطُّ ؟

Whose good offices shall I seek if You withhold Your support from me? What a shame will it be when tomorrow I am brought to stand before You and when those not encumbered with sins are told to pass on and those laded with sins are told to fall (into hell)! Will I pass on with the light-footed or fall with the laden?

وَيْلِي كُلَّمَا كَبُرَ سِنِّي كَثُرَتْ ذُنُوبِي! وَيْلِي كُلَّمَا طَالَ عُمْرِي كَثُرَتْ مَعَاصِيَّ! فَكَمْ أَتُوبُ وَ كَمْ أَعُودُ ؟ أَ مَا آنَ لِي أَنْ أَسْتَحْيِيَ مِنْ رَبِّي ؟

Woe to me! With growing age my sins multiply! Woe to me! The longer I live the more numerous are my offences! How often shall I repent and how often shall I relapse? Has not time yet come when I should be ashamed before my Lord?!!

اَللّٰهُمَّ فَبِحَقِّ مُحَمَّدٍ وَ آلِ مُحَمَّدٍ اغْفِرْ لِي وَ ارْحَمْنِي يَا أَرْحَمَ الرَّاحِمِينَ وَ خَيْرَ الْغَافِرِينَ

O Allah, by the right of Muḥammad and the Family of Muḥammad, forgive me and have mercy on me, O Most Merciful of the merciful and the Best of forgivers! Then, mournfully, put your face on the ground say,

اِرْحَمْ مَنْ أَسَاءَ وَ اقْتَرَفَ، وَ اسْتَكَانَ وَ اعْتَرَفَ.

Have mercy on someone who having been guilty of misconduct and sin, now surrenders and confesses his sins!

Then placing the right cheek on the ground, say:

إِنْ كُنْتُ بِئْسَ الْعَبْدُ، فَأَنْتَ نِعْمَ الرَّبُّ

If I have been a bad servant, You are indeed an excellent Lord!

Then place the left cheek on the ground, and say:

عَظُمَ الذَّنْبُ مِنْ عَبْدِكَ فَلْيَحْسُنِ الْعَفْوُ مِنْ عِنْدِكَ يَا كَرِيمُ.

Inasmuch as Your servant's sin is great, it will be gracious of You to pardon him! O Munificent One!

Then returning to the position of prostration, say 100 times "Al-'afw, al-'afw..."

This is one of the celebrated mosques of Kūfah and is known after Zayd b. Ṣūḥān, one of the distinguished companions of the Commander of the Faithful ('a). He was considered one of his eminent votaries (abdāl). He was martyred in the Battle of the Camel while fighting in the Imam's camp. The supplication cited above is ascribed to him, and he used to recite it in nightly prayers.

The Mosque of Sa'sa'ah

Near the Mosque of Zayd is another ascribed to his brother Ṣa'sa'ah b. Ṣūḥān, who was also one of Imam 'Alī's companions. Ṣa'ṣa'ah was one of those who knew the Imam's station and was a leading figure among the faithful. A gifted and eloquent speaker, the Commander of the Faithful ('a) highly regarded his talent in oratory as well as his austere piety and support for the cause of the truth.

On the night of the Imam's martyrdom, when his body was carried from Kūfah to Najaf, Ṣa'ṣa'ah was also among those who attended the funeral. After the burial, standing at the graveside, Ṣa'ṣa'ah smeared his head with a handful of dust and spoke, saying, "You are dearer to me than my own parents, O Commander of the Faithful! Rejoice in the dignity that God has granted you! O Abul Ḥasan! Immaculate was your birth, formidable was your patience and great was your jihād. You attained what you had longed for, making a profitable deal with God, and departed to His vicinage ..." He wept bitterly as he spoke, making all listeners weep as well. It was really a mourning ceremony that was held in the dark of that night at the Imam's graveside. Ṣa'ṣa'ah's was a sermon delivered in this mourning session, attended by Imam al-Ḥasan, Imam al-Ḥusayn, Muḥammad ibn Ḥanafiyyah, Abū al-Faḍl al-'Abbās and other sons and relatives of the Imam ('a). After his speech those present offered condolences to Imam al-

Ḥasan, Imam al-Ḥusayn and other sons of the Imam ('a). Then they returned to Kūfah.

The Mosque of Ṣa'ṣa'ah is one of the celebrated mosques of Kūfah and the Imam of the Era—may Allah's blessings be upon him—was seen there by a group of people during the month of Rajab. The Imam offered two rak'ahs and recited the supplication "Allāhumma, yā dhal minanis sābighah, wal ālâ'il wāzi 'ah...,".

ZIYARAH MUSLIM IBN AQEEL (A)

The Visitation

Muslim ibn Aqeel was the son of Aqeel ibn Abi Talib, and therefore was a first cousin to Imam Husayn (peace be upon him). The Imam (peace be upon him) sent Muslim as his ambassador to Kufa, where Muslim (peace be upon him) was brutally murdered by the Umayyads on the 9th of Dhul-hijjah. His shrine is within the Premises of the Masjid Kufa near Najaf Iraq

الْحَمْدُ لِلَّهِ ٱلْمَلِكِ ٱلْحَقِّ ٱلْمُبِينِ

alhamdu lillahi almaliki alhaqqi almubini

All praise be to Allah: the Lord and the evident Truth.

ٱلْمُتَصَاغِرِ لِعَظَمَتِهِ جَبَابِرَةُ ٱلطَّاغِينَ

almutasaghiri li`azamatihi jababiratu alttaghina

All the tyrannical oppressors are subservient to His almightiness

ٱلْمُعْتَرِفِ بِرُبُوبِيَّتِهِ جَمِيعُ أَهْلِ ٱلسَّمَاوَاتِ وَٱلأَرَضِينَ

almu`tarifi birububiyyatihi jami`u ahli alssamawati wal-aradina

All the inhabitants of the heavens and the layers of the earth admit His Godhead

ٱلْمُقِرِّ بِتَوْحِيدِهِ سَائِرُ ٱلْخَلْقِ أَجْمَعِينَ

almuqirri bitawhidihi sa'iru alkhalqi ajma`ina

All the created beings confess of His Oneness.

وَصَلَّىٰ ٱللَّهُ عَلَىٰ سَيِّدِ ٱلأَنَامِ

wa salla allahu `ala sayyidi al-anami

May Allah send blessings upon the master of all created beings

وَأَهْلِ بَيْتِهِ ٱلْكِرَامِ

wa ahli baytihi alkirami

and upon the members of his Household; the noble ones,

صَلاةً تَقَرُّ بِهَا أَعْيُنُهُمْ

salatan taqarru biha a`yunuhum

such blessings that delight them

وَيَرْغَمُ بِهَا أَنْفُ شَانِئِهِمْ

wa yarghamu biha anfu shani'ihim
and humiliate all those who antagonize them

مِنَ ٱلْجِنِّ وَٱلإِنْسِ أَجْمَعِينَ

min aljinni wal-insi ajma`ina
from all jinn and mankind.

سَلامُ ٱللَّهِ ٱلْعَلِيِّ ٱلْعَظِيمِ

salamu allahi al`aliyyi al`azimi
Peace of Allah the All-high and All-great,

وَسَلاَمُ مَلاَئِكَتِهِ ٱلْمُقَرَّبِينَ

wa salamu mala'ikatihi almuqarrabina
and peace of His favorite angels,

وَأَنْبِيَائِهِ ٱلْمُرْسَلِينَ

wa anbiya'ihi almursalina
His missioned Prophets,

وَأَئِمَّتِهِ ٱلْمُنْتَجَبِينَ

wa a'immatihi almuntajabina
His choice Imams,

وَعِبَادِهِ ٱلصَّالِحِينَ

wa `ibadihi alssalihina
His righteous servants,

وَجَمِيعِ ٱلشُّهَدَاءِ وَٱلصِّدِّيقِينَ

wa jami`i alshshuhada'i walssiddiqina
and all the martyrs and veracious ones,

وَٱلزَّاكِيَاتُ ٱلطَّيِّبَاتُ

walzzakiyatu alttayyibatu
and all blessings that are pure and delightful,

فِيمَا تَغْتَدِي وَتَرُوحُ

fima taghtadi wa taruhu
that are coming and going,

عَلَيْكَ يَا مُسْلِمُ بْنَ عَقِيلِ بْنِ أَبِي طَالِبٍ

`alayka ya muslimu bna `aqili bni abi talibin
be upon you, Muslim the son of `Aqil the son of Abu-Talib.

وَرَحْمَةُ ٱللَّهِ وَبَرَكَاتُهُ

wa rahmatu allahi wa barakatuhu
Allah's mercy and benedictions be upon you.

أَشْهَدُ أَنَّكَ أَقَمْتَ ٱلصَّلاَةَ

ashhadu annaka aqamta alssalata
I bear witness that you performed the prayers,

وَآتَيْتَ ٱلزَّكَاةَ

wa atayta alzzakata
defrayed the zakat,

وَأَمَرْتَ بِٱلْمَعْرُوفِ

wa amarta bilma`rufi
enjoined the right

وَنَهَيْتَ عَنِ ٱلْمُنْكَرِ

wa nahayta `an almunkari
forbade the wrong,

وَجَاهَدْتَ فِي ٱللَّهِ حَقَّ جِهَادِهِ

wa jahadta fi allahi haqqa jihadihi
strove in the way of Allah in the best manner of striving

وَقُتِلْتَ عَلَىٰ مِنْهَاجِ ٱلْمُجَاهِدِينَ فِي سَبِيلِهِ

wa qutilta `ala minhaji almujahidina fi sabilihi
and you were slain following the course of those who strive in Allah's way

حَتَّىٰ لَقِيتَ ٱللَّهَ عَزَّ وَجَلَّ وَهُوَ عَنْكَ رَاضٍ

hatta laqita allaha `azza wa jalla wa huwa `anka radin

until you met Allah, to Whom belong all might and majesty, while He is pleased with you.

وَأَشْهَدُ أَنَّكَ وَفَيْتَ بِعَهْدِ ٱللَّهِ

wa ashhadu annaka wafayta bi`ahdi allahi

And I bear witness that you fulfilled your covenant with Allah

وَبَذَلْتَ نَفْسَكَ فِي نُصْرَةِ حُجَّةِ ٱللَّهِ وَٱبْنِ حُجَّتِهِ

wa badhalta nafsaka fi nusrati hujjati allahi wabni hujjatihi

and sacrificed yourself for the sake of supporting Allah's argument and the son of Allah's argument (namely, Imam al-Husayn)

حَتَّىٰ أَتَاكَ ٱلْيَقِينُ

hatta ataka alyaqinu

until death came upon you

أَشْهَدُ لَكَ بِٱلتَّسْلِيمِ وَٱلْوَفَاءِ

ashhadu laka bilttaslimi walwafa'i

I bear witness that you submitted and acted loyally to him

وَٱلنَّصِيحَةِ لِخَلَفِ ٱلنَّبِيِّ ٱلْمُرْسَلِ

walnnasihati likhalafi alnnabiyyi almursali

and that you acted sincerely to the successor of the missioned Prophet,

وَٱلسِّبْطِ ٱلْمُنْتَجَبِ

walssibti almuntajabi

the select grandson (of the Prophet),

وَٱلدَّلِيلِ ٱلْعَالِمِ

walddalili al`alimi

the guide (to the right path), the knowledgeable,

وَٱلْوَصِيِّ ٱلْمُبَلِّغِ

walwasiyyi almuballighi

the Prophet's successor, the conveyor (of his mission),

وَٱلْمَظْلُومِ ٱلْمُهْتَضَمِ

walmazlumi almuhtadami

the wronged, and the oppressed Imam.

فَجَزَاكَ ٱللَّهُ عَنْ رَسُولِهِ

fajazaka allahu `an rasulihi

May Allah reward you on behalf of His Messenger,

وَعَنْ أَمِيرِ ٱلْمُؤْمِنِينَ

wa `an amiri almu'minina

on behalf of the Commander of the Faithful,

وَعَنِ ٱلْحَسَنِ وَٱلْحُسَيْنِ

wa `an alhasani walhusayni

and on behalf of al-Hasan and al-Husayn

أَفْضَلَ ٱلْجَزَاءِ

afdala aljaza'i

with the best of rewarding

بِمَا صَبَرْتَ وَٱحْتَسَبْتَ وَأَعَنْتَ

bima sabarta wa ihtasabta wa a`anta

that befits your steadfastness, reliance (on Allah), and assistance.

فَنِعْمَ عُقْبَىٰ ٱلدَّارِ

fani`ma `uqba alddari

How excellent is the final home!

لَعَنَ ٱللَّهُ مَنْ قَتَلَكَ

la`ana allahu man qatalaka

May Allah curse him who slew you.

وَلَعَنَ ٱللَّهُ مَنْ أَمَرَ بِقَتْلِكَ

wa la`ana allahu man amara biqatlika

May Allah curse him who ordered of slaying you.

وَلَعَنَ ٱللَّهُ مَنْ ظَلَمَكَ

wa la`ana allahu man zalamaka

May Allah curse him who wronged you.

وَلَعَنَ ٱللَّهُ مَنِ ٱفْتَرَىٰ عَلَيْكَ

wa la`ana allahu man iftara `alayka

May Allah curse him who forged lies against you.

وَلَعَنَ ٱللَّهُ مَنْ جَهِلَ حَقَّكَ

wa la`ana allahu man jahila haqqaka

May Allah curse him who underestimated your position

وَٱسْتَخَفَّ بِحُرْمَتِكَ

wastakhaffa bihurmatika

and belittled your sanctity.

وَلَعَنَ ٱللَّهُ مَنْ بَايَعَكَ وَغَشَّكَ

wa la`ana allahu man baya`aka wa ghashshaka

May Allah curse those who cheated you after they had sworn allegiance to you,

وَخَذَلَكَ وَأَسْلَمَكَ

wa khadhalaka wa aslamaka

those who disappointed and let you down,

وَمَنْ أَلَّبَ عَلَيْكَ وَلَمْ يُعِنْكَ

wa man allaba `alayka wa lam yu`inka

and those who allied against you instead of assisting you.

ٱلْحَمْدُ لِلَّهِ ٱلَّذِي جَعَلَ ٱلنَّارَ مَثْوَاهُمْ

alhamdu lillahi alladhi ja`ala alnnara mathwahum

All praise be to Allah Who decided Hellfire to be the eternal abode of those peoples.

وَبِئْسَ ٱلْوِرْدُ ٱلْمَوْرُودُ

wa bi'sa alwirdu almawrudu

Woeful indeed will be the place to which they are led!

أَشْهَدُ أَنَّكَ قُتِلْتَ مَظْلُوماً

ashhadu annaka qutilta mazluman
I bear witness that you were slain wrongly

وَأَنَّ ٱللَّهَ مُنْجِزٌ لَكُمْ مَا وَعَدَكُمْ

wa anna allaha munjizun lakum ma wa`adakum
and that Allah shall fulfill His promise to you.

جِئْتُكَ زَائِراً عَارِفاً بِحَقِّكُمْ

ji'tuka za'iran `arifan bihaqqikum
As I am visiting you, I recognize your right,

مُسَلِّماً لَكُمْ

musalliman lakum
I am submissive to you,

تَابِعاً لِسُنَّتِكُمْ

tabi`an lisunnatikum
I am imitating your course,

وَنُصْرَتِي لَكُمْ مُعَدَّةٌ

wa nusrati lakum mu`addatun
and I am preparing myself for supporting you

حَتَّىٰ يَحْكُمَ ٱللَّهُ وَهُوَ خَيْرُ ٱلْحَاكِمِينَ

hatta yahkuma allahu wa huwa khayru alhakimina
until Allah judges, and He is the best of judges.

فَمَعَكُمْ مَعَكُمْ

fama`akum ma`akum
So, I am always with you

لاَ مَعَ عَدُوِّكُمْ

la ma`a `aduwwikum
and I never am with your enemies.

صَلوَاتُ ٱللَّهِ عَلَيْكُمْ

salwatu allahi `alaykum
May Allah's peace be upon you

وَعَلَىٰ أَرْوَاحِكُمْ وَأَجْسَادِكُمْ

wa `ala arwahikum wa ajsadikum
and upon your souls and bodies

وَشَاهِدِكُمْ وَغَائِبِكُمْ

wa shahidikum wa gha'ibikum
and upon the present from you and the absent one.

وَٱلسَّلاَمُ عَلَيْكُمْ وَرَحْمَةُ ٱللَّهِ وَبَرَكَاتُهُ

wa alssalamu `alaykum wa rahmatu allahi wa barakatuhu
Peace and Allah's mercy and blessings be upon you.

قَتَلَ ٱللَّهُ أُمَّةً قَتَلَتْكُمْ بِٱلأَيْدِي وَٱلأَلْسُنِ

qatala allahu ummatan qatalatkum bilaydi wal-alsuni
May Allah kill the groups that have killed you with deeds and words.

You may then enter, approach the tomb -or point to the tomb, according to the previous narration- and say the following words

ٱلسَّلاَمُ عَلَيْكَ أَيُّهَا ٱلْعَبْدُ ٱلصَّالِحُ

alssalamu `alayka ayyuha al`abdu alssalihu
Peace be upon you, O righteous servant (of Allah),

ٱلْمُطِيعُ لِلَّهِ وَلِرَسُولِهِ وَلأَمِيرِ ٱلْمُؤْمِنِينَ

almuti`u lillahi wa lirasulihi wa li'amiri almu'minina
who is obedient to Allah, to His Messenger, to the Commander of the Faithful,

وَٱلْحَسَنِ وَٱلْحُسَيْنِ عَلَيْهِمُ ٱلسَّلاَمُ

walhasani walhusayni `alayhim alssalamu
to al-Hasan, and to al-Husayn, peace be upon them.

ٱلْحَمْدُ لِلَّهِ

alhamdu lillahi
All praise be to Allah

وَسَلاَمٌ عَلَىٰ عِبَادِهِ ٱلَّذِينَ ٱصْطَفَىٰ

wa salamun `ala `ibadihi alladhina istafa
and all peace be upon His servants whom He has chosen:

مُحَمَّدٍ وَآلِهِ

muhammadin wa alihi
Muhammad and his Household.

وَٱلسَّلاَمُ عَلَيْكُمْ وَرَحْمَةُ ٱللَّهِ

wa alssalamu `alaykum wa rahmatu allahi
Peace, Allah's mercy,

وَبَرَكَاتُهُ وَمَغْفِرَتُهُ

wa barakatuhu wa maghfiratuhu
blessings, and forgiveness be upon you

وَعَلَىٰ رُوحِكَ وَبَدَنِكَ

wa `ala ruhika wa badanika
and upon your soul and your body.

أَشْهَدُ أَنَّكَ مَضَيْتَ عَلَىٰ مَا مَضَىٰ عَلَيْهِ ٱلْبَدْرِيُّونَ

ashhadu annaka madayta `ala ma mada `alayhi albadriyyuna
I bear witness that you died for the same principles for which the martyrs of the Battle of Badr died:

ٱلْمُجَاهِدُونَ فِي سَبِيلِ ٱللَّهِ

almujahiduna fi sabili allahi
those who strove in Allah's way

ٱلْمُبَالِغُونَ فِي جِهَادِ أَعْدَائِهِ

almubalighuna fi jihadi a`da'ihi
and did their best in struggling against Allah's enemies

وَنُصْرَةِ أَوْلِيَائِهِ

wa nusrati awliya'ihi
and in supporting Allah's friends.

فَجَزَاكَ ٱللَّهُ أَفْضَلَ ٱلْجَزَاءِ

fajazaka allahu afdala aljaza'i
So, may Allah reward you with the best rewarding,

وَأَكْثَرَ ٱلْجَزَاءِ

wa akthara aljaza'i
with the most abundant rewarding,

وَأَوْفَرَ جَزَاءِ أَحَدٍ مِمَّنْ وَفَىٰ بِبَيْعَتِهِ

wa awfara jaza'i ahadin mimman wafa bibay`atihi
and with the most affluent rewarding that He grants to one who fulfilled his allegiance to Him,

وَٱسْتَجَابَ لَهُ دَعْوَتَهُ

wastajaba lahu da`watahu
responded to His invitation,

وَأَطَاعَ وُلاَةَ أَمْرِهِ

wa ata`a wulata amrihi
and obeyed His representatives.

أَشْهَدُ أَنَّكَ قَدْ بَالَغْتَ فِي ٱلنَّصِيحَةِ

ashhadu annaka qad balaghta fi alnnasihati
I bear witness that you exerted all efforts in acting sincerely

وَأَعْطَيْتَ غَايَةَ ٱلْمَجْهُودِ

wa a`tayta ghayata almajhudi
and you put forth all possible endeavors

حَتَّىٰ بَعَثَكَ ٱللَّهُ فِي ٱلشُّهَدَاءِ

hatta ba`athaka allahu fi alshshuhada'i
so that Allah has included you with the martyrs,

وَجَعَلَ رُوحَكَ مَعَ أَرْوَاحِ ٱلسُّعَدَاءِ

wa ja`ala ruhaka ma`a arwahi alssu`ada'i
put your soul with the souls of the delighted ones,

وَأَعْطَاكَ مِنْ جِنَانِهِ أَفْسَحَهَا مَنْزِلاً

wa a`taka min jinanihi afsahaha manzilan
has decided for you the most spacious abode in the gardens of His Paradise

وَأَفْضَلَهَا غُرَفاً

wa afdalaha ghurafan
and the best rooms therein,

وَرَفَعَ ذِكْرَكَ فِي ٱلْعِلِّيِّينَ

wa rafa`a dhikraka fi al`illiyyina
raised your name to the `illiyyin (the loftiest place),

وَحَشَرَكَ مَعَ ٱلنَّبِيِّينَ وَٱلصِّدِّيقِينَ

wa hasharaka ma`a alnnabiyyina walssiddiqina
and added you to the group of the Prophets, the veracious ones,

وَٱلشُّهَدَاءِ وَٱلصَّالِحِينَ

walshshuhada'i walssalihina
the martyrs, and the righteous ones.

وَحَسُنَ أُولٰئِكَ رَفِيقاً

wa hasuna ula'ika rafiqan
How excellent is the company of these.

أَشْهَدُ أَنَّكَ لَمْ تَهِنْ وَلَمْ تَنْكُلْ

ashhadu annaka lam tahin wa lam tankul
I bear witness that you never slackened or recoiled (from your duty)

وَأَنَّكَ قَدْ مَضَيْتَ عَلَىٰ بَصِيرَةٍ مِنْ أَمْرِكَ

wa annaka qad madayta `ala basiratin min amrika
and that you died while you are certain of your doctrine

مُقْتَدِياً بِٱلصَّالِحِينَ

muqtadiyan bilssalihina
as you followed the righteous ones

وَمُتَّبِعاً لِلنَّبِيِّينَ

wa muttabi`an lilnnabiyyina
and imitated the Prophets.

فَجَمَعَ ٱللَّهُ بَيْنَنَا وَبَيْنَكَ

fajama`a allahu baynana wa baynaka
So, may Allah gather us with you

وَبَيْنَ رَسُولِهِ وَأَوْلِيَائِهِ

wa bayna rasulihi wa awliya'ihi
and with His Messenger and intimate servants

فِي مَنَازِلِ ٱلْمُخْبِتِينَ

fi manazili almukhbitina
in the abodes of the modest ones.

فَإِنَّهُ أَرْحَمُ ٱلرَّاحِمِينَ

fa'innahu arhamu alrrahimina
Surely, He is the most merciful of all those who show mercy.

The Prayers

You may then offer a two-unit prayer at the side of his head and present this prayer as your gift to him. Then, you may say the prayer which is said at the end of the Ziyarah recited in holy shrine of al-`Abbas (sa)

ٱللَّهُمَّ صَلِّ عَلَىٰ مُحَمَّدٍ وَآلِ مُحَمَّدٍ

allahumma salli `ala muhammadin wa ali muhammadin
O Allah, send blessings upon Muhammad and the Household of Muhammad,

وَلاَ تَدَعْ لِي فِي هٰذَا ٱلْمَكَانِ ٱلْمُكَرَّمِ...

wa la tada` li fi hadha almakani almukarrami...
and, as I am in this noble place...

ZIYARAH OF HANI' IBN `URWAH

The Visitation

When you stop at the tomb of Hani' ibn `Urwah, you may greet the Holy Prophet (s) and then say the following:

سَلاَمُ ٱللَّهِ ٱلْعَظِيمِ وَصَلَوَاتُهُ

salamu allahi al`azimi wa salawatuhu

Peace of Allah the All-great and His blessings

عَلَيْكَ يَا هَانِئُ بْنَ عُرْوَةَ

`alayka ya hani'u bna `urwata

be upon you, Hani' the son of `Urwah.

اَلسَّلاَمُ عَلَيْكَ ايُّهَا ٱلْعَبْدُ ٱلصَّالِحُ

alssalamu `alayka ayyuha al`abdu alssalihu

Peace be upon you, O righteous servant (of Allah),

اَلنَّاصِحُ لِلَّهِ وَلِرَسُولِهِ وَلامِيرِ ٱلْمُؤْمِنِينَ

alnnasihu lillahi wa lirasulihi wa li'amiri almu'minina

who acted sincerely for the sake of Allah, His Messenger, the Commander of the Faithful,

وَٱلْحَسَنِ وَٱلْحُسَيْنِ عَلَيْهِمُ ٱلسَّلاَمُ

walhasani walhusayni `alayhim alssalamu

al-Hasan, and al-Husayn, peace be upon them.

اشْهَدُ انَّكَ قُتِلْتَ مَظْلُوماً

ashhadu annaka qutilta mazluman

I bear witness that you were slain wrongly.

فَلَعَنَ ٱللَّهُ مَنْ قَتَلَكَ وَٱسْتَحَلَّ دَمَكَ

fala`ana allahu man qatalaka wastahalla damaka

So, may Allah curse those who slew you and dared to shed your blood

وَحَشَىٰ قُبُورَهُمْ نَاراً

wa hasha quburahum naran
and may He stuff their graves with fire.

اشْهَدُ انَّكَ لَقِيتَ ٱللَّهَ وَهُوَ رَاضٍ عَنْكَ

ashhadu annaka laqita allaha wa huwa radin `anka
I bear witness that you met Allah while He is pleased with You

بِمَا فَعَلْتَ وَنَصَحْتَ

bima fa`alta wa nasahta
for what you did and acted sincerely.

وَاشْهَدُ انَّكَ قَدْ بَلَغْتَ دَرَجَةَ ٱلشُّهَدَاءِ

wa ashhadu annaka qad balaghta darajata alshsuhada'i
And I bear witness that you have attained the rank of the martyrs,

وَجُعِلَ رُوحُكَ مَعَ ارْوَاحِ ٱلسُّعَدَاءِ

wa ju`ila ruhuka ma`a arwahi alssu`ada'i
your soul has been included with the souls of the delighted ones

بِمَا نَصَحْتَ لِلَّهِ وَلِرَسُولِهِ مُجْتَهِداً

bima nasahta lillahi wa lirasulihi mujtahidan
for you painstakingly acted with sincerity for Allah and for His Messenger,

وَبَذَلْتَ نَفْسَكَ فِي ذَاتِ ٱللَّهِ وَمَرْضَاتِهِ

wa badhalta nafsaka fi dhati allahi wa mardatihi
and sacrificed yourself for the sake of Allah and for the sake of attaining His pleasure.

فَرَحِمَكَ ٱللَّهُ وَرَضِيَ عَنْكَ

farahimaka allahu wa radiya `anka
So, may Allah have mercy upon you and be pleased with you,

وَحَشَرَكَ مَعَ مُحَمَّدٍ وَآلِهِ ٱلطَّاهِرِينَ

wa hasharaka ma`a muhammadin wa alihi alttahirina
may He include you with the group of Muhammad and his Immaculate Household,

وَجَمَعَنَا وَإِيَّاكُمْ مَعَهُمْ فِي دَارِ ٱلنَّعِيمِ

wa jama`ana wa iyyakum ma`ahum fi dari alnna`imi
and may He gather us with you and them in the Abode of Bliss.

وَسَلامٌ عَلَيْكَ وَرَحْمَةُ ٱللَّهِ وَبَرَكَاتُهُ

wa salamun `alayka wa rahmatu allahi wa barakatuhu
Peace and Allah's mercy and blessings be upon you.

The Prayers

You may then offer a two-unit prayer and present it as a gift to Hani' ibn `Urwah. Then, you may pray Almighty Allah to grant you your requests. As for bidding farewell to him, you may say the same form of wada` (bidding farewell) that is said to Muslim ibn `Aqil.

IMAM MUSA AL-KADHIM (A) & IMAM MUHAMMAD AL-JAWAD (A)

The Visitation

اَلسَّلاَمُ عَلَيْكُمَا يَا وَلِيَّيِ ٱللَّهِ

alssalamu `alaykuma ya waliyyay allahi

Peace be upon both of you, O Allah's most intimate servants.

اَلسَّلاَمُ عَلَيْكُمَا يَا حُجَّتَيِ ٱللَّهِ

alssalamu `alaykuma ya hujjatay allahi

Peace be upon both of you, O Allah's arguments.

اَلسَّلاَمُ عَلَيْكُمَا يَا نُورَيِ ٱللَّهِ فِي ظُلُمَاتِ ٱلارْضِ

alssalamu `alaykuma ya nuray allahi fi zulumati al-ardi

Peace be upon both of you, O Allah's lights in the darkness of the earth.

اشْهَدُ انَّكُمَا قَدْ بَلَّغْتُمَا عَنِ ٱللَّهِ مَا حَمَّلَكُمَا

ashhadu annakuma qad ballaghtuma `an allahi ma hammalakuma

I bear witness that you both conveyed faithfully that which Allah ordered You to convey,

وَحَفِظْتُمَا مَا ٱسْتُودِعْتُمَا

wa hafiztuma ma istudi`tuma

safeguarded that which He entrusted with you,

وَحَلَّلْتُمَا حَلاَلَ ٱللَّهِ

wa hallaltuma halala allahi

decided as lawful all that which Allah has deemed lawful,

وَحَرَّمْتُمَا حَرَامَ ٱللَّهِ

wa harramtuma harama allahi

decided as unlawful all that which Allah has deemed unlawful,

وَاقَمْتُمَا حُدُودَ ٱللَّهِ

wa aqamtuma hududa allahi

carried out the decrees of Allah,

وَتَلَوْتُمَا كِتَابَ ٱللَّهِ

wa talawtuma kitaba allahi
recited the Book of Allah,

وَصَبَرْتُمَا عَلَىٰ ٱلاذَىٰ فِي جَنْبِ ٱللَّهِ

wa sabartuma `ala al-adha fi janbi allahi
endured harm for the sake of Allah,

مُحْتَسِبَيْنِ حَتَّىٰ اتَاكُمَا ٱلْيَقِينُ

muhtasibayni hatta atakuma alyaqinu
expecting His reward, until death came upon you.

ابْرَا إِلَىٰ ٱللَّهِ مِنْ اعْدَائِكُمَا

abra'u ila allahi min a`da'ikuma
I repudiate your enemies in the presence of Allah

وَاتَقَرَّبُ إِلَىٰ ٱللَّهِ بِوِلاَيَتِكُمَا

wa ataqarrabu ila allahi biwilayatikuma
and I seek nearness to Allah through declaring loyalty to you both.

اتَيْتُكُمَا زَائِرا

ataytukuma za'iran
I have come to you both, visiting you,

عَارِفاً بِحَقِّكُمَا

`arifan bihaqqikuma
recognizing your rights,

مُوَالِياً لاوْلِيَائِكُمَا

miwaliyan li'awliya'ikuma
declaring loyalty to your loyalists,

مُعَادِياً لاعْدَائِكُمَا

mu`adiyan li'a`da'ikuma
showing enmity toward your enemies,

مُسْتَبْصِراً بِٱلْهُدَىٰ ٱلَّذِي انْتُمَا عَلَيْهِ

mustabsiran bilhuda alladhi antuma `alayhi
acknowledging the true guidance that you both follow,

عَارِفاً بِضَلاَلَةِ مَنْ خَالَفَكُمَا

`arifan bidalalati man khalafakuma
and understanding the deviation (from the right path) of any one who disagrees with you.

فَٱشْفَعَا لِي عِنْدَ رَبِّكُمَا

fashfa`a li `inda rabbikuma
So, (please) intercede for me with your Lord,

فَإِنَّ لَكُمَا عِنْدَ ٱللَّهِ جَاهاً عَظِيماً

fa'inna lakuma `inda allahi jahan `aziman
for you both enjoy with Allah a great standing

وَمَقَاماً مَحْمُوداً

wa maqaman mahmudan
and a praiseworthy position.

At this point, you may then turn to the side of the Imam's head and say the following words:

اَلسَّلاَمُ عَلَيْكُمَا يَا حُجَّتَيِ ٱللَّهِ فِي ارْضِهِ وَسَمَائِهِ

alssalamu `alaykuma ya hujjatay allahi fi ardihi wa sama'ihi
Peace be upon both of you, O Allah's arguments in His land and in His heavens.

عَبْدُكُمَا وَوَلِيُّكُمَا زَائِرُكُمَا

`abdukuma wa waliyyukuma za'irukuma
I—your servant and loyalist—have visited you both,

مُتَقَرِّباً إِلَىٰ ٱللَّهِ بِزِيَارَتِكُمَا

mutaqarriban ila allahi biziyaratikuma
seeking nearness to Allah through my visit to you both.

اَللَّهُمَّ ٱجْعَلْ لِي لِسَانَ صِدْقٍ فِي اوْلِيَائِكَ ٱلْمُصْطَفَيْنَ

allahumma ij`al li lisana sidqin fi awliya'ika almustafayna
O Allah, (please) ordain for me a goodly mention among your well-chosen, intimate servants,

وَحَبِّبْ إِلَيَّ مَشَاهِدَهُمْ

wa habbib ilayya mashahidahum
endear to me their shrines,

وَٱجْعَلْنِي مَعَهُمْ فِي ٱلدُّنْيَا وَٱلآخِرَةِ

waj`alni ma`ahum fi alddunya wal-akhirati
and include me with them in this world and in the Hereafter,

يَا ارْحَمَ ٱلرَّاحِمِينَ

ya arhama alrrahimina
O most merciful of all those who show mercy.

The Prayers

You may then offer a two-unit prayer for each Imam and then pray Almighty Allah for anything you wish.

The Farewell

When you intend to bid farewell to the two holy Imams, you may stop at the holy tomb and say the following words:

اَلسَّلاَمُ عَلَيْكُمَا يَا وَلِيَّيِ ٱللَّهِ

alssalamu `alaykuma ya waliyyay allahi
Peace be upon both of you, O Allah's representatives.

اسْتَوْدِعُكُمَا ٱللَّهَ

astawdi`ukuma allaha
I entrust you both with Allah

وَاقْرَا عَلَيْكُمَا ٱلسَّلاَمَ

wa aqra'u `alaykuma alssalama
and invoke His peace upon you both.

آمَنَّا بِٱللَّهِ وَبِٱلرَّسُولِ

amanna billah wa bilrrasuli
We believe in Allah, in the Messenger,

وَبِمَا جِئْتُمَا بِهِ وَدَلَلْتُمَا عَلَيْهِ

wa bima ji'tuma bihi wa dalaltuma `alayhi
and in that which you both have come with and instructed.

ٱللَّهُمَّ ٱكْتُبْنَا مَعَ ٱلشَّاهِدِينَ

allahumma iktubna ma`a alshshahidina
O Allah, write us down with those who bear witness.

ٱللَّهُمَّ لاَ تَجْعَلْهُ آخِرَ ٱلْعَهْدِ

allahumma la taj`alhu akhira al`ahdi
O Allah, (please) do not decide this visit

مِنْ زِيَارَتِي إِيَّاهُمَا

min ziyarati iyyahuma
to be the last visit of mine to them;

وَٱرْزُقْنِي ٱلْعَوْدَ إِلَيْهِمَا

warzuqni al`awda ilayhima
rather, grant me more chances to re-visit them

وَٱحْشُرْنِي مَعَهُمَا

wahshurni ma`ahuma
and include me with both of them,

وَمَعَ آبَائِهِمَا ٱلطَّاهِرِينَ

wa ma`a aba'ihima alttahirina
with their immaculate fathers,

وَٱلْقَائِمِ ٱلْحُجَّةِ مِنْ ذُرِّيَّتِهِمَا

walqa'imi alhujjati min dhurriyyatihima
and with the Rising, Argument Imam from their offspring.

يَا أرْحَمَ ٱلرَّاحِمِينَ

ya arhama alrrahimina

O most merciful of all those who show mercy.

You may then pray to Almighty Allah for your personal requests, and they shall be granted, Allah willing.

IMAM ALI AL-NAQI (A) & IMAM HASAN AL-ASKARI (A)

The Visitation

اَلسَّلاَمُ عَلَيْكُمَا يَا وَلِيَّيِ ٱللَّهِ

alssalamu `alaykuma ya waliyyy allahi
Peace be upon both of you, O representatives of Allah.

اَلسَّلاَمُ عَلَيْكُمَا يَا حُجَّتَيِ ٱللَّهِ

alssalamu `alaykuma ya hujjatay allahi
Peace be upon both of you, O Arguments of Allah (against His created beings).

اَلسَّلاَمُ عَلَيْكُمَا يَا نُورَيِ ٱللَّهِ فِي ظُلُمَاتِ ٱلارْضِ

alssalamu `alaykuma ya nuray allahi fi zulumati al-ardi
Peace be upon both of you, O Light of Allah in the darkness of the earth.

اَلسَّلاَمُ عَلَيْكُمَا يَا مَنْ بَدَا لِلَّهِ فِي شَانِكُمَا

alssalamu `alaykuma ya man bada lillahi fi sha'nikuma
Peace be upon both of you, O they about whom Allah has decided.

اتَيْتُكُمَا زَائِراً

ataytukuma za'iran
I have come to you visiting (your tombs),

وعَارِفاً بِحَقِّكُمَا

`arifan bihaqqikuma
recognizing your right,

مُعَادِياً لاِعْدَائِكُمَا

mu`adiyan li'a`da'ikuma
showing enmity towards your enemies,

مُوَالِياً لاوْلِيَائِكُمَا

muwaliyan li'awliya'ikuma
declaring loyalty to your loyalists,

مُؤْمِناً بِمَا آمَنْتُمَا بِهِ

mu'minan bima amantuma bihi
believing in that which you both believed in,

كَافِراً بِمَا كَفَرْتُمَا بِهِ

kafiran bima kafartuma bihi
disbelieving in all that which you both disbelieved in,

مُحَقِّقاً لِمَا حَقَّقْتُمَا

muhaqqiqan lima haqqaqtuma
deeming right all that which you deemed right,

مُبْطِلاً لِمَا ابْطَلْتُمَا

mubtilan lima abtaltuma
and deeming wrong all that which you deemed wrong.

اسْالُ ٱللَّهَ رَبِّي وَرَبَّكُمَا

as'alu allaha rabbi wa rabbakuma
I thus beseech Allah, my and your Lord,

انْ يَجْعَلَ حَظِّي مِنْ زِيَارَتِكُمَا

an yaj`ala hazzi min ziyaratikuma
to decide that my rewards for my visit to you both

ٱلصَّلاَةَ عَلَىٰ مُحَمَّدٍ وَآلِهِ

alssalata `ala muhammadin wa alihi
to be His sending blessings upon Muhammad and his Household

وَانْ يَرْزُقَنِي مُرَافَقَتَكُمَا فِي ٱلْجِنَانِ

wa an yarzuqani murafaqatakuma fi aljinani
and to grant me the favor of accompanying you both in the gardens of Paradise

مَعَ آبَائِكُمَا ٱلصَّالِحِينَ

ma`a aba'ikuma alssalihina
with your righteous fathers.

وَاسْأَلُهُ انْ يُعْتِقَ رَقَبَتِي مِنَ ٱلنَّارِ

wa as'aluhu an yu`tiqa raqabati min alnnari
I also beseech Him to save me from Hellfire,

وَيَرْزُقَنِي شَفَاعَتَكُمَا وَمُصَاحَبَتَكُمَا

wa yarzuqani shafa`atakuma wa musahabatakuma
to grant me your intercession and your company,

وَيُعَرِّفَ بَيْنِي وَبَيْنَكُمَا

wa yu`arrifa bayni wa baynakuma
to introduce me to you,

وَلاَ يَسْلُبَنِي حُبَّكُمَا

wa la yaslubani hubbakuma
not to take out from my heart love for you both

وَحُبَّ آبَائِكُمَا ٱلصَّالِحِينَ

wa hubba aba'ikuma alssalihina
and for your righteous fathers at all,

وَانْ لاَ يَجْعَلَهُ آخِرَ ٱلْعَهْدِ مِنْ زِيَارَتِكُمَا

wa an la yaj`alahu akhira al`ahdi min ziyaratikuma
not to decide this time of my visit to you as the last,

وَيَحْشُرَنِي مَعَكُمَا فِي ٱلْجَنَّةِ بِرَحْمَتِهِ

wa yahshurani ma`akuma fi aljannati birahmatihi
and to include me with your group in Paradise, out of His mercy .

اَللَّهُمَّ ٱرْزُقْنِي حُبَّهُمَا

allahumma irzuqni hubbahuma
O Allah, (please do) grant me love for them

وَتَوَفَّنِي عَلَىٰ مِلَّتِهِمَا

wa tawaffani `ala millatihima
and make me die following their faith.

اَللَّهُمَّ ٱلْعَنْ ظَالِمِي آلِ مُحَمَّدٍ حَقَّهُمْ وَٱنْتَقِمْ مِنْهُمْ

allahumma il`an zalimi ali muhammadin haqqahum wantaqim minhum

O Allah, curse and punish those who usurped the right of the Household of Muhammad wrongfully.

اَللَّهُمَّ ٱلْعَنِ ٱلاوَّلِينَ مِنْهُمْ وَٱلآخِرِينَ

allahumma il`an al-awwalina minhum wal-akhirina

O Allah, curse the past and the coming generations of those people,

وَضَاعِفْ عَلَيْهِمُ ٱلْعَذَابَ

wa da`if `alayhim al`adhaba

apply to them many folds of torture,

وَابْلِغْ بِهِمْ وَبِاشْيَاعِهِمْ

wa abligh bihim wa bi'ashya`ihim

and send them, their fans,

وَمُحِبِّيهِمْ وَمُتَّبِعِيهِمْ

wa muhibbihim wa muttabi`ihim

their adherents, and the followers

اسْفَلَ دَرْكٍ مِنَ ٱلْجَحِيمِ

asfala darkin min aljahimi

to the deepest area of Hellfire.

إِنَّكَ عَلَىٰ كُلِّ شَيْءٍ قَدِيرٌ

innaka `ala kulli shay'in qadirun

Verily, You have power over all things.

اَللَّهُمَّ عَجِّلْ فَرَجَ وَلِيِّكَ وَٱبْنِ وَلِيِّكَ

allahumma `ajjil faraja waliyyika wabni waliyyika

O Allah, (please do) hasten the Relief of Your representative and the son of Your representative

وَٱجْعَلْ فَرَجَنَا مَعَ فَرَجِهِمْ

waj`al farajana ma`a farajihim

and cause our relief to accompany his relief,

يَا ارْحَمَ ٱلرَّاحِمِينَ

ya arhama alrrahimina
O most merciful of all those who show mercy.

You may then pray for yourself and your parents.

The Prayers

If you can reach their tombs, you may offer a two-unit prayer there. or in the mosque which is adjacent to the house of the two Imams, peace of Allah be upon them, where they used to perform the prayers.

The Farewell

When you intend to bid farewell to the two holy Imams, you may stop at the holy tomb and say the following words:

ٱلسَّلاَمُ عَلَيْكُمَا يَا وَلِيَّيِ ٱللَّهِ

alssalamu `alaykuma ya waliyyay allahi
Peace be upon both of you, O Allah's representatives.

اسْتَوْدِعُكُمَا ٱللَّهَ

astawdi`ukuma allaha
I entrust you both with Allah

وَاقْرَا عَلَيْكُمَا ٱلسَّلاَمَ

wa aqra'u `alaykuma alssalama
and invoke His peace upon you both.

آمَنَّا بِٱللَّهِ وَبِٱلرَّسُولِ

amanna billah wa bilrrasuli
We believe in Allah, in the Messenger,

وَبِمَا جِئْتُمَا بِهِ وَدَلَلْتُمَا عَلَيْهِ

wa bima ji'tuma bihi wa dalaltuma `alayhi
and in that which you both have come with and instructed.

اَللَّهُمَّ ٱكْتُبْنَا مَعَ ٱلشَّاهِدِينَ

allahumma iktubna ma`a alshshahidina

O Allah, write us down with those who bear witness.

اَللَّهُمَّ لاَ تَجْعَلْهُ آخِرَ ٱلْعَهْدِ مِنْ زِيَارَتِي إِيَّاهُمَا

allahumma la taj`alhu akhira al`ahdi min ziyarati iyyahuma

O Allah, (please) do not decide this visit to be my last visit to them;

وَٱرْزُقْنِي ٱلْعَوْدَ إِلَيْهِمَا

warzuqni al`awda ilayhima

rather, grant me more chances to re-visit them

وَٱحْشُرْنِي مَعَهُمَا وَمَعَ آبَائِهِمَا ٱلطَّاهِرِينَ

wahshurni ma`ahuma wa ma`a aba'ihima alttahirina

and include me with both of them, with their immaculate fathers,

وَٱلْقَائِمِ ٱلْحُجَّةِ مِنْ ذُرِّيَّتِهِمَا

walqa'imi alhujjati min dhurriyyatihima

and with the Rising, Argument Imam from their offspring.

يَا ارْحَمَ ٱلرَّاحِمِينَ

ya arhama alrrahimina

O most merciful of all those who show mercy.

ZIYARAH OF LADY NARGIS (R)

The mother of Imam al-Qa'im whose tomb is situated behind the tomb of our master Imam al-Hasan al-`Askari (a). You should thus say the following words while visiting her tomb:

اَلسَّلاَمُ عَلَىٰ رَسُولِ ٱللَّهِ

alssalamu `ala rasuli allahi

Peace be upon Allah's Messenger,

صَلَّىٰ ٱللَّهُ عَلَيْهِ وَآلِهِ

salla allahu `alayhi wa alihi

Allah's blessings be upon him,

اَلصَّادِقِ ٱلامِينِ

alssadiqi al-amini

the veracious and honest.

اَلسَّلاَمُ عَلَىٰ مَوْلاَنَا امِيرِ ٱلْمُؤْمِنِينَ

alssalamu `ala mawlana amiri almu'minina

Peace be upon our master the Commander of the Faithful.

اَلسَّلاَمُ عَلَىٰ ٱلائِمَّةِ ٱلطَّاهِرِينَ

alssalamu `ala al-a'immati alttahirina

Peace be upon the Immaculate Imams

اَلْحُجَجِ ٱلْمَيَامِينِ

alhujaji almayamini

and the blessed Arguments (of Allah).

اَلسَّلاَمُ عَلَىٰ وَالِدَةِ ٱلإِمَامِ

alssalamu `ala walidati al-imami

Peace be upon the mother of the Imam;

وَٱلْمُودَعَةِ اسْرَارَ ٱلْمَلِكِ ٱلْعَلاَّمِ

walmuda`ati asrara almaliki al`allami

the lady entrusted with the secrets of the All-knowing King

وَٱلْحَامِلَةِ لاِشْرَفِ ٱلانَامِ

walhamilati li'ashrafi al-anami
and the bearer of the most honorable of all beings.

اَلسَّلاَمُ عَلَيْكِ ايَّتُهَا ٱلصِّدِّيقَةُ ٱلْمَرْضِيَّةُ

alssalamu `alayki ayyatuha alssiddiqatu almardiyyatu
Peace be upon you, O veracious and well-pleased lady.

اَلسَّلاَمُ عَلَيْكِ يَا شَبِيهَةَ امِّ مُوسَىٰ

alssalamu `alayki ya shabihata ummi musa
Peace be upon you, O equivalent of (Prophet) Moses' mother

وَٱبْنَةَ حَوَارِيِّ عِيسَىٰ

wabnata hawariyyi `isa
and daughter of (Prophet) Jesus' Disciple.

اَلسَّلاَمُ عَلَيْكِ ايَّتُهَا ٱلتَّقِيَّةُ ٱلنَّقِيَّةُ

alssalamu `alayki ayyatuha alttaqiyyatu alnnaqiyyatu
Peace be upon you, O pious and bright.

اَلسَّلاَمُ عَلَيْكِ ايَّتُهَا ٱلرَّضِيَّةُ ٱلْمَرْضِيَّةُ

alssalamu `alayki ayyatuha alrradiyyatu almardiyyatu
Peace be upon you, O well-pleased and well-contented.

اَلسَّلاَمُ عَلَيْكِ ايَّتُهَا ٱلْمَنْعُوتَةُ فِي ٱلإِنْجِيلِ

alssalamu `alayki ayyatuha alman`utatu fi al-injili
Peace be upon you, O described in the Gospel,

ٱلْمَخْطُوبَةُ مِنْ رُوحِ ٱللَّهِ ٱلامِينِ

almakhtubatu min ruhi allahi al-amini
betrothed from the Honest Spirit of Allah,

وَمَنْ رَغِبَ فِي وُصْلَتِهَا مُحَمَّدٌ سَيِّدُ ٱلْمُرْسَلِينَ

wa man raghiba fi wuslatiha muhammadun sayyidu almursalina
desired for relationship by Muhammad the chief of the Messenger,

وَٱلْمُسْتَوْدَعَةُ اسْرَارَ رَبِّ ٱلْعَالَمِينَ

walmustawda`atu asrara rabbi al`alamina
and entrusted with the secrets of the Lord of the Worlds.

اَلسَّلاَمُ عَلَيْكِ وَعَلَىٰ آبَائِكِ ٱلْحَوَارِيِّينَ

alssalamu `alayki wa `ala aba'iki alhawariyyina
Peace be upon you and upon your fathers the Disciples.

اَلسَّلاَمُ عَلَيْكِ وَعَلَىٰ بَعْلِكِ وَوَلَدِكِ

alssalamu `alayki wa `ala ba`liki wa waladiki
Peace be upon you, your husband, and your son.

اَلسَّلاَمُ عَلَيْكِ وَعَلَىٰ رُوحِكِ وَبَدَنِكِ ٱلطَّاهِرِ

alssalamu `alayki wa `ala ruhiki wa badaniki alttahiri
Peace be upon you and upon your pure spirit and body.

اشْهَدُ انَّكِ احْسَنْتِ ٱلْكَفَالَةَ

ashhadu annaki ahsanti alkafalata
I bear witness that you acted excellently in custody (of your son),

وَادَّيْتِ ٱلامَانَةَ

wa addayti al-amanata
fulfilled the trust,

وَٱجْتَهَدْتِ فِي مَرْضَاتِ ٱللَّهِ

wajtahadti fi mardati allahi
worked painstakingly for gaining Allah's pleasure,

وَصَبَرْتِ فِي ذَاتِ ٱللَّهِ

wa sabarti fi dhati allahi
acted steadfastly for the sake of Allah,

وَحَفِظْتِ سِرَّ ٱللَّهِ

wa hafizti sirra allahi
kept the secret of Allah,

وَحَمَلْتِ وَلِيَّ ٱللَّهِ

wa hamalti waliyya allahi

born the representative of Allah,

وَبَالَغْتِ فِي حِفْظِ حُجَّةِ ٱللَّهِ

wa balaghti fi hifzi hujjati allahi

did meticulously in the safeguarding of the Argument of Allah,

وَرَغِبْتِ فِي وُصْلَةِ ابْنَاءِ رَسُولِ ٱللَّهِ

wa raghibti fi wuslati abna'i rasuli allahi

and desired for maintaining the descendants of the Messenger of Allah

عَارِفَةً بِحَقِّهِمْ

`arifatan bihaqqihim

as you had full recognition of their rights,

مُؤْمِنَةً بِصِدْقِهِمْ

mu'minatan bisidqihim

believed in their honesty,

مُعْتَرِفَةً بِمَنْزِلَتِهِمْ

mu`tarifatan bimanzilatihim

professed their status,

مُسْتَبْصِرَةً بِامْرِهِمْ

mustabsiratan bi'amrihim

acknowledged their matter,

مُشْفِقَةً عَلَيْهِمْ

mushfiqatan `alayhim

sympathized with them,

مُؤْثِرَةً هَوَاهُمْ

mu'thiratan hawahum

and preceded their inclination to yours.

وَاشْهَدُ انَّكِ مَضَيْتِ عَلَىٰ بَصِيرَةٍ مِنْ امْرِكِ

wa ashhadu annaki madayti `ala basiratin min amriki

I also bear witness that you passed away with full awareness of the truth,

مُقْتَدِيَةً بِٱلصَّالِحِينَ

muqtadiyatan bilssalihina

following the examples of the righteous ones,

رَاضِيَةً مَرْضِيَّةً

radiyatan mardiyyatan

well-pleased, well-contented,

تَقِيَّةً نَقِيَّةً زَكِيَّةً

taqiyyatan naqiyyatan zakiyyatan

pious, bright, and pure.

فَرَضِيَ ٱللَّهُ عَنْكِ وَارْضَاكِ

faradiya allahu `anki wa ardaki

So, may Allah be pleased with you and may He please you

وَجَعَلَ ٱلْجَنَّةَ مَنْزِلَكِ وَمَاوَاكِ

wa ja`ala aljannata manzilaki wa ma'waki

and decide Paradise to be your abode and dwelling.

فَلَقَدْ اوْلاَكِ مِنَ ٱلْخَيْرَاتِ مَا اوْلاَكِ

falaqad awlaki min alkhayrati ma awlaki

He has endued you with lots of the good things with which He has bestowed upon you

وَاعْطَاكِ مِنَ ٱلشَّرَفِ مَا بِهِ اغْنَاكِ

wa a`taki min alshsharafi ma bihi aghnaki

and He has given you the honorable position that made you dispense with everything else.

فَهَنَاكِ ٱللَّهُ بِمَا مَنَحَكِ

fahannaki allahu bima manahaki

May Allah delight and gratify you

مِنَ ٱلْكَرَامَةِ وَامْرَاكِ

min alkaramati wa amraki

with the dignity that He has granted you.

You may then raise your head towards the heavens and say the following dua:

اَللَّهُمَّ إِيَّاكَ اَعْتَمَدْتُ

allahumma iyyaka i`tamadtu

O Allah, to You alone have I had recourse.

وَلِرِضَاكَ طَلَبْتُ

wa liridaka talabtu

Your pleasure alone have I sought.

وَبِاوْلِيَائِكَ إِلَيْكَ تَوَسَّلْتُ

wa bi'awliya'ika ilayka tawassaltu

Through Your representatives have I sought means to You.

وَعَلَىٰ غُفْرَانِكَ وَحِلْمِكَ اَتَّكَلْتُ

wa `ala ghufranika wa hilmika ittakaltu

On Your forgiveness and forbearance have I relied.

وَبِكَ اَعْتَصَمْتُ

wa bika i`tasamtu

By You alone have I held fast.

وَبِقَبْرِ امِّ وَلِيِّكَ لُذْتُ

wa biqabri ummi waliyyika ludhtu

In the tomb of the mother of Your representative have I taken refuge.

فَصَلِّ عَلَىٰ مُحَمَّدٍ وَآلِ مُحَمَّدٍ

fasalli `ala muhammadin wa ali muhammadin

So, (please) send blessings upon Muhammad and Muhammad's Household,

وَٱنْفَعْنِي بِزِيَارَتِهَا

wanfa`ni biziyaratiha

make me benefit by my visit to her,

وَثَبِّتْنِي عَلَىٰ مَحَبَّتِهَا

wa thabbitni `ala mahabbatiha

keep me firm on love for her,

وَلاَ تَحْرِمْنِي شَفَاعَتَهَا

wa la tahrimni shafa`ataha

do not deprive me of her intercession

وَشَفَاعَةَ وَلَدِهَا

wa shafa`ata waladiha

and her son's intercession,

وَٱرْزُقْنِي مُرَافَقَتَهَا

warzuqni murafaqataha

provide me with being in her companionship,

وَٱحْشُرْنِي مَعَهَا وَمَعَ وَلَدِهَا

wahshurni ma`aha wa ma`a waladiha

and include me with the group of her and her son

كَمَا وَفَّقْتَنِي لِزِيَارَةِ وَلَدِهَا وَزِيَارَتِهَا

kama waffaqtani liziyarati waladiha wa ziyaratiha

as You have grant me success to visit her son and her.

اَللَّهُمَّ إِنِّي اتَوَجَّهُ إِلَيْكَ بِالائِمَّةِ ٱلطَّاهِرِينَ

allahumma inni atawajjahu ilayka bil-a'immati alttahirina

O Allah, I do turn my face towards You by means of the immaculate Imams

وَاتَوَسَّلُ إِلَيْكَ بِٱلْحُجَجِ ٱلْمَيَامِينِ

wa atawassalu ilayka bilhujaji almayamini

and I choose as my mediation to You the blessed Arguments

مِنْ آلِ طٰهٰ وَيٰس

min ali taha wa yasin

from the descendants of Taha and Yasin,

انْ تُصَلِّيَ عَلَىٰ مُحَمَّدٍ وَآلِ مُحَمَّدٍ ٱلطَّيِّبِينَ

an tusalliya `ala muhammadin wa ali muhammadin alttayyibina
(beseeching You) to bless Muhammad and Muhammad's Household the pure

وَانْ تَجْعَلَنِي مِنَ ٱلْمُطْمَئِنِّينَ ٱلْفَائِزِينَ

wa an taj`alani min almutma'innina alfa'izina
and to make me of the tranquil, triumphant,

ٱلْفَرِحِينَ ٱلْمُسْتَبْشِرِينَ

alfarihina almustabshirina
blissful, and glorious ones

ٱلَّذِينَ لاَ خَوْفٌ عَلَيْهِمْ وَلاَ هُمْ يَحْزَنُونَ

alladhina la khawfun `alayhim wa la hum yahzanuna
on whom there is neither fear nor shall they be aggrieved.

وَٱجْعَلْنِي مِمَّنْ قَبِلْتَ سَعْيَهُ

waj`alni mimman qabilta sa`yahu
And (please) make me one of those whose deeds are admitted by You,

وَيَسَّرْتَ امْرَهُ

wa yassarta amrahu
whose affairs will be made easy by You,

وَكَشَفْتَ ضُرَّهُ

wa kashafta durrahu
whose distress will be relieved by You,

وَآمَنْتَ خَوْفَهُ

wa amanta khawfahu
and whose fear will be secured by You.

اَللَّهُمَّ بِحَقِّ مُحَمَّدٍ وَآلِ مُحَمَّدٍ

allahumma bihaqqi muhammadin wa ali muhammadin
O Allah [I beseech You] in the name of Muhammad and the Household of Muhammad,

صَلِّ عَلَىٰ مُحَمَّدٍ وَآلِ مُحَمَّدٍ

salli `ala muhammadin wa ali muhammadin
(please) send blessings upon Muhammad and the Household of Muhammad,

وَلاَ تَجْعَلْهُ آخِرَ الْعَهْدِ مِنْ زِيَارَتِي إِيَّاهَا

wa la taj`alhu akhira al`ahdi min ziyarati iyyaha
do not decide this visit to be the last time of my visits to her;

وَٱرْزُقْنِي ٱلْعَوْدَ إِلَيْهَا ابداً مَا ابْقَيْتَنِي

warzuqni al`awda ilayha abadan ma abqaytani
rather, endue me with other chances to re-visit her as long as You keep me alive.

وَإِذَا تَوَفَّيْتَنِي فَٱحْشُرْنِي فِي زُمْرَتِهَا

wa idha tawaffaytani fahshurni fi zumratiha
If You decide to grasp my soul, then (please) include me with her group,

وَادْخِلْنِي فِي شَفَاعَةِ وَلَدِهَا وَشَفَاعَتِهَا

wa adkhilni fi shafa`ati waladiha wa shafa`atiha
bring me in the intercession of her son and her,

وَٱغْفِرْ لِي وَلِوَالِدَيَّ

waghfir li wa liwalidayya
forgive me and my parents

وَلِلْمُؤْمِنِينَ وَٱلْمُؤْمِنَاتِ

wa lilmu'minina walmu'minati
as well as the believing men and women,

وَآتِنَا فِي ٱلدُّنْيَا حَسَنَةً

wa atina fi alddunya hasanatan
give us good in this world

وَفِي ٱلآخِرَةِ حَسَنَةً

wa fi al-akhirati hasanatan
and good in the Hereafter,

وَقِنَا بِرَحْمَتِكَ عَذَابَ ٱلنَّارِ

wa qina birahmatika `adhaba alnnari
and save us, out of Your mercy, from the chastisement of Fire.

وَٱلسَّلاَمُ عَلَيْكُمْ يَا سَادَاتِي

walssalamu `alaykum ya sadati
Peace be upon you all, O my masters.

وَرَحْمَةُ ٱللَّهِ وَبَرَكَاتُهُ

wa rahmatu allahi wa barakatuhu
Allah's mercy and blessings, too, be upon you.

ZIYARAH OF LADY HAKIMAH (R)

Lady Ḥakīmah, the daughter of Imam Muḥammad al-Taqī ('a), whose grave is at the feet of the tomb of the two Imams. The following text is to be recited while facing in the direction of the qiblah.

اَلسَّلاٰمُ عَلىٰ آدَمَ صِفْوَةِ اللهِ، اَلسَّلاٰمُ عَلىٰ نُوحٍ نَبِيِّ اللهِ، اَلسَّلاٰمُ عَلىٰ إِبْرَاهِيمَ خَلِيلِ اللهِ، اَلسَّلاٰمُ عَلىٰ مُوسَى كَلِيمِ اللهِ، اَلسَّلاٰمُ عَلىٰ عِيسَى رُوحِ اللهِ،

Peace be to Adam, the chosen of Allah. Peace be to Noah, the prophet of Allah. Peace be to Abraham, the dedicated friend of Allah. Peace be to Moses, Allah's interlocutor. Peace be to Jesus, the spirit of Allah.

اَلسَّلاٰمُ عَلَيْكَ يَا رَسُولَ اللهِ، اَلسَّلاٰمُ عَلَيْكَ يَا خَيْرَ خَلْقِ اللهِ، اَلسَّلاٰمُ عَلَيْكَ يَا صَفِيَّ اللهِ، اَلسَّلاٰمُ عَلَيْكَ يَا مُحَمَّدَ بْنَ عَبْدِ اللهِ خَاتَمَ النَّبِيِّينَ، اَلسَّلاٰمُ عَلَيْكَ يَا أَمِيرَ الْمُؤْمِنِينَ عَلِيَّ بْنَ أَبِي طَالِبٍ وَصِيَّ رَسُولِ اللهِ، اَلسَّلاٰمُ عَلَيْكِ يَا فَاطِمَةُ سَيِّدَةَ نِسَاءِ الْعَالَمِينَ،

Peace be to you, O Apostle of Allah! Peace be to you, O best of Allah's creation! Peace be to you, O favorite of Allah! Peace be to you, O Muḥammad ibn 'Abd Allah, the Seal of the Prophets! Peace be to you, O 'Alī ibn Abī Ṭālib, the Commander of the Faithful and legatee of the Apostle of Allah! Peace be to you, O Fāṭimah, mistress of the world's womankind!

اَلسَّلاٰمُ عَلَيْكُمَا يَا سِبْطَيِ الرَّحْمَةِ، وَسَيِّدَيْ شَبَابِ أَهْلِ الْجَنَّةِ، اَلسَّلاٰمُ عَلَيْكَ يَا عَلِيَّ بْنَ الْحُسَيْنِ سَيِّدَ الْعَابِدِينَ، وَقُرَّةَ عَيْنِ النَّاظِرِينَ، اَلسَّلاٰمُ عَلَيْكَ يَا مُحَمَّدَ بْنَ عَلِيٍّ بَاقِرَ الْعِلْمِ بَعْدَ النَّبِيِّ، اَلسَّلاٰمُ عَلَيْكَ يَا جَعْفَرَ بْنَ مُحَمَّدٍ الصَّادِقَ الْبَارَّ الْأَمِينَ،

Peace be to you, O grandsons of the Prophet of Mercy and doyens of the youth of paradise. Peace be to you, O 'Ali ibn al-Ḥusayn, foremost of the devout and delight of the onlookers! Peace be to you, O Muḥammad ibn 'Alī, exponent of Divine knowledge after the Prophet! Peace be to you, O Ja'far ibn Muḥammad, the truthful, pious and trustworthy Imam!

اَلسَّلاٰمُ عَلَيْكَ يٰا مُوسَى بْنَ جَعْفَرٍ الطّٰاهِرَ الطُّهْرَ، اَلسَّلاٰمُ عَلَيْكَ يٰا عَلِيَّ بْنَ مُوسَى الرِّضَا الْمُرْتَضىٰ، اَلسَّلاٰمُ عَلَيْكَ يٰا مُحَمَّدَ بْنَ عَلِيٍّ التَّقِيَّ، اَلسَّلاٰمُ عَلَيْكَ يٰا عَلِيَّ بْنَ مُحَمَّدٍ النَّقِيَّ النّٰاصِحَ الْأَمِينَ، اَلسَّلاٰمُ عَلَيْكَ يٰا حَسَنَ بْنَ عَلِيٍّ، اَلسَّلاٰمُ عَلَى الْوَصِيِّ مِنْ بَعْدِهِ .

Peace be to you, O Mūsā ibn Ja'far, the pure and immaculate Imam! Peace be to you, O 'Alī ibn Mūsā, the approved and favoured Imam! Peace be to you, O Muḥammad ibn 'Alī, the Godwary Imam. Peace be to you, O 'Alī ibn Muḥammad, the blameless and trustworthy advisor! Peace be to you, O Ḥasan ibn 'Alī! Peace be to the legatee after him!

اَللّٰهُمَّ صَلِّ عَلىٰ نُورِكَ وَسِرَاجِكَ، وَ وَلِيِّ وَلِيِّكَ وَ وَصِيِّ وَصِيِّكَ، وَ حُجَّتِكَ عَلىٰ خَلْقِكَ،

O Allah, bless Your light and lamp, the walī of Your walī, the legatee of Your legatee and Your testament to Your creation!

اَلسَّلاٰمُ عَلَيْكِ يٰا بِنْتَ رَسُولِ اللّٰهِ، اَلسَّلاٰمُ عَلَيْكِ يٰا بِنْتَ فَاطِمَةَ وَخَدِيجَةَ، اَلسَّلاٰمُ عَلَيْكِ يٰا بِنْتَ أَمِيرِ الْمُؤْمِنِينَ، اَلسَّلاٰمُ عَلَيْكِ يٰا بِنْتَ الْحَسَنِ وَ الْحُسَيْنِ،

Peace be to you, O daughter of the Apostle of Allah! Peace be to you, O daughter of Fāṭimah and Khadījah! Peace be to you, O daughter of the Commander of the Faithful! Peace be to you, O daughter of al-Ḥasan and al-Ḥusayn!

اَلسَّلاٰمُ عَلَيْكِ يٰا بِنْتَ وَلِيِّ اللّٰهِ، اَلسَّلاٰمُ عَلَيْكِ يٰا أُخْتَ وَلِيِّ اللّٰهِ، اَلسَّلاٰمُ عَلَيْكِ يٰا عَمَّةَ وَلِيِّ اللّٰهِ، اَلسَّلاٰمُ عَلَيْكِ يٰا بِنْتَ مُحَمَّدِ بْنِ عَلِيٍّ التَّقِيِّ، وَ رَحْمَةُ اللّٰهِ وَ بَرَكَاتُهُ،

Peace be to you, O daughter of Allah's walī! Peace be to you, O sister of Allah's walī! Peace be to you, O aunt of Allah's walī! Peace be to you, O daughter of Muḥammad ibn 'Alī al-Taqī, and may Allah's mercy and His bounties be upon you!

اَلسَّلاٰمُ عَلَيْكِ عَرَّفَ اللّٰهُ بَيْنَنَا وَبَيْنَكُمْ فِي الْجَنَّةِ، وَ حَشَرَنَا فِي زُمْرَتِكُمْ، وَ أَوْرَدَنَا حَوْضَ نَبِيِّكُمْ، وَ سَقَانَا بِكَأْسِ جَدِّكُمْ، مِنْ يَدِ عَلِيِّ بْنِ أَبِي طَالِبٍ، صَلَوَاتُ اللّٰهِ عَلَيْكُمْ،

Peace be to you, may Allah acquaint us and you with one another in paradise and gather us in your fold and admit us at the Pool of the Prophet and give us to drink from the cup of your ancestor, by the hand of 'Alī ibn Abī Ṭālib! May Allah's blessings be upon you.

أَسْأَلُ اللهَ أَنْ يُرِيَنَا فِيكُمُ السُّرُورَ والْفَرَجَ، وَ أَنْ يَجْمَعَنَا وَ إِيَّاكُمْ فِي زُمْرَةِ جَدِّكُمْ مُحَمَّدٍ صَلَّى اللهُ عَلَيْهِ وَ آلِهِ، وَ أَنْ لاٰ يَسْلُبَنَا مَعْرِفَتَكُمْ، إِنَّهُ وَلِيٌّ قَدِيرٌ،

I beseech Allah to show us delight and relief in you and to gather us and you in the fold of your ancestor, Muḥammad, may Allah bless him and his Family, and not to divest us of your knowledge. Indeed He is the all-powerful guardian.

أَتَقَرَّبُ إِلَى اللهِ بِحُبِّكُمْ، والْبَرَاءَةِ مِنْ أَعْدَائِكُمْ، وَ التَّسْلِيمِ إِلَى اللهِ، رَاضِيًا بِهِ غَيْرَ مُنْكِرٍ وَ لاٰ مُسْتَكْبِرٍ، وَ عَلىٰ يَقِينِ مَا أَتَى بِهِ مُحَمَّدٌ وَ بِهِ رَاضٍ، نَطْلُبُ بِذَلِكَ وَجْهَكَ يٰا سَيِّدِي، اَللّٰهُمَّ وَ رِضَاكَ وَ الدَّارَ الْآخِرَةَ،

I seek nearness to Allah through my love for you and my repudiation of your enemies, through my submission to Allah out of compliance to Him, without denial and defiance, and through my conviction in the teachings brought by Muḥammad, while I am satisfied and pleased with them, and with that I seek Your pleasure, O my Master., O Allah, our fate in the abode of the Hereafter depends on Your approval!

يٰا حَكِيمَةُ اشْفَعِي لِي فِي الْجَنَّةِ، فَإِنَّ لَكِ عِنْدَ اللهِ شَأْنًا مِنَ الشَّأْنِ

O Ḥakīmah, intercede for me in paradise, for you have indeed an eminent station with Allah!

اَللّٰهُمَّ إِنِّي أَسْأَلُكَ أَنْ تَخْتِمَ لِي بِالسَّعَادَةِ، فَلاٰ تَسْلُبَ مِنِّي مَا أَنَا فِيهِ، ولاٰ حَوْلَ وَ لاٰ قُوَّةَ إِلّٰا بِاللهِ الْعَلِيِّ الْعَظِيمِ،

O Allah, I beseech You to conclude my life with felicity, and do not take away from me what (faith) I presently possess. There is no power or force except what derives from Allah, the All-exalted and the All-great!

اَللّٰهُمَّ اسْتَجِبْ لَنَا، وتَقَبَّلْهُ بِكَرَمِكَ وعِزَّتِكَ، وَ بِرَحْمَتِكَ وَ عَافِيَتِكَ، وَ صَلَّى اللهُ عَلىٰ مُحَمَّدٍ وَ آلِهِ أَجْمَعِينَ، وَ سَلَّمَ تَسْلِيمًا يٰا أَرْحَمَ الرَّاحِمِينَ .

O Allah, answer our petitions and accept our devotions with Your generosity, Your might, Your mercy, and Your gift of well-being. May Allah bless Muḥammad and all his Family and greet them with the worthiest greetings! O Most Merciful of the merciful.

THE 12TH HOLY IMAM (A)

سَلاَمٌ عَلَىٰ آلِ يٰس

salamun `ala ale yasin
Peace be upon the Household of Yasin.

اَلسَّلاَمُ عَلَيْكَ يَا دَاعِيَ ٱللَّهِ وَرَبَّانِيَّ آيَاتِهِ

alssalamu `alayka ya da`iya allahi wa rabbaniyya ayatihi
Peace be upon you, O caller to Allah and interpreter of His Verses.

اَلسَّلاَمُ عَلَيْكَ يَا بَابَ ٱللَّهِ وَدَيَّانَ دِينِهِ

alssalamu `alayka ya baba allahi wa dayyana dinihi
Peace be upon you, O door to Allah and applier of His religion.

اَلسَّلاَمُ عَلَيْكَ يَا خَلِيفَةَ ٱللَّهِ وَنَاصِرَ حَقِّهِ

alssalamu `alayka ya khalifata allahi wa nasira haqqihi
Peace be upon you, O viceroy of Allah and backer of His right.

اَلسَّلاَمُ عَلَيْكَ يَا حُجَّةَ ٱللَّهِ وَدَلِيلَ إِرَادَتِهِ

alssalamu `alayka ya hujjata allahi wa dalila iradatihi
Peace be upon you, O Argument of Allah and sign of His volition.

اَلسَّلاَمُ عَلَيْكَ يَا تَالِيَ كِتَابِ ٱللَّهِ وَتَرْجُمَانَهُ

alssalamu `alayka ya taliya kitabi allahi wa tarjumanihi
Peace be upon you, O reciter of the Book of Allah and its interpreter.

اَلسَّلاَمُ عَلَيْكَ فِي آنَاءِ لَيْلِكَ وَأَطْرَافِ نَهَارِكَ

alssalamu `alayka fi ana'i laylika wa atrafi naharika
Peace be upon you at the hours of Your night and the two ends of Your day.

اَلسَّلاَمُ عَلَيْكَ يَا بَقِيَّةَ ٱللَّهِ فِي أَرْضِهِ

alssalamu `alayka ya baqiyyata allahi fi ardihi
Peace be upon you, O herald of Allah on His lands.

ٱلسَّلاَمُ عَلَيْكَ يَا مِيثَاقَ ٱللَّهِ ٱلَّذِي أَخَذَهُ وَوَكَّدَهُ

alssalamu `alayka ya mithaqa allahi alladhi akhadhahu wa wakkadahu

Peace be upon you, O covenant of Allah that He has made and confirmed.

ٱلسَّلاَمُ عَلَيْكَ يَا وَعْدَ ٱللَّهِ ٱلَّذِي ضَمِنَهُ

alssalamu `alayka ya wa`da allahi alladhi daminahu

Peace be upon you, O Promise of Allah that He has assured.

ٱلسَّلاَمُ عَلَيْكَ أَيُّهَا ٱلْعَلَمُ ٱلْمَنْصُوبُ

alssalamu `alayka ayyuha al`alamu almansubu

Peace be upon you, O appointed pennon,

وَٱلْعِلْمُ ٱلْمَصْبُوبُ

wal`ilmu almasbubu

poured knowledge,

وَٱلْغَوْثُ وَٱلرَّحْمَةُ ٱلْوَاسِعَةُ

walghawthu walrrahmatu alwasi`atu

aid, and expansive mercy.

وَعْداً غَيْرَ مَكْذُوبٍ

wa`dan ghayra makdhubin

This is verily a promise that shall never be belied.

ٱلسَّلاَمُ عَلَيْكَ حِينَ تَقُومُ

alssalamu `alayka hina taqumu

Peace be upon you whenever you rise (to undertake the mission).

ٱلسَّلاَمُ عَلَيْكَ حِينَ تَقْعُدُ

alssalamu `alayka hina taq`udu

Peace be upon you whenever you sit.

ٱلسَّلاَمُ عَلَيْكَ حِينَ تَقْرَأُ وَتُبَيِّنُ

alssalamu `alayka hina taqra'u wa tubayyinu

Peace be upon you whenever you recite and elucidate.

اَلسَّلاَمُ عَلَيْكَ حِينَ تُصَلِّي وَتَقْنُتُ

alssalamu `alayka hina tusalli wa taqnutu

Peace be upon you whenever you offer prayer and supplicate.

اَلسَّلاَمُ عَلَيْكَ حِينَ تَرْكَعُ وَتَسْجُدُ

alssalamu `alayka hina tarka`u wa tasjudu

Peace be upon you whenever you genuflect and prostrate (yourself for Allah).

اَلسَّلاَمُ عَلَيْكَ حِينَ تُهَلِّلُ وَتُكَبِّرُ

alssalamu `alayka hina tuhallilu wa tukabbiru

Peace be upon you whenever you profess Allah's Godhead and profess His All-greatness.

اَلسَّلاَمُ عَلَيْكَ حِينَ تَحْمَدُ وَتَسْتَغْفِرُ

alssalamu `alayka hin tahmadu wa tastaghfiru

Peace be upon you whenever you praise Allah and implore for His forgiveness.

اَلسَّلاَمُ عَلَيْكَ حِينَ تُصْبِحُ وَتُمْسِي

alssalamu `alayka hina tusbihu wa tumsi

Peace be upon you whenever you begin and end your day.

اَلسَّلاَمُ عَلَيْكَ فِي ٱللَّيْلِ إِذَا يَغْشَىٰ

alssalamu `alayka fi allayli idha yaghsha

Peace be upon you in the night when it draws a veil

وَٱلنَّهَارِ إِذَا تَجَلَّىٰ

walnnahari idha tajalla

and the day when it shines in brightness.

اَلسَّلاَمُ عَلَيْكَ أَيُّهَا ٱلإِمَامُ ٱلْمَأْمُونُ

alssalamu `alayka ayyuha al-imamu alma'munu

Peace be upon you, O entrusted leader.

اَلسَّلاَمُ عَلَيْكَ أَيُّهَا ٱلْمُقَدَّمُ ٱلْمَأْمُولُ

alssalamu `alayka ayyuha almuqaddamu alma'mulu

Peace be upon you, O favored and expected.

اَلسَّلاَمُ عَلَيْكَ بِجَوَامِعِ ٱلسَّلاَمِ

alssalamu `alayka bijawami`i alssalami

Peace be upon you to the ultimate meaning of peace.

أُشْهِدُكَ يَا مَوْلاَيَ

ushhiduka ya mawlaya

I solicit you, O my master,

أَنِّي أَشْهَدُ أَنْ لاَ إِلٰهَ إِلاَّ ٱللَّهُ

anni ashhadu an la ilaha illa allahu

to testify to me that I bear witness that there is no god but Allah;

وَحْدَهُ لاَ شَرِيكَ لَهُ

wahdahu la sharika lahu

One and Only Lord and having no associate,

وَأَنَّ مُحَمَّداً عَبْدُهُ وَرَسُولُهُ

wa anna muhammadan `abduhu wa rasuluhu

and that Muhammad is His servant and messenger.

لاَ حَبِيبَ إِلاَّ هُوَ وَأَهْلُهُ

la habiba illa huwa wa ahluhu

There is no one more beloved by Allah than him and his household.

وَأُشْهِدُكَ يَا مَوْلاَيَ

wa ushhiduka ya mawlaya

And I solicit you, O my master, to testify to me that I bear witness

أَنَّ عَلِيّاً أَمِيرَ ٱلْمُؤْمِنِينَ حُجَّتُهُ

anna `aliyyan amira almu'minina hujjatuhu

that `Ali the Commander of the Faithful is His argument,

وَٱلْحَسَنَ حُجَّتُهُ

walhasana hujjatuhu

al-Hasan is His argument,

وَٱلْحُسَيْنَ حُجَّتُهُ

walhusayna hujjatuhu
al-Husayn is His argument,

وَعَلِيَّ بْنَ ٱلْحُسَيْنِ حُجَّتُهُ

wa `aliyya bna alhusayni hujjatuhu
`Ali the son of al-Husayn is His argument,

وَمُحَمَّدَ بْنَ عَلِيٍّ حُجَّتُهُ

wa muhammada bna `aliyyin hujjatuhu
Muhammad the son of `Ali is His argument,

وَجَعْفَرَ بْنَ مُحَمَّدٍ حُجَّتُهُ

wa ja`fara bna muhammadin hujjatuhu
Ja`far the son of Muhammad is His argument,

وَمُوسَىٰ بْنَ جَعْفَرٍ حُجَّتُهُ

wa musa bna ja`farin hujjatuhu
Musa the son of Ja`far is His argument,

وَعَلِيَّ بْنَ مُوسَىٰ حُجَّتُهُ

wa `aliyya bna musa hujjatuhu
`Ali the son of Musa is His argument,

وَمُحَمَّدَ بْنَ عَلِيٍّ حُجَّتُهُ

wa muhammada bna `aliyyin hujjatuhu
Muhammad the son of `Ali is His argument,

وَعَلِيَّ بْنَ مُحَمَّدٍ حُجَّتُهُ

wa `aliyya bna muhammadin hujjatuhu
`Ali the son of Muhammad is His argument,

وَٱلْحَسَنَ بْنَ عَلِيٍّ حُجَّتُهُ

walhasana bna `aliyyin hujjatuhu
and al-Hasan the son of `Ali is His argument.

وَأَشْهَدُ أَنَّكَ حُجَّةُ ٱللَّهِ

wa ashhadu annaka hujjatu allahi
I also bear witness that you are verily the argument of Allah.

أَنْتُمُ ٱلأَوَّلُ وَٱلآخِرُ

antum al-awwalu wal-akhiru
You all are the first and the last.

وَأَنَّ رَجْعَتَكُمْ حَقٌّ لاَ رَيْبَ فِيهَا

wa anna raj`atakum haqqun la rayba fiha
And (I bear witness) that your (promised) Return is undoubtedly true

يَوْمَ لاَ يَنْفَعُ نَفْساً إِيمَانُهَا

yawma la yanfa`u nafsan imanuha
"On the day when its belief avails not a soul

لَمْ تَكُنْ آمَنَتْ مِنْ قَبْلُ

lam takun amanat min qablu
which theretofore believed not,

أَوْ كَسَبَتْ فِي إِيمَانِهَا خَيْراً

aw kasabat fi imaniha khayran
nor in its belief earned good by works,"

وَأَنَّ ٱلْمَوْتَ حَقٌّ

wa anna almawta haqqun
death is true,

وَأَنَّ نَاكِراً وَنَكِيراً حَقٌّ

wa anna nakiran wa nakiran haqqun
and Nakir and Nakir are true.

وَأَشْهَدُ أَنَّ ٱلنَّشْرَ حَقٌّ

wa ashhadu anna alnnashra haqqun
And I bear witness that the Raising for death is true,

وَٱلْبَعْثَ حَقٌّ

walba`tha haqqun
the Resurrection is true,

وَأَنَّ ٱلصِّرَاطَ حَقٌّ

wa anna alssirata haqqun
the Discriminating Bridge is true,

وَٱلْمِرْصَادَ حَقٌّ

walmirsada haqqun
the Watchtower is true,

وَٱلْمِيزَانَ حَقٌّ

walmizana haqqun
the Balance (of deeds) is true,

وَٱلْحَشْرَ حَقٌّ

walhashra haqqun
the Gathering is true,

وَٱلْحِسَابَ حَقٌّ

walhisaba haqqun
the Reckoning is true,

وَٱلْجَنَّةَ وَٱلنَّارَ حَقٌّ

waljannata walnnara haqqun
Paradise and Hell are true,

وَٱلْوَعْدَ وَٱلْوَعِيدَ بِهِمَا حَقٌّ

walwa`da walwa`ida bihima haqqun
and the promise of Paradise and the threat with Hell are true.

يَا مَوْلاَيَ شَقِيَ مَنْ خَالَفَكُمْ

ya mawlaya shaqiya man khalafakum
O My master! Certainly wretched is he who opposes you

وَسَعِدَ مَنْ أَطَاعَكُمْ

wa sa`ida man ata`akum
and certainly happy is he who obeys you.

فَأَشْهَدْ عَلَىٰ مَا أَشْهَدْتُكَ عَلَيْهِ

fashhad `ala ma ashhadtuka `alayhi
So, testify to me all that which I have besought you to testify.

وَأَنَا وَلِيٌّ لَكَ

wa ana waliyyun laka
I am verily an ally of you

بَرِيءٌ مِنْ عَدُوِّكَ

bari'un min `aduwwika
and denouncing your enemy.

فَٱلْحَقُّ مَا رَضِيتُمُوهُ

falhaqqu ma raditumuhu
The truth is only that which you accept,

وَٱلْبَاطِلُ مَا أَسْخَطْتُمُوهُ

walbatilu ma askhattumuhu
the wrong is only that which you disallow,

وَٱلْمَعْرُوفُ مَا أَمَرْتُمْ بِهِ

walma`rufu ma amartum bihi
the good is only that which you enjoin,

وَٱلْمُنْكَرُ مَا نَهَيْتُمْ عَنْهُ

walmunkaru ma nahaytum `anhu
and the evil is only that which you forbid.

فَنَفْسِي مُؤْمِنَةٌ بِٱللَّهِ

fanafsi mu'minatun billahi
My soul is thus believing in Allah;

وَحْدَهُ لاَ شَرِيكَ لَهُ

wahdahu la sharika lahu

One and Only Lord and having no associate,

وَبِرَسُولِهِ وَبِأَمِيرِ ٱلْمُؤْمِنِينَ

wa birasulihi wa bi'amiri almu'minina

and also in His Messenger, in the Commander of the Faithful,

وَبِكُمْ يَا مَوْلاَيَ أَوَّلِكُمْ وَآخِرِكُمْ

wa bikum ya mawlaya awwalikum wa akhirikum

and in you all, O my master, from the beginning to the end.

وَنُصْرَتِي مُعَدَّةٌ لَكُمْ

wa nusrati mu`addatun lakum

I have prepared myself to back you

وَمَوَدَّتِي خَالِصَةٌ لَكُمْ

wa mawaddati khalisatun lakum

and my love is sincerely dedicated to you.

آمِينَ آمِينَ

amina amina

Respond! Respond!

General Supplications

KUMAYL

بِسْمِ اللّٰهِ الرَّحْمَنِ الرَّحِيمِ

bis-millahir-rahmanir-rahim

In the Name of Allah, the All-merciful, the All-compassionate

اللَّهُمَّ إِنِّي أَسْأَلُكَ بِرَحْمَتِكَ الَّتِي وَسِعَتْ كُلَّ شَيْءٍ

allahumma in-ni as-aluka bi-rah-matikal-lati wasi`at kul-la shay

O Allah, I ask You by Your mercy, which embraces all things.

وَبِقُوَّتِكَ الَّتِي قَهَرْتَ بِهَا كُلَّ شَيْءٍ

wa bi-qu-watikal-lati qahar-ta biha kul-la shay

And by Your strength, through which You dominatest all things,

وَخَضَعَ لَهَا كُلُّ شَيْءٍ

wa khada`a laha kul-lu shay

And toward which all things are humble

وَذَلَّ لَهَا كُلُّ شَيْءٍ

wa dhal-la laha kul-lu shay

And before which all things are lowly;

وَبِجَبَرُوتِكَ الَّتِي غَلَبْتَ بِهَا كُلَّ شَيْءٍ

wa bi-jabarutikal-lati ghalab-ta biha kul-la shay

And by Your invincibility through which You overwhelmest all things,

وَبِعِزَّتِكَ الَّتِي لا يَقُومُ لَهَا شَيْءٌ

wa bi`izzatikal-lati la yaqumu laha shay

And by Your might, which nothing can resist;

وَبِعَظَمَتِكَ الَّتِي مَلأَتْ كُلَّ شَيْءٍ

wa bi`azamatikal-lati mala-at kul-la shay

And by Your tremendousness, which has filled all things;

وَبِسُلْطَانِكَ الَّذِي عَلاَ كُلَّ شَيْءٍ

wa bisul-tanikal-ladhi `ala kul-la shay

by Your force, which towers over all things;

وَبِوَجْهِكَ الْبَاقِي بَعْدَ فَنَاءِ كُلِّ شَيْء

wa bi-waj-hikal-baqi ba`da fana-i kul-li shay

And by Your face, which subsists after the annihilation of all things,

وَبِأَسْمَائِكَ الَّتِي مَلأَتْ أَرْكَانَ كُلِّ شَيْء

wa bi-as-ma-ikal-lati malat ar-kana kul-li shay

And by Your Names, which have filled the foundations of all things;

وَبِعِلْمِكَ الَّذِي أَحَاطَ بِكُلِّ شَيْء

wa bi`il-mikal-ladhi ahata bikul-li shay

And by Your knowledge, which encompasses all things;

وَبِنُورِ وَجْهِكَ الَّذِي أَضَاءَ لَهُ كُلُّ شَيْء

wa bi-nuri waj-hikal-ladhi ada-a lahu kul-lu shay

And by the light of Your face, through which all things are illumined!

يَا نُورُ يَا قُدُّوسُ

ya nuru ya qud-dus

O Light! O All-holy!

يَا أَوَّلَ الأَوَّلِينَ

ya aw-walal-aw-walin

O First of those who are first

وَيَا آخِرَ الآخِرِينَ

wa ya a-khiral-a-khirin

And O Last of those who are last!

اللَّهُمَّ اغْفِرْ لِي الذُّنُوبَ الَّتِي تَهْتِكُ الْعِصَمَ

allahumma-igh-fir liyadh-dhunubal-lati tah-tikul`isam

O Allah, forgive me those sins which tear apart safeguards!

اللَّهُمَّ اغْفِرْ لِي الذُّنُوبَ الَّتِي تُنْزِلُ النِّقَمَ

allahumma-igh-fir liyadh-dhunubal-lati tunzilun-niqam

O Allah, forgive me those sins which draw down adversities!

اللَّهُمَّ اغْفِرْ لِي الذُّنُوبَ الَّتِي تُغَيِّرُ النِّعَمَ

allahumma-igh-fir liyadh-dhunubal-lati tughy-yirun-ni`am

O Allah, forgive me those sins which alter blessings!

اللَّهُمَّ اغْفِرْ لِي الذُّنُوبَ الَّتِي تَحْبِسُ الدُّعَاءَ

allahumma-igh-fir liyadh-dhunubal-lati tah-bisud-du'a

O Allah forgive me those sins which hold back supplication!

اللَّهُمَّ اغْفِرْ لِي الذُّنُوبَ الَّتِي تَقْطَعُ الرَّجَاءَ

allahumma-igh-fir liyadh-dhunubal-lati taq-tau'r-raja

O Allah forgive me those sins which cut down the hopes!

اللَّهُمَّ اغْفِرْ لِي الذُّنُوبَ الَّتِي تُنْزِلُ البَلاءَ

allahumma-igh-fir liyadh-dhunubal-lati tunzilul-bala

O Allah, forgive me those sins which draw down tribulation!

اللَّهُمَّ اغْفِرْ لِي كُلَّ ذَنْبٍ أَذْنَبْتُهُ وَكُلَّ خَطِيئَةٍ أَخْطَأْتُهَا

allahumma-igh-fir liya kul-la dham-bin adhnabtuhu wa kul-la khati-atin akh-tatuha

O Allah, forgive me every sin I have committed and every mistake I have made!

اللَّهُمَّ إِنِّي أَتَقَرَّبُ إِلَيْكَ بِذِكْرِكَ

allahumma inni ataqarrabu ilayka bi-dhik-rik

O Allah, verily I seek nearness to You through remembrance of You,

وَأَسْتَشْفِعُ بِكَ إِلَى نَفْسِكَ

wa as-tash-fiu' bika ila naf-sik

And I seek intercession from You with Yourself,

وَأَسْأَلُكَ بِجُودِكَ أَن تُدْنِيَنِي مِن قُرْبِكَ

wa as-aluka bi-judika an tud-ni-yani min qur-bik

And I ask You through Your munificence to bring me near to Your proximity,

وَأَن تُوزِعَنِي شُكْرَكَ

wa an tuzi`ani shuk-rak

And to provide me with gratitude toward You

وَأَن تُلْهِمَنِي ذِكْرَكَ

wa an tul-himani dhik-rak

And to inspire me with Your remembrance.

اللّهُمَّ إنِّي أَسْأَلُكَ سُؤَالَ خَاضِعٍ مُّتَذَلِّلٍ خَاشِعٍ أَن تُسَامِحَنِي وَتَرْحَمَنِي

allahumma in-ni as-luka suala khadii'm-mutadhal-lilin kha-shii'n an tusamihani wa tar-hamani

O Allah, verily I ask You with the asking of a submissive, abased and lowly man to show me forbearance, to have mercy on me

وَتَجْعلَنِي بِقَسَمِكَ رَاضِياً قَانِعاً، وَفِي جَمِيعِ الأَحْوَالِ مُتَوَاضِعاً

wa taj-`alani bi-qasamika radiyan qani`n wa fi jamii'l-ah-wali mutawadi`aa

And to make me satisfied and content with Your appointment and [make me] humble in every state.

اللّهُمَّ وَأَسْأَلُكَ سُؤَالَ مَنِ اشْتَدَّتْ فَاقَتُهُ

allahumma wa as-aluka suala manish-tad-dat faqatuh

O Allah, I ask You the question of one whose indigence is extreme,

وَأَنزَلَ بِكَ عِنْدَ الشَّدَائِدِ حَاجَتَهُ

wa anzala bika i'ndash-shada-idi hajatahu

And who has stated to You in difficulties his need

وَعَظُمَ فِيمَا عِنْدَكَ رَغْبَتُهُ

wa `azuma fima i'ndaka ragh-batuhu

And whose desire for what is with You has become great.

اللّهُمَّ عَظُمَ سُلْطَانُكَ وَعَلاَ مَكَانُكَ

allahumma `azuma sul-tanuka wa `ala makanuk

O Allah, Your force is tremendous, Your place is lofty,

وَخَفِي مَكْرُكَ وَظَهَرَ أَمْرُكَ

wa khafiya mak-ruka wazahara am-ruk

And Your plan is hidden, Your command is manifest,

وَغَلَبَ قَهْرُكَ وَجَرَتْ قُدْرَتُكَ

wa ghalaba qah-ruka wa jarat qud-ratuk

And Your domination is overwhelming, Your power is unhindered

وَلا يُمْكِنُ الْفِرَارُ مِنْ حُكُومَتِكَ

wa-la yum-kinul-firaru min huku-matik

And escape from Your governance is impossible.

اللَّهُمَّ لا أَجِدُ لِذُنُوبِي غَافِراً

allahumma la ajidu lidhunubi ghafira

O Allah, I find no forgiver of my sins,

وَّلا لِقَبَائِحِي سَاتِراً

wa-la liqaba-ihi satira

Nor concealer of my ugly acts

وَّلا لِشَيْءٍ مِّنْ عَمَلِي الْقَبِيحِ بِالْحَسَنِ مُبَدِّلاً غَيْرَكَ

wa-la lishayim-min `amali-yal-qabihi bil-hasani mubad-dilan ghayrak

Nor transformer of any of my ugly acts into good acts but You

لا إِلَهَ إِلاَّ أَنتَ

la ilaha il-la anta

There is no god but You!

سُبْحَانَكَ وَبِحَمْدِكَ

sub-hanaka wa biham-dika

Glory be to You, and Thine is the praise!

ظَلَمْتُ نَفْسِي

zalam-tu naf-si

I have wronged myself,

وَتَجَرَّأْتُ بِجَهْلِي

wa tajar-ratu bijah-li

And I have been audacious in my ignorance

وَسَكَنتُ إِلَي قَدِيمِ ذِكْرِكَ لِي وَمَنِّكَ عَلَيَّ

wa sakan-tu ila qadimi dhik-rika li wa man-nika `alay

And I have depended upon Your ancient remembrance of me and Your favour toward me.

اللَّهُمَّ مَوْلايَ

allahumma maw-lay

O Allah! O my Protector!

كَم مِّن قَبِيحٍ سَتَرْتَهُ

kam-min qabihin satar-tah

How many ugly things You hast concealed!

وَكَمْ مِّن فَادِحٍ مِّنَ الْبَلاءِ أَقَلْتَهُ

wa kam-min fadihim-minal-bala-i aqal-tah

How many burdensome tribulations You hast abolished!

وَكَمْ مِّنْ عِثَارٍ وَّقَيْتَهُ

wa kam-min i'thariw-waqaytah

And how many stumbles You hast prevented!

وَكَمْ مِّن مَّكْرُوهٍ دَفَعْتَهُ

wa kam-mim-mak-ruhin dafa`tah

And how many ordeals You hast repelled!

وَكَمْ مِّن ثَنَاءٍ جَمِيلٍ لَّسْتُ أَهْلاً لَّهُ نَشَرْتَهُ

wa kam-min thana-in jamilil-las-tu ah-lal-lahu nashar-tah

And how much beautiful praise, for which I was unworthy, You hast spread abroad!

اللَّهُمَّ عَظُمَ بَلائِي

allahumma `azuma balai

O Allah, my tribulation is tremendous,

وَأَفْرَطَ بِي سُوءُ حَالِي

wa af-rata bi suo-u hali

And my bad state is excessive,

وَقَصُرَتْ بِي أَعْمَالِي

wa qasurat bi a`mali

And my acts are inadequate,

وَقَعَدَتْ بِي أَغْلاَلِي

wa qa`adat bi agh-la-li

And my fetters have tied me down,

وَحَبَسَنِي عَن نَّفْعِي بُعْدُ آمَالِي

wa habasani `an-naf-e'e bu`a-du a-ma-li

And my far-fetched hopes have held me back from my gain

وَخَدَعَتْنِي الدُّنْيَا بِغُرُورِهَا وَنَفْسِي بِجِنَايَتِهَا وَمِطَالِي

wa khada`at-nid-dunya bi-ghururi-ha wa naf-si bi-jinayatiha wa mita-li

And this world with its delusions, my own soul with its offences and my delay have deceived me.

يَا سَيِّدِي فَأَسْأَلُكَ بِعِزَّتِكَ أَن لا يَحْجُبَ عَنْكَ دُعَائِي سُوءُ عَمَلِي وَفِعَالِي

ya say-yidi fa-as-aluka bi-i'z-zatika an la yah-juba `an-ka du`aa-i suo-u `amali wa fi`ali

O my Master! So I ask You by Your might not to let my evil works and acts veil my supplication from You,

وَلا تَفْضَحَنِي بِخَفِيِّ مَا اطَّلَعْتَ عَلَيْهِ مِنْ سِرِّي

wa-la taf-dah-ni bi-khafi-yi mat-tala`ta `ailayhi min sir-ri

And not to disgrace me through the hidden things You knowest of my secrets

وَلا تُعَاجِلْنِي بِالْعُقُوبَةِ عَلَى مَا عَمِلْتُهُ فِي خَلَوَاتِي

wa-la tu`ajil-ni bil-u'qubati `ala ma `amil-tuhu fi khalawati

And not to hasten me to punishment for what I have done in private:

مِنْ سُوءِ فِعْلِي وَإِسَاءَتِي

min suo-i fi`a-li wa isa-ati

My evil acts in secrecy and my misdeeds

وَدَوَامِ تَفْرِيطِي وَجَهَالَتِي

wa dawami taf-riti wa jahalati

And my continuous negligence and my ignorance

وَكَثْرَةِ شَهَوَاتِي وَغَفْلَتِي

wa kath-rati sha-hawati wa ghaf-lati

And my manifold passions and my forgetfulness.

وَكُنِ اللَّهُمَّ بِعِزَّتِكَ لِي فِي كُلِّ الأَحْوَالِ رَؤُوفاً

wa kunil-lahumma bi-i'z-zatika li fi kul-lil-ah-wali ra'ufa

And by Your might, O Allah, be kind to me in all states

وَعَلَيَّ فِي جَمِيعِ الأُمُورِ عَطُوفاً

wa `alay-ya fi jamii'l-umuri `atufa

And be gracious to me in all affairs!

إِلَهِي وَرَبِّي مَن لِّي غَيْرُكَ أَسْأَلُهُ كَشْفَ ضُرِّي وَالنَّظَرَ فِي أَمْرِي

ilahi wa rab-bi mal-li ghayruka as-aluhu kash-fa dur-ri wan-nazara fi am-ri!

My God and my Lord! Have I any but You from whom to ask removal of my affliction and regard for my affairs!

إِلَهِي وَمَوْلاَي أَجْرَيْتَ عَلَيَّ حُكْماً اتَّبَعْتُ فِيهِ هَوَى نَفْسِي

ilahi wa maw-laya aj-rayta `alay-ya huk-mant-taba`tu fihi hawa naf-si

My God and my Protector! You put into effect through me a decree in which I followed the caprice of my own soul

وَلَمْ أَحْتَرِسْ فِيهِ مِن تَزْيِينِ عَدُوِّي

wa lam ah-taris fihi min tazyini `adu-wi

And [I] did not remain wary of adorning my enemy.

فَغَرَّنِي بِمَا أَهْوَى وَأَسْعَدَهُ عَلَى ذَلِكَ الْقَضَاءُ

fa-ghar-rani bi-ma ah-wa wa as-`adahu `ala dha-likal-qada

So he deluded me through my soul's caprice and therein destiny favoured him

فَتَجَاوَزْتُ بِمَا جَرَى عَلَيَّ مِنْ ذَلِكَ بَعْضَ حُدُودِكَ

fa-taja-waztu bi-ma jara `alay-ya min dha-lika ba`da hududik

So, in what was put into effect through me in that situation, I transgressed some of Your statutes

وَخَالَفْتُ بَعْضَ أَوَامِرِكَ

wa khalaf-tu ba`da awamirik

And disobeyed some of Your commands.

فَلَكَ الْحُجَّةُ عَلَيَّ فِي جَمِيعِ ذَلِكَ

falakal-huj-jatu `alay-ya fi jamii' dhalik

So Thine is the argument against me in all of that

،وَلا حُجَّةَ لِي فِيمَا جَرَى عَلَيَّ فِيهِ قَضَاؤُكَ

wa-la huj-jata li fima jara `alay-ya fihi qadauka

I have no argument in what Your destiny put into effect through me therein

وَأَلْزَمَنِي حُكْمُكَ وَبَلاؤُكَ

wa alzamani huk-muka wa balauk

nor in what Your decree and Your tribulation imposed upon me.

وَقَدْ أَتَيْتُكَ يَا إِلَهِي بَعْدَ تَقْصِيرِي وَإِسْرَافِي عَلَى نَفْسِي

wa qad ataytuka ya ilahi ba`da taq-siri wa is-rafi `ala naf-si

Now I have come to You, My God, after my shortcoming and my immoderation toward myself,

مُعْتَذِراً نَّادِماً

mu`a-tadhiran-nadiman

Proffering my excuse, regretful,

مُّنْكَسِراً مُّسْتَقِيلاً

mun-kasiram-mus-taqilama

Broken, apologizing,

مُّسْتَغْفِراً مُّنِيباً

mus-tagh-firam-muniban

Asking forgiveness, repenting,

مُّقِرّاً مُّذْعِناً مُّعْتَرِفاً

muqir-ram-mudhi'nam-mu`a-tarifa

Acknowledging, submissive, confessing.

لا أَجِدُ مَفَرّاً مِّمَّا كَانَ مِنِّي

la ajidu mafar-ram-mim-ma kana min-ni

I find no place to flee from what occurred through me,

وَلا مَفْزَعاً أَتَوَجَّهُ إِلَيْهِ فِي أَمْرِي

wa-la mafza'an atawaj-jahu ilayhi fi am-ri

Nor any place of escape to which I may turn in my affairs,

غَيْرَ قَبُولِكَ عُذْرِي، وَإِدخَالِكَ إِيَايَ فِي سَعَةٍ مِّن رَّحْمَتِكَ

ghayra qabulika u'dhri wa id-khalika i-yaya fi sa'tim-mir-rah-matik

Other than Your acceptance of my excuse and Your entering me into the compass of Your mercy.

اللَّهُمَّ فَاقْبَل عُذْرِي

allahumma faq-bal u'dhri

O Allah, so accept my excuse,

وَارْحَمْ شِدَّةَ ضُرِّي

war-ham shid-data duri

Have mercy upon the severity of my affliction

وَفُكَّنِي مِن شَدِّ وَثَاقِي

wa fuk-kani min shad-di wathaqi

And release me from the tightness of my fetters,

يَا رَبِّ ارْحَمْ ضَعْفَ بَدَنِي وَرِقَّةَ جِلْدِي وَدِقَّةَ عَظْمِي

ya rab-bir-ham da`fa badani wa riq-qata jil-di wa diq-qata `azmi

My Lord, have mercy upon the weakness of my body, the thinness of my skin and the frailty of my bones.

يَا مَنْ بَدَأَ خَلْقِي وَذِكْرِي وَتَرْبِيَتِي وَبِرِّي وَتَغْذِيَتِي

ya mam bada khal-qi wa dhik-ri wa tar-bi-yati wa biri wa tagh-dhi-yati

O You who gave rise to my creation, to the remembrance of me, to the nurture of me, to goodness toward me and to nourishment on me,

هَبْنِي لابْتِدَاءِ كَرَمِكَ وَسَالِفِ بِرِّكَ بِي

hab-ni lb-tida-i karamika wa salifi bir-rika bi

Bestow upon me for the sake of Your having given rise [to me] with generosity and Your previous goodness to me!

يَا إِلَهِي وَسَيِّدِي وَرَبِّي

ya ilahi wa say-yidi wa rab-bi

O Allah, my Master and my Lord!

أَتُرَاكَ مُعَذِّبِي بِنَارِكَ بَعْدَ تَوْحِيدِكَ

aturaka mu`adh-dhibi binarika ba`da taw-hidik

Canst You see Yourself tormenting me with Your fire after I have professed Your Unity

وَبَعْدَ مَا انْطَوَى عَلَيْهِ قَلْبِي مِن مَّعْرِفَتِكَ

wa ba`da man-tawa `ailayhi qal-bi mim-ma`rifatik

And after the knowledge of You my heart has embraced,

وَلَهِجَ بِهِ لِسَانِي مِنْ ذِكْرِكَ

wa lahija bihi lisani min dhik-rik

And the remembrance of You my tongue has constantly mentioned

وَاعْتَقَدَهُ ضَمِيرِي مِنْ حُبِّكَ

wa a`taqadahu zamiri min hub-bik

And the love of You to which my mind has clung,

وَبَعْدَ صِدْقِ اعْتِرَافِي وَدُعَائِي خَاضِعاً لِرُبُوبِيَّتِكَ

wa ba`da sid-qi-`a-tirafi wa du`aa-i khadi`aal-li-rububi-yatika

And after the sincerity of my confession and my supplication, humble before Your lordship?

هَيْهَاتَ أَنتَ أَكْرَمُ مِنْ أَن تُضَيِّعَ مَن رَّبَّيْتَهُ

hayhata anta ak-ramu min an tuday-yi`a mar-rab-baytah

Far be it from You! You art more generous than that You shouldst squander him whom You hast nurtured,

أَوْ تُبْعِدَ مَنْ أَدْنَيْتَهُ

aw tub-i'da man ad-naytah

Or banish him whom You hast brought nigh,

أَوْ تُشَرِّدَ مَنْ آوَيْتَهُ

aw tushar-rida man a-aytah

Or drive away him whom You hast given an abode

أَوْ تُسَلِّمَ إِلَى الْبَلاَءِ مَن كَفَيْتَهُ وَرَحِمْتَهُ

aw tus-s-lima ilal-bala-i man kafay-tahu wa rahim-tah

Or submit to tribulation him whom You hast spared and shown mercy.

وَلَيْتَ شِعْرِي يَا سَيِّدِي وَإِلَهِي وَمَوْلاَي

wa layta shi`a-ri yay say-yidi wa ilahi wa maw-lay

Would that I knew, my Master, My God and my Protector,

أَتُسَلِّطُ النَّارَ عَلَى وُجُوهٍ خَرَّتْ لِعَظَمَتِكَ سَاجِدَةً

atusal-litun-nara `ala wujuhin khar-rat li-`azamatika sajidah

Whether You wilt give the Fire dominion over faces fallen down prostrate before Your Tremendousness,

وَّعَلَى أَلْسُنٍ نَّطَقَتْ بِتَوْحِيدِكَ صَادِقَةً وَّبِشُكْرِكَ مَادِحَةً

wa `ala al-sunin-nataqat bi-taw-hidika sadiqataw-wa bishuk-rika madihah

And over tongues voicing sincerely the profession of Your Unity and giving thanks to You in praise,

وَّعَلَى قُلُوبٍ اعْتَرَفَتْ بِإِلَهِيَّتِكَ مُحَقِّقَةً

wa `ala qulubin-`a-tarafat bi-ilhi-yatika muhaq-qiqah

And over hearts acknowledging Your Divinity through verification,

وَّعَلَى ضَمَائِرَ حَوَتْ مِنَ الْعِلْمِ بِكَ حَتَّى صَارَتْ خَاشِعَةً

wa `ala dama-ira hawat minal-i'l-mi bika hat-ta sarat khashi`ah

And over minds encompassing knowledge of You until they have become humble

وَّعَلَى جَوارِحَ سَعَتْ إِلَى أَوْطَانِ تَعَبُّدِكَ طَائِعَةً وَّأَشَارَتْ بِاسْتِغْفَارِكَ مُذْعِنَةً

wa `ala jawariha sa't ila aw-tani ta'b-budika ta-i`ataw-wa asharat bis-tigh-farika mudhi'nah

And over bodily members speeding to the places of Your worship in obedience and beckoning for Your forgiveness in submission.

مَّا هَكَذَا الظَّنُّ بِكَ وَلا أُخْبِرْنَا بِفَضْلِكَ عَنكَ

ma hkadhaz-zan-nu bika wa-la ukh-bir-na bi-fadlika `anka

No such opinion is held of You! Nor has such been reported - thanks to Your bounty — concerning You,

يَا كَرِيمُ، يَا رَبِّ

ya karimu ya rab

O All-generous! My Lord,

وَأَنتَ تَعْلَمُ ضَعْفِي عَن قَلِيلٍ مِّن بَلاءِ الدُّنْيَا وَعُقُوبَاتِهَا

wa anta ta`lamu da`fi `an qalilim-min bala-id-dun-ya wa u'qubatiha

And You knowest my weakness before a little of this world's tribulations and punishments,

وَمَا يَجْرِي فِيهَا مِنَ الْمَكَارِهِ عَلَى أَهْلِهَا

wa ma yaj-ri fiha minal-makarihi `ala ah-liha

And before those ordeals which befall its inhabitants,

عَلَى أَنَّ ذَلِكَ بَلاءٌ وَّمَكْرُوهٌ، قَلِيلٌ مَّكْثُهُ، يَسِيرٌ بَقَاؤُهُ، قَصِيرٌ مُّدَّتُهُ

`ala an-na dha-lika bala-uw-wa mak-ruhun, qalilum-mak-thuhu, yasirum baqa-uhu, qasirum-mud-datuh

Even though it is a tribulation and ordeal whose stay is short, whose subsistence is but little and, whose period is but fleeting.

فَكَيْفَ احْتِمَالِي لِبَلاءِ الآخِرَةِ وَجَلِيلِ وُقُوعِ الْمَكَارِهِ فِيهَا

fa-kayfah-timali li-bala-il-akhirati wa jalili wuqui'l-makarihi fiha!

So how can I endure the tribulations of the next world and the great ordeals that occur within it?

وَهُوَ بَلاءٌ تَطُولُ مُدَّتُهُ، وَيَدُومُ مَقَامُهُ، وَلا يُخَفَّفُ عَنْ أَهْلِهِ

wa huwa bala-un tatulu mud-datuhu, wa yadumu maqamuhu, wa-la yukhaf-fafu `an ah-lih

For it is a tribulation whose period is long, whose station endures and whose sufferers are given no respite,

لأَنَّهُ لا يَكُونُ إِلاَّ عَنْ غَضَبِكَ وَانتِقَامِكَ وَسَخَطِكَ

li-an-nahu la yakunu il-la `an ghadabika wan-tiqamika wa sakhatik

Since it only occurs as a result of Your wrath, Your vengeance and Your anger,

وَهَذَا مَا لا تَقُومُ لَهُ السَّمَاوَاتُ وَالأَرْضُ

wa hadha ma la taqumu lahus-samawatu wal-ardu

And these cannot be withstood by the heavens and the earth.

يَا سَيِّدِي فَكَيْفَ بِي

ya say-yidi fakayfa bi

O Master, so what about me?!

وَأَنَا عَبْدُكَ الضَّعِيفُ الذَّلِيلُ الْحَقِيرُ الْمِسْكِينُ الْمُسْتَكِينُ

wa ana `abukad-dae'efudh-dhalilul-haqirul-mis-kinul-mus-takin

For I am Your weak, lowly, base, wretched and miserable slave.

يَا إِلَهِي وَرَبِّي وَسَيِّدِي وَمَوْلايَ

ya ilahi wa rab-bi wa say-yidi wa maw-lay

My God! My Lord! My Master! My Protector!

لأَيِّ الأُمُورِ إِلَيْكَ أَشْكُو

li-ay-yil-umuri ilayka ash-ku

For which things would I complain to You?

وَلِمَا مِنْهَا أَضِجُّ وَأَبْكِي

wa lima minha adij-ju wa ab-ki

And for which of them would I lament and weep?

لأَلِيمِ الْعَذَابِ وَشِدَّتِهِ

li-alimil-`adhabi wa shid-datih

For the pain and severity of chastisement?

أَمْ لِطُولِ الْبَلاءِ وَمُدَّتِهِ

am litulil-bala-i wa mud-datih

Or for the length and period of tribulation?

فَلَئِن صَيَّرْتَنِي لِلْعُقُوبَاتِ مَعَ أَعْدَائِكَ

fa-la-in say-yar-tani lil-u'qubati ma' a`da-ik

So if You takest me to the punishments with Your enemies,

وَجَمَعْتَ بَيْنِي وَبَيْنَ أَهْلِ بَلائِكَ

wa jama`ta bayni wa bayna ahli bala-ik

And gatherest me with the people of Your tribulation

وَفَرَّقْتَ بَيْنِي وَبَيْنَ أَحِبَّائِكَ وَأَوْلِيَائِكَ

wa far-raq-ta bay-ni wa bay-na ahib-ba-ika wa aw-li-ya-ik

And separatest me from Your friends and saints,

فَهَبْنِي يَا إِلَهِي وَسَيِّدِي وَمَوْلايَ وَرَبِّي صَبَرْتُ عَلَى عَذَابِكَ

fa-hab-ni ya ilahi wasay-yidi wa mawlaya wa rab-bi sabar-tu `ala `adhabika

Then suppose, My God, my Master, my Protector and my Lord that I am able to endure Your chastisement,

فَكَيْفَ أَصْبِرُ عَلَى فِرَاقِكَ

fakayfa as-biru `ala firaqika

How can I endure separation from You?

وَهَبْنِي صَبَرْتُ عَلَى حَرِّ نَارِكَ

wa hab-ni sabar-tu `ala har-ri narika

And suppose that I am able to endure the heat of Your fire,

فَكَيْفَ أَصْبِرُ عَنِ النَّظَرِ إِلَى كَرَامَتِكَ

fakayfa as-biru `an-nazari ila karamatik

How can I endure not gazing upon Your generosity?

أَمْ كَيْفَ أَسْكُنُ فِي النَّارِ وَرَجَائِي عَفْوُكَ

am kayfa as-kunu fin-nari wa raja-i `af-wuk

Or how can I dwell in the Fire while my hope is Your pardon?

فَبِعِزَّتِكَ يَا سَيِّدِي وَمَوْلايَ أُقْسِمُ صَادِقاً، لَئِن تَرَكْتَنِي نَاطِقاً

fabi-i'z-zatika ya say-yidi wa mawlaya uq-simu sadiqal-la-in tarak-tani natiqan

So by Your might, my Master and my protector, I swear sincerely, if You leavest me with speech,

لأَضِجَّنَّ إِلَيْكَ بَيْنَ أَهْلِهَا ضَجِيجَ الآمِلِينَ

ladij-jan-na ilayka bayna ah-liha dajijal-amilin

I will lament to You from the midst of the Fire's inhabitants with lamentation of the hopeful;

وَلأَصْرُخَنَّ إِلَيكَ صُرَاخَ المُسْتَصْرِخِينَ

wa lasrukhan-na ilayka surakhal-mus-tas-rikhin

I will cry to You with the cry of those crying for help;

وَلأَبْكِيَنَّ عَلَيْكَ بُكَاءَ الفَاقِدِينَ

wa-la-ab-ki-yan-na `ailayka buka-al-faqidin

I will weep to You with the weeping of the bereft;

وَلأُنَادِيَنَّكَ أَيْنَ كُنتَ يَا وَلِيَّ الْمُؤْمِنِينَ

wa la-unadi-yan-naka ay-na kun-ta ya wali-yal-mu-minin

And I will call to You, Where art You, O Sponsor of the believers,

يَا غَايَةَ آمَالِ العَارِفِينَ

ya ghayata a-malil-`arifin

O Goal of the hopes of Your knowers,

يَا غِيَاثَ المُسْتَغِيثِينَ

ya ghiyathal-mus-taghithin

O Aid of those who seek assistance,

يَا حَبِيبَ قُلُوبِ الصَّادِقِينَ

ya habiba qulubis-sadiqin

O Friend of the hearts of the sincere

وَيَا إِلَهَ العَالَمِينَ

wa ya ilhal-`alamin

And O God of all the world's inhabitants!

أَفَتُرَاكَ، سُبْحَانَكَ يَا إِلَهِي وَبِحَمْدِكَ، تَسْمَعُ فِيهَا صَوْتَ عَبْدٍ مُسْلِمٍ

afaturaka sub-hanaka ya ilahi wa biham-dika tas-mau' fiha saw-ta `ab-dim-mus-limin

Canst You see Yourself — Glory be to You My God, and Thine is the praised — hearing within the Fire the voice of a slave surrendered to You,

سُجِنَ فِيهَا بِمُخَالَفَتِهِ

sujina fiha bi-mukhalafatih

Imprisoned there because of his violations,

وَذَاقَ طَعْمَ عَذَابِهَا بِمَعْصِيَتِهِ

wa dhaqa ta`ma `adhabiha bi-ma`si-yatih

Tasting the favour of its torment because of his disobedience,

وَحُبِسَ بَيْنَ أَطْبَاقِهَا بِجُرْمِهِ وَجَرِيرَتِهِ

wa hubisa bayna at-baqiha bijur-mih wa jariratih

And confined within its levels because of his sin and crime,

وَهُوَ يَضِجُّ إِلَيْكَ ضَجِيجَ مُؤَمِّلٍ لِرَحْمَتِكَ

wa huwa yadij-ju ilayka dajija muammilil-lirah-mat-k

While he laments to You with the lament of one hopeful for Your mercy,

وَيُنَادِيكَ بِلِسَانِ أَهْلِ تَوْحِيدِكَ

wa yunadika bi-lisani ahli taw-hidik

And calls to You with the tongue of those who profess Your Unity

وَيَتَوَسَّلُ إِلَيْكَ بِرُبُوبِيَّتِكَ

wa yatawas-salu ilayka bi-rububi-yatik

And entreats You by Your lordship!

يَا مَوْلاَيَ فَكَيْفَ يَبْقَى فِي الْعَذَابِ وَهُوَ يَرْجُو مَا سَلَفَ مِنْ حِلْمِكَ

ya mawlay fa-kayfa yabqa fil-`adhabi wa huwa yar-ju ma salafa min hil-mik

My Protector, so how should he remain in the chastisement, while he has hope for Your previous clemency?

أَمْ كَيْفَ تُؤْلِمُهُ النَّارُ وَهُوَ يَأمَلُ فَضْلَكَ وَرَحْمَتَكَ

am kayfa tu-limuhun-naru wa huwa ya-malu fadlaka wa rah-mataka

Or how should the Fire cause him pain while he expects Your bounty and mercy?

أَمْ كَيْفَ يُحْرِقُهُ لَهِيبُهَا وَأَنتَ تَسْمَعُ صَوْتَهُ وَتَرَى مَكَانَهُ

am kayfa yuh-riquhu lahibuha wa anta tas-mau' saw-tahu wa tara makanah

Or how should its flames burn him, while You hearest his voice and seest his place?

أَمْ كَيْفَ يَشْتَمِلُ عَلَيْهِ زَفِيرُهَا وَأَنتَ تَعْلَمُ ضَعْفَهُ

am kayfa yash-tamilu `ailayhi zafiruha wa anta ta`lamu da`fah

Or how should its groaning encompass him, while You knowest his weakness?

أَمْ كَيْفَ يَتَقَلْقَلُ بَيْنَ أَطْبَاقِهَا وَأَنتَ تَعْلَمُ صِدْقَهُ

am kayfa yataqalqalu bayna at-baqiha wa anta ta`lamu sid-qah

Or how should he be convulsed among its levels, while You knowest his sincerity?

أَمْ كَيْفَ تَزْجُرُهُ زَبَانِيَتُهَا وَهُوَ يُنَادِيكَ يَا رَبَّهُ

am kayfa tazjuruhu zabani-yatuha wa huwa yunadika ya rab-bah

Or how should its keepers torture him while he calls out to You, O Lord?

أَمْ كَيْفَ يَرْجُو فَضْلَكَ فِي عِتْقِهِ مِنْهَا فَتَتْرُكُهُ فِيهَا

am kayfa yar-ju fadlaka fi i't-qihi minha fatat-rukuhu fiha

Or how should he have hope of Your bounty in freeing him from it, while You abandonest him within it?

هَيهَاتَ مَا ذَلِكَ الظَّنُّ بِكَ

hayhat ma dhalikaz-zan-nu bik

Far be it from You! That is not what is expected of You,

وَلا الْمَعْرُوفُ مِن فَضْلِكَ

wa-lal-ma`rufu min fadlik

Nor what is well-known of Your bounty,

وَلا مُشْبِهٌ لِمَا عَامَلْتَ بِهِ الْمُوَحِّدِينَ مِنْ بِرِّكَ وَإِحْسَانِكَ

wa-la mush-biha lima `amal-ta bihil-muah-hidina mim bir-rika wa ih-sanik

Nor it is similar to the goodness and kindness You hast shown to those who profess Your Unity.

فَبِالْيَقِينِ أَقْطَعُ لَوْلا مَا حَكَمْتَ بِهِ مِن تَعْذِيبِ جَاحِدِيكَ

fa-bial-yaqini aq-tau' law-la ma hakam-ta bihi min ta`dhibi jahidik

So I declare with certainty that were it not for what You hast decreed concerning the chastisement of Your deniers

وَقَضَيْتَ بِهِ مِنْ إِخْلاَدِ مُعَانِدِيكَ

wa qadayta bihi min ikh-laydi mu`anidik

And what You hast foreordained concerning the everlasting home of those who stubbornly resist,

لَجَعَلْتَ النَّارَ كُلَّهَا بَرْداً وَّسَلاَماً

laja'l-tan-nara kul-laha bar-daw-wa salama

You wouldst make the Fire, all of it, coolness and safety,

وَمَا كَانَ لأَحَدٍ فِيهَا مَقَرّاً وَّلا مُقَاماً

wa ma kana li-ahadin fiha maqar-raw-wa-la muqama

And no one would have a place of rest or abode within it.

لَكِنَّكَ تَقَدَّسَتْ أَسْمَاؤُكَ أَقْسَمْتَ أَنْ تَمْلأَهَا مِنَ الْكَافِرِينَ

lakin-naka taqad-dasat as-ma-uka aq-sam-ta an tam-laha minal-kafirina;

But You—holy are Your Names—hast sworn that You wilt fill it with the unbelievers,

مِنَ الْجِنَّةِ وَالنَّاسِ أَجْمَعِينَ

minal-jin-nati wan-nasi aj-m`ain

Both Jinn and men together,

وَأَن تُخَلِّدَ فِيهَا الْمُعَانِدِينَ

wa-an tukhal-lida fihal-mu`anidin

And that You wilt place those who stubbornly resist therein forever

وَأَنتَ جَلَّ ثَنَاؤُكَ قُلْتَ مُبْتَدِئاً، وَتَطَوَّلْتَ بِالإِنْعَامِ مُتَكَرِّماً

wa anta jal-la thana-uka qul-ta mub-tadiwaw-wa tataw-wal-ta bil-in-`ami mutakar-rima

And You— majestic is Your eulogy— said at the beginning and wernt gracious through kindness as a favour,

أَفَمَن كَانَ مُؤْمِنًا كَمَن كَانَ فَاسِقًا ۚ لَّا يَسْتَوُونَ

afaman kana muminan kaman kana fasiqal-la yas-tawun

(What? Is he who has been believer like unto him who has been ungodly? They are not equal)

إِلَهِي وَسَيِّدِي فَأَسْأَلُكَ بِالْقُدْرَةِ الَّتِي قَدَّرْتَهَا

ilahi wa say-yidi fa-as-aluka bial-qud-ratil-lati qad-dartaha

My God and my Master! So I ask You by the power You hast apportioned

وَبِالْقَضِيَّةِ الَّتِي حَتَمْتَهَا وَحَكَمْتَهَا وَغَلَبْتَ مَنْ عَلَيْهِ أَجْرَيْتَهَا

wa bil-qadi-yatil-lati hatam-taha wa hakam-taha wa ghalab-ta man `ailayhi aj-raytaha

And by the decision which You hast determined and imposed and through which You hast overcome him toward whom it has been put into effect,

أَن تَهَبَ لِي، فِي هذِهِ اللَّيْلَةِ، وَفِي هَذِهِ السَّاعَةِ

an tahaba li fi hadhihil-laylati wa fi hadhihis-sa'ah

That You forgivest me in this night and at this hour

كُلَّ جُرْمٍ أَجْرَمْتُهُ

kul-la jur-min aj-ram-tuh

Every offence I have committed,

وَكُلَّ ذَنْبٍ أَذْنَبْتُهُ

wa kul-la dham-bin adhnab-tuh

And every sin I have performed,

وَكُلَّ قَبِيحٍ أَسْرَرْتُهُ

wa kul-la qabihin as-rar-tuh

And every ugly thing I have concealed

وَكُلَّ جَهْلٍ عَمِلْتُهُ

wa kul-la jah-lin `amil-tuhu,
And every folly I have enacted

كَتَمْتُهُ أَوْ أَعْلَنتُهُ

katam-tuhuo aw a`lan-tuhu,
Whether I have hidden or announced it,

أَخفَيْتُهُ أَوْ أَظْهَرْتُهُ

akhfaytuhuo aw azhar-tuh
Or I have concealed it or manifested it

وَكُلَّ سَيِّئَةٍ أَمَرْتَ بِإِثْبَاتِهَا الْكِرَامَ الكَاتِبِينَ

wa kul-la say-yi-atin amarta bi-ith-batihayal-kiramal-katibin
And every evil act which You hast commanded the Noble Writers to record,

الَّذِينَ وَكَّلْتَهُم بِحِفْظِ مَا يَكُونُ مِنِّي

al-ladhina wak-kal-tahum bi-hif-zi ma yakunu min-ni
Those whom You hast appointed to watch over what appears from me

وَجَعَلْتَهُمْ شُهُوداً عَلَيَّ مَعَ جَوَارِحِي

wa ja'l-tahum shuhudan `alay-ya ma' jawarihi
And whom You hast made, along with my bodily members, witness against me.

وَكُنتَ أَنتَ الرَّقِيبَ عَلَيَّ مِن وَّرَائِهِمْ

wa kunta antar-raqiba `alay-ya miw-wara-ihim
And You wast Yourself the Watcher over me from behind them,

وَالشَّاهِدَ لِمَا خَفِيَ عَنْهُمْ

wash-shahida lima khafiya `an-hum
And the Witness of what is hidden from them

وَبِرَحْمَتِكَ أَخْفَيْتَهُ

wa bi-rah-matika akh-faytahu
But through Your mercy You concealed it

وَبِفَضْلِكَ سَتَرْتَهُ

wa bifadlika satar-tah
And through Your bounty You veiled it.

وَأَن تُوَفِّرَ حَظِّي مِن كُلِّ خَيْرٍ تُنْزِلُهُ

wa an tuwf-fira haz-zi min kul-li khayrin tunziluh
[And I ask You] that You bestowest upon me an abundant share of every good You sendest down,

أَوْ إِحْسَانٍ تُفْضِلُهُ

aw ih-sanin tuf-diluh
Or kindness You conferrest,

أَوْ بِرٍّ تَنْشِرُهُ

aw bir-rin tan-shiruhu
Or goodness You unfoldest,

أَوْ رِزْقٍ تَبْسُطُهُ

aw rizqin tab-sutuh
Or provision You spreadest out,

أَوْ ذَنْبٍ تَغْفِرُهُ

aw dham-bin tagh-firuyhu
Or sin You forgivest,

أَوْ خَطَأٍ تَسْتُرُهُ

aw khatain tas-turuhu
Or error You coverest.

يَا رَبِّ يَا رَبِّ يَا رَبِّ

ya rab-bi ya rab-bi ya rabb
My Lord! My Lord! My Lord!

يَا إِلَهِي وَسَيِّدِي وَمَوْلاي وَمَالِكَ رِقِّي

ya ilahi wa say-yidi wa maw-laya wa malika riq-qi
My God! My Master! My Protector! Owner of my bondage!

يَا مَنْ بِيَدِهِ نَاصِيَتِي

ya mam bi-yadihi nasi-yati
O He in whose hand is my forelock!

يَا عَلِيماً بِضُرِّي وَمَسْكَنَتِي

ya `alimam biduri wa mas-kanati

O He who knows my affliction and my misery!

يَا خَبِيراً بِفَقْرِي وَفَاقَتِي

ya khabiram bi-faq-ri wa faqati

O He who is aware of my poverty and indigence!

يَا رَبِّ يَا رَبِّ يَا رَبِّ

ya rab-bi ya ya rab-bi ya rabb

My Lord! My Lord! My Lord!

أَسْأَلُكَ بِحَقِّكَ وَقُدْسِكَ

as-aluka bi-haq-qika wa qud-sik

I ask You by Your Truth and Your Holiness

وَأَعْظَمِ صِفَاتِكَ وَأَسْمَائِكَ

wa a`zami sifatika wa as-ma-ika

And the greatest of Your Attributes and Names,

أَن تَجْعَلَ أَوْقَاتِي فِي اللَّيلِ وَالنَّهَارِ بِذِكْرِكَ مَعْمُورَةً

an taj-`ala aw-qati fil-layli wan-nahari bi-dhik-rika ma`murah

That You makest my times in the night and the day inhabited by Your remembrance,

وَبِخِدْمَتِكَ مَوْصُولَةً

wa bikhid-matika maw-sulah

And joined to Your service

وَأَعْمَالِي عِنْدَكَ مَقْبُولَةً

wa a`mali i'ndaka maq-bulah

And my works acceptable to You,

حَتَّى تَكُونَ أَعْمَالِي وَأَوْرَادِي كُلُّهَا وِرْداً وَاحِداً

hat-ta takuna a`mali wa aw-radi kul-luha wir-daw-wahidan

So that my works and my litanies may all be a single litany

وَحَالِي فِي خِدْمَتِكَ سَرْمَداً

wa hali fi khid-matika sar-mada

And my occupation with Your service everlasting.

يَا سَيِّدِي، يَا مَنْ عَلَيْهِ مُعَوَّلِي

ya say-yidi ya man `ailayhi mu`aw-wali

My Master! O He upon whom I depend!

يَا مَنْ إِلَيْهِ شَكَوْتُ أَحْوَالِي

ya man ilayhi shakaw-tu ah-wali

O He to whom I complain about my states!

يَا رَبِّ يَا رَبِّ يَا رَبِّ

ya rab-bi ya rab-bi ya rabb

My Lord! My Lord! My Lord!

قَوِّ عَلَى خِدْمَتِكَ جَوَارِحِي

qaw-wi `ala khid-matika jawarihi

Strengthen my bodily members in Your service,

وَاشْدُدْ عَلَى الْعَزِيمَةِ جَوَانِحِي

wash-dud `alal-`azimati jawanihi

And fortify my ribs in determination

وَهَبْ لِي الْجِدَّ فِي خَشْيَتِكَ

wa hab liyal-jid-da fi khash-yatik

And bestow upon me earnestness in my fear of You

وَالدَّوَامَ فِي الإتِّصَالِ بِخِدْمَتِكَ

wad-dawama fil-at-itisali bikhid-matik

And continuity in my being joined to Your service

حَتَّى أَسْرَحَ إِلَيكَ فِي مَيَادِينِ السَّابِقِينَ

hat-ta as-raha ilayka fi maya-dinis-sabiqin

So that I may move easily toward You in the battlefields of the foremost

وَأُسْرِعَ إِلَيْكَ فِي الْمبُادِرِينَ

wa us-ri`a ilayka fil-mubadirin

And hurry to You among the prominent

وَأَشْتَاقَ إِلَى قُرْبِكَ فِي الْمُشْتَاقِينَ

wa ash-taqa ila qur-bika fil-mush-taqin

And desire fervently Your proximity among the fervently desirous

وَأَدْنُو مِنْكَ دُنُوَّ الْمُخْلِصِينَ

wa ad-nua minka dunu-wal-mukh-lisin

And move nearer to You with the nearness of the sincere

وَأَخَافَكَ مَخَافَةَ الْمُوقِنِينَ

wa akhafaka makhafatal-muqinin

And fear You with the fear of those who have certitude

وَأَجْتَمِعَ فِي جِوَارِكَ مَعَ الْمُؤْمِنِينَ

wa aj-tami`a fi jiwarika ma'l-mu-mnin

And gather with the believers in Your vicinity.

اللَّهُمَّ وَمَنْ أَرَادَنِي بِسُوءٍ فَأَرِدْهُ

allahumma wa man aradani bisuo-in farid-hu

O Allah, whoever desires evil for me, desire [it] for him!

وَمَن كَادَنِي فَكِدْهُ

wa man kadani fakid-hu

whoever deceives me-deceive him!

وَاجْعَلْنِي مِنْ أَحْسَنِ عَبِيدِكَ نَصِيباً عِنْدَكَ

waj-`alni min ahasani `abidika nasiban i'ndaka

And make me one of the most excellent of Your slaves in Portion from You,

وَأَقْرَبِهِم مَّنْزِلَةً مِّنْكَ

wa aq-rabihim-manzilatam-mink

And the nearest of them in station to You

وَأَخَصِّهِمْ زُلْفَةً لَّدَيْكَ

wa akhas-sihim zul-fatal-ladayk

And the most elected of them in proximity to You.

فَإِنَّهُ لا يُنَالُ ذَلِكَ إِلاَّ بِفَضْلِكَ

fa-in-nahu la yunalu dha-lika il-la bi-fadlik

For that cannot be attained except by Your bounty.

وَجُدْ لِي بِجُودِكَ

wa jud li bijudik

And grant generously to me through Your munificence,

وَاعْطِفْ عَلَيَّ بِمَجْدِكَ

w`a-tif `alay-ya bi-maj-dik

And incline toward me with Your splendour

وَاحْفَظْنِي بِرَحْمَتِكَ

wah-fazni birah-matik

And protect me with Your mercy!

وَاجْعَل لِّسَانِي بِذِكْرِكَ لَهِجاً

waj-`al-lisani bidhik-rika lahija

And make my tongue remember You without ceasing

وَّقَلْبِي بِحُبِّكَ مُتَيَّماً

wa qal-bi bi-hub-bika mutay-yama

And my heart enthralled by Your love!

وَّمُنَّ عَلَيَّ بِحُسْنِ إجَابَتِكَ

wa mun-na `alay-ya bihus-ni ijabatik

And be gracious to me by answering me favourably,

وَأَقِلْنِي عَثْرَتِي وَاغْفِرْ زَلَّتِي

wa aqil-ni `ath-rati wagh-fir zal-lati

And nullify my slips And forgive my lapses!

فَإِنَّكَ قَضَيْتَ عَلَى عِبَادِكَ بِعِبَادَتِكَ

fa-in-naka qadayta `ala i'badika bi-i'badatik

For You hast decreed Your worship for Your servants

وَأَمَرْتَهُم بِدُعَائِكَ

wa amar-tahum bidu`aa-ika

And commanded them to supplicate You

وَضَمِنتَ لَهُمُ الإِجَابَةَ

wa daminta lahumul-ijabah

And assured them that they would be answered.

فَإِلَيْكَ يَا رَبِّ نَصَبْتُ وَجْهِي

fa-ilayka ya rab-bi nasab-tu waj-hi

So toward You, my Lord, I have turned my face

وَإِلَيْكَ يَا رَبِّ مَدَدتُّ يَدِي

wa ilayka ya rab-bi madad-tu yadi

And toward You, my Lord, I have extended my hand.

فَبِعِزَّتِكَ اسْتَجِبْ لِي دُعَائِي

fa-bi-i'z-zatikas-tajib li du`aa-i

So by Your might, comply with my supplication

وَبَلِّغْنِي مُنَايَ

wa bal-ligh-ni munay

And make me attain my desires!

وَلا تَقْطَعْ مِن فَضْلِكَ رَجَائِي

wa-la taq-ta' min fadlika raja-i

Do not severe my hoping for Your Favours

وَاكْفِنِي شَرَّ الْجِنِّ وَالإِنْسِ مِنْ أَعْدَائِي

wak-fini shar-ral-jin-ni wal-in-si min a`da-i

And spare me the evil of my enemies from among the jinn and men!

يَا سَرِيعَ الرِّضَا

ya sari-y`ar-rida

O He, whose pleasure is quickly achieved!

اغْفِرْ لِمَن لا يَمْلِكُ إِلاَّ الدُّعَاءَ

igh-fir liman-la yam-liku il-lad-du`aa

Forgive him who owns nothing but supplication

فَإِنَّكَ فَعَّالٌ لِّمَا تَشَاءُ

fa-in-naka fa`alul-lima tasha

For You dost what You wilt.

يَا مَنْ اسْمُهُ دَوَاءٌ

ya manis-muhu dawa-un

O He whose Name is a remedy,

وَذِكْرُهُ شِفَاءٌ وَطَاعَتُهُ غِنًى

wa dhik-ruhu shifa-un wa ta'tuhu ghinan

And whose remembrance is a cure, and whose obedience is wealth!

ارْحَم مَّن رَّأْسُ مَالِهِ الرَّجَاءُ

ir-ham-mar-ra-su malihir-raja

Have mercy upon him whose capital is hope

وَسِلاَحُهُ الْبُكَاءُ

wa silahuhul-buka-u

And whose weapon is tears!

يَا سَابِغَ النِّعَمِ يَا دَافِعَ النِّقَمِ

ya sabighan-ni`am ya dafi`an-niqam

O Ample in blessings! O Repeller of adversities!

يَا نُورَ الْمُسْتَوْحِشِينَ فِي الظُّلَمِ

ya nural-mus-taw-hishina fiz-zulami

O Light of those who are lonely in the darkness!

يَا عَالِماً لا يُعَلَّمُ

ya `alimal-la yu`al-lam

O Knower who was never taught!

صَلِّ عَلَى مُحَمَّدٍ وَّآلِ مُحَمَّدٍ

sal-li `ala muhammad wa a-li muhammadin

Bless Muhammad and Muhammad's household!

وافْعَلْ بِي مَا أَنتَ أَهْلُهُ

waf-`al bi ma anta ah-luh

And do with me what is worthy of You!

وَصَلَّى اللَّهُ عَلَى رَسُولِهِ وَالأَئِمَّةِ الْمَيَامِينَ مِنْ آلِهِ

wa sal-lallahu `ala rasulihi wal-aimmatil-mayamina min a-lihi

And Allah bless His messenger and the holy Imams of his household

وَسَلَّمَ تَسْلِيماً كَثِيراً

wa sal-lama tas-liman kathira

And give them abundant peace!

TAWASSUL

اَللَّهُمَّ إِنِّي أَسْأَلُكَ وَأَتَوَجَّهُ إِلَيْكَ

allahumma inni as'aluka wa atawajjahu ilayka

O Allah, I beseech You and turn my face toward You

بِنَبِيِّكَ نَبِيِّ ٱلرَّحْمَةِ

binabiyyika nabiyyi alrrahmati

in the name of Your Prophet; the Prophet of Mercy,

مُحَمَّدٍ صَلَّىٰ ٱللَّهُ عَلَيْهِ وَآلِهِ

muhammadin salla allahu `alayhi wa alihi

Muhammad—may Allah send blessings to him and his Household.

يَا أَبَا ٱلْقَاسِمِ

ya aba alqasimi

O Abu'l-Qasim!

يَا رَسُولَ ٱللَّهِ

ya rasula allahi

O Allah's Messenger!

يَا إِمَامَ ٱلرَّحْمَةِ

ya imama alrrahmati

O Chief of Mercy!

يَا سَيِّدَنَا وَمَوْلاَنَا

ya sayyidana wa mawlana

O our master and chief!

إِنَّا تَوَجَّهْنَا وَٱسْتَشْفَعْنَا

inna tawajjahana wastashfa`na

We are turning our faces toward you, seeking your intercession

وَتَوَسَّلْنَا بِكَ إِلَىٰ ٱللَّهِ

wa tawassalna bika ila allahi

and your advocacy for us before Allah;

وَقَدَّمْنَاكَ بَيْنَ يَدَيْ حَاجَاتِنَا

wa qaddamnaka bayna yaday hajatina
and we are presenting you [as our intermediary] for the settlement of our needs.

يَا وَجِيهاً عِنْدَ ٱللَّهِ

ya wajihan `inda allahi
O well-esteemed with Allah,

إِشْفَعْ لَنَا عِنْدَ ٱللَّهِ

ishfa` lana `inda allahi
intercede for us before Allah.

يَا أَبَا ٱلْحَسَنِ

ya aba alhasani
O Abu'l-Hasan!

يَا أَمِيرَ ٱلْمُؤْمِنِينَ

ya amira almu'minina
O commander of the Believers!

يَا عَلِيُّ بْنَ أَبِي طَالِبٍ

ya `aliyyu bna abi talibin
O `Ali, son of Abu-Talib!

يَا حُجَّةَ ٱللَّهِ عَلَىٰ خَلْقِهِ

ya hujjata allahi `ala khalqihi
O Allah's Argument against His creatures!

يَا سَيِّدَنَا وَمَوْلاَنَا

ya sayyidana wa mawlana
O our master and chief!

إِنَّا تَوَجَّهْنَا وَٱسْتَشْفَعْنَا

inna tawajjahana wastashfa`na
We are turning our faces toward you, seeking your intercession

وَتَوَسَّلْنَا بِكَ إِلَىٰ اللهِ

wa tawassalna bika ila allahi
and your advocacy for us before Allah;

وَقَدَّمْنَاكَ بَيْنَ يَدَيْ حَاجَاتِنَا

wa qaddamnaka bayna yaday hajatina
and we are presenting you [as our intermediary] for the settlement of our needs.

يَا وَجِيهاً عِنْدَ ٱللَّهِ

ya wajihan `inda allahi
O well-esteemed with Allah,

إِشْفَعْ لَنَا عِنْدَ ٱللَّهِ

ishfa` lana `inda allahi
intercede for us before Allah.

يَا فَاطِمَةُ ٱلزَّهْرَاءُ

ya fatimatu alzzahra'u
O Fatimah, the Luminous Lady!

يَا بِنْتَ مُحَمَّدٍ

ya binta muhammadin
O daughter of Muhammad!

يَا قُرَّةَ عَيْنِ ٱلرَّسُولِ

ya qurrata `ayni alrrasuli
O delight of the Messenger's eyes!

يَا سَيِّدَتَنَا وَمَوْلاَتَنَا

ya sayyidatana wa mawlatana
O our chief!

إِنَّا تَوَجَّهْنَا وَٱسْتَشْفَعْنَا

inna tawajjahana wastashfa`na
We are turning our faces toward you, seeking your intercession

وَتَوَسَّلْنَا بِكِ إِلَىٰ ٱللَّهِ

wa tawassalna biki ila allahi
and your advocacy for us before Allah;

وَقَدَّمْنَاكِ بَيْنَ يَدَيْ حَاجَاتِنَا

wa qaddamnaki bayna yaday hajatina
and we are presenting you [as our intermediary] for the settlement of our needs.

يَا وَجِيهَةً عِنْدَ ٱللَّهِ

ya wajihatan `inda allahi
O well-esteemed with Allah,

إِشْفَعي لَنَا عِنْدَ ٱللَّهِ

ishfa`i lana `inda allahi
intercede for us before Allah.

يَا أَبَا مُحَمَّدٍ

ya aba muhammadin
O Abu-Muhammad!

يَا حَسَنُ بْنَ عَلِيٍّ

ya hasanu bna `aliyyin
O Hasan the son of `Ali!

أَيُّهَا ٱلْمجْتَبَىٰ

ayyuha almujtaba
O well-Chosen one!

يَا بْنَ رَسُولِ ٱللَّهِ

yabna rasuli allahi
O son of Allah's Messenger!

يَا حُجَّةَ ٱللَّهِ عَلَىٰ خَلْقِهِ

ya hujjata allahi `ala khalqihi
O Allah's Argument against His creatures!

يَا سَيِّدَنَا وَمَوْلاَنَا

ya sayyidana wa mawlana
O our master and chief!

إِنَّا تَوَجَّهْنَا وَٱسْتَشْفَعْنَا

inna tawajjahana wastashfa`na
we are turning our faces toward you, seeking your intercession

وَتَوَسَّلْنَا بِكَ إِلَىٰ ٱللَّهِ

wa tawassalna bika ila allahi
and your advocacy for us before Allah;

وَقَدَّمْنَاكَ بَيْنَ يَدَيْ حَاجَاتِنَا

wa qaddamnaka bayna yaday hajatina
and we are presenting you [as our intermediary] for the settlement of our needs.

يَا وَجِيهاً عِنْدَ ٱللَّهِ

ya wajihan `inda allahi
O well-esteemed with Allah,

إِشْفَعْ لَنَا عِنْدَ ٱللَّهِ

ishfa` lana `inda allahi
intercede for us before Allah.

يَا أَبَا عَبْدِ ٱللَّهِ

ya aba `abdillahi
O Abu-`Abdullah!

يَا حُسَيْنُ بْنَ عَلِيٍّ

ya husaynu bna `aliyyin
O Husayn the son of `Ali!

أَيُّهَا ٱلشَّهِيدُ

ayyuha alshshahidu
O Martyr!

يَا بْنَ رَسُولِ ٱللَّهِ

yabna rasuli allahi
O son of Allah's Messenger!

يَا حُجَّةَ ٱللَّهِ عَلَىٰ خَلْقِهِ

ya hujjata allahi `ala khalqihi
O Allah's Argument against His creatures!

يَا سَيِّدَنَا وَمَوْلاَنَا

ya sayyidana wa mawlana
O our master and chief!

إِنَّا تَوَجَّهْنَا وَٱسْتَشْفَعْنَا

inna tawajjahana wastashfa`na
we are turning our faces toward you, seeking your intercession

وَتَوَسَّلْنَا بِكَ إِلَىٰ ٱللَّهِ

wa tawassalna bika ila allahi

and your advocacy for us before Allah;

وَقَدَّمْنَاكَ بَيْنَ يَدَيْ حَاجَاتِنَا

wa qaddamnaka bayna yaday hajatina

and we are presenting you [as our intermediary] for the settlement of our needs.

يَا وَجِيهاً عِنْدَ ٱللَّهِ

ya wajihan `inda allahi

O well-esteemed with Allah,

إِشْفَعْ لَنَا عِنْدَ ٱللَّهِ

ishfa` lana `inda allahi

intercede for us before Allah.

يَا أَبَا ٱلْحَسَنِ

ya aba alhasani

O Abu'l-Hasan!

يَا عَلِيُّ بْنَ ٱلْحُسَيْنِ

ya `aliyyu bna alhusayni

O `Ali the son of al-Husayn!

يَا زَيْنَ ٱلْعَابِدِينَ

ya zayna al`abidina

O Ornament of the Worshippers!

يَا بْنَ رَسُولِ ٱللَّهِ

yabna rasuli allahi

O son of Allah's Messenger!

يَا حُجَّةَ ٱللَّهِ عَلَىٰ خَلْقِهِ

ya hujjata allahi `ala khalqihi

O Allah's Argument against His creatures!

يَا سَيِّدَنَا وَمَوْلاَنَا

ya sayyidana wa mawlana

O our master and chief!

إِنَّا تَوَجَّهْنَا وَٱسْتَشْفَعْنَا

inna tawajjahana wastashfa`na

we are turning our faces toward you, seeking your intercession

وَتَوَسَّلْنَا بِكَ إِلَىٰ ٱللَّهِ

wa tawassalna bika ila allahi

and your advocacy for us before Allah;

وَقَدَّمْنَاكَ بَيْنَ يَدَيْ حَاجَاتِنَا

wa qaddamnaka bayna yaday hajatina

and we are presenting you [as our intermediary] for the settlement of our needs.

يَا وَجِيهاً عِنْدَ ٱللَّهِ

ya wajihan `inda allahi

O well-esteemed with Allah,

إِشْفَعْ لَنَا عِنْدَ ٱللَّهِ

ishfa` lana `inda allahi

intercede for us before Allah.

يَا أَبَا جَعْفَرٍ

ya aba ja`farin

O Abu-Ja`far!

يَا مُحَمَّدُ بْنَ عَلِيٍّ

ya muhammadu bna `aliyyin

O Muhammad the son of `Ali!

أَيُّهَا ٱلْبَاقِرُ

ayyuha albaqiru

O Cleaver [of knowledge]!

يَا بْنَ رَسُولِ ٱللَّهِ

yabna rasuli allahi

O son of Allah's Messenger!

يَا حُجَّةَ ٱللَّهِ عَلَىٰ خَلْقِهِ

ya hujjata allahi `ala khalqihi

O Allah's Argument against His creatures!

يَا سَيِّدَنَا وَمَوْلاَنَا

ya sayyidana wa mawlana
O our master and chief!

إِنَّا تَوَجَّهْنَا وَٱسْتَشْفَعْنَا

inna tawajjahana wastashfa`na
we are turning our faces toward you, seeking your intercession

وَتَوَسَّلْنَا بِكَ إِلَىٰ ٱللَّهِ

wa tawassalna bika ila allahi
and your advocacy for us before Allah;

وَقَدَّمْنَاكَ بَيْنَ يَدَيْ حَاجَاتِنَا

wa qaddamnaka bayna yaday hajatina
and we are presenting you [as our intermediary] for the settlement of our needs.

يَا وَجِيهاً عِنْدَ ٱللَّهِ

ya wajihan `inda allahi
O well-esteemed with Allah,

إِشْفَعْ لَنَا عِنْدَ ٱللَّهِ

ishfa` lana `inda allahi
intercede for us before Allah.

يَا أَبَا عَبْدِ ٱللَّهِ

ya aba `abdillahi
O Abu-`Abdullah!

يَا جَعْفَرُ بْنَ مُحَمَّدٍ

ya ja`faru bna muhammadin
O Ja`far the son of Muhammad!

أَيُّهَا ٱلصَّادِقُ

ayyuha alssadiqu
O Veracious!

يَا بْنَ رَسُولِ ٱللَّهِ

yabna rasuli allahi
O son of Allah's Messenger!

يَا حُجَّةَ ٱللَّهِ عَلَىٰ خَلْقِهِ

ya hujjata allahi `ala khalqihi

O Allah's Argument against His creatures!

يَا سَيِّدَنَا وَمَوْلاَنَا

ya sayyidana wa mawlana

O our master and chief!

إِنَّا تَوَجَّهْنَا وَٱسْتَشْفَعْنَا

inna tawajjahana wastashfa`na

we are turning our faces toward you, seeking your intercession

وَتَوَسَّلْنَا بِكَ إِلَىٰ ٱللَّهِ

wa tawassalna bika ila allahi

and your advocacy for us before Allah;

وَقَدَّمْنَاكَ بَيْنَ يَدَيْ حَاجَاتِنَا

wa qadamnaka bayna yaday hajatina

and we are presenting you [as our intermediary] for the settlement of our needs.

يَا وَجِيهاً عِنْدَ ٱللَّهِ

ya wajihan `inda allahi

O well-esteemed with Allah,

إِشْفَعْ لَنَا عِنْدَ ٱللَّهِ

ishfa` lana `inda allahi

intercede for us before Allah.

يَا أَبَا ٱلْحَسَنِ

ya aba alhasani

O Abu'l-Hasan!

يَا مُوسَىٰ بْنَ جَعْفَرٍ

ya musa bna ja`farin

O Musa the son of Ja`far!

أَيُّهَا ٱلْكَاظِمُ

ayyuha alkazimu

O Suppressor [of rage]!

يَا بْنَ رَسُولِ ٱللَّهِ

yabna rasuli allahi
O son of Allah's Messenger!

يَا حُجَّةَ ٱللَّهِ عَلَىٰ خَلْقِهِ

ya hujjata allahi `ala khalqihi
O Allah's Argument against His creatures!

يَا سَيِّدَنَا وَمَوْلاَنَا

ya sayyidana wa mawlana
O our master and chief!

إِنَّا تَوَجَّهْنَا وَٱسْتَشْفَعْنَا

inna tawajjahana wastashfa`na
we are turning our faces toward you, seeking your intercession

وَتَوَسَّلْنَا بِكَ إِلَىٰ ٱللَّهِ

wa tawassalna bika ila allahi
and your advocacy for us before Allah;

وَقَدَّمْنَاكَ بَيْنَ يَدَيْ حَاجَاتِنَا

wa qaddamnaka bayna yaday hajatina
and we are presenting you [as our intermediary] for the settlement of our needs.

يَا وَجِيهاً عِنْدَ ٱللَّهِ

ya wajihan `inda allahi
O well-esteemed with Allah,

إِشْفَعْ لَنَا عِنْدَ ٱللَّهِ

ishfa` lana `inda allahi
intercede for us before Allah.

يَا أَبَا ٱلْحَسَنِ

ya aba alhasani
O Abu'l-Hasan!

يَا عَلِيَّ بْنَ مُوسَىٰ

ya `aliyyu bna musa
O `Ali the son of Musa!

أَيُّهَا ٱلرِّضَا

ayyuha alrrida
O Amicable!

يَا بْنَ رَسُولِ ٱللَّهِ

yabna rasuli allahi
O son of Allah's Messenger!

يَا حُجَّةَ ٱللَّهِ عَلَىٰ خَلْقِهِ

ya hujjata allahi `ala khalqihi
O Allah's Argument against His creatures!

يَا سَيِّدَنَا وَمَوْلاَنَا

ya sayyidana wa mawlana
O our master and chief!

إِنَّا تَوَجَّهْنَا وَٱسْتَشْفَعْنَا

inna tawajjahana wastashfa`na
we are turning our faces toward you, seeking your intercession

وَتَوَسَّلْنَا بِكَ إِلَىٰ ٱللَّهِ

wa tawassalna bika ila allahi
and your advocacy for us before Allah;

وَقَدَّمْنَاكَ بَيْنَ يَدَيْ حَاجَاتِنَا

wa qaddamnaka bayna yaday hajatina
and we are presenting you [as our intermediary] for the settlement of our needs.

يَا وَجِيهاً عِنْدَ ٱللَّهِ

ya wajihan `inda allahi
O well-esteemed with Allah,

إِشْفَعْ لَنَا عِنْدَ ٱللَّهِ

ishfa` lana `inda allahi
intercede for us before Allah.

يَا أَبَا جَعْفَرٍ

ya aba ja`farin
O Abu-Ja`far!

يَا مُحَمَّدُ بْنَ عَلِيٍّ

ya muhammadu bna `aliyyin

O Muhammad the son of `Ali!

أَيُّهَا ٱلتَّقِيُّ ٱلْجَوَادُ

ayyuha alttaqiyyu aljawadu

O pious and magnanimous!

يَا بْنَ رَسُولِ ٱللَّهِ

yabna rasuli allahi

O son of Allah's Messenger!

يَا حُجَّةَ ٱللَّهِ عَلَىٰ خَلْقِهِ

ya hujjata allahi `ala khalqihi

O Allah's Argument against His creatures!

يَا سَيِّدَنَا وَمَوْلاَنَا

ya sayyidana wa mawlana

O our master and chief!

إِنَّا تَوَجَّهْنَا وَٱسْتَشْفَعْنَا

inna tawajjahana wastashfa`na

we are turning our faces toward you, seeking your intercession

وَتَوَسَّلْنَا بِكَ إِلَىٰ ٱللَّهِ

wa tawassalna bika ila allahi

and your advocacy for us before Allah;

وَقَدَّمْنَاكَ بَيْنَ يَدَيْ حَاجَاتِنَا

wa qaddamnaka bayna yaday hajatina

and we are presenting you [as our intermediary] for the settlement of our needs.

يَا وَجِيهاً عِنْدَ ٱللَّهِ

ya wajihan `inda allahi

O well-esteemed with Allah,

إِشْفَعْ لَنَا عِنْدَ ٱللَّهِ

ishfa` lana `inda allahi

intercede for us before Allah.

يَا أَبَا ٱلْحَسَنِ

ya aba alhasani
O Abu'l-Hasan!

يَا عَلِيُّ بْنَ مُحَمَّدٍ

ya `aliyyu bna muhammadin
O `Ali the son of Muhammad!

أَيُّهَا ٱلْهَادِي ٱلنَّقِيُّ

ayyuha alhadi alnnaqiyyu
O guide and pure!

يَا بْنَ رَسُولِ ٱللَّهِ

yabna rasuli allahi
O son of Allah's Messenger!

يَا حُجَّةَ ٱللَّهِ عَلَىٰ خَلْقِهِ

ya hujjata allahi `ala khalqihi
O Allah's Argument against His creatures!

يَا سَيِّدَنَا وَمَوْلاَنَا

ya sayyidana wa mawlana
O our master and chief!

إِنَّا تَوَجَّهْنَا وَٱسْتَشْفَعْنَا

inna tawajjahana wastashfa`na
we are turning our faces toward you, seeking your intercession

وَتَوَسَّلْنَا بِكَ إِلَىٰ ٱللَّهِ

wa tawassalna bika ila allahi
and your advocacy for us before Allah;

وَقَدَّمْنَاكَ بَيْنَ يَدَيْ حَاجَاتِنَا

wa qaddamnaka bayna yaday hajatina
and we are presenting you [as our intermediary] for the settlement of our needs.

يَا وَجِيهاً عِنْدَ ٱللَّهِ

ya wajihan `inda allahi
O well-esteemed with Allah,

إِشْفَعْ لَنَا عِنْدَ ٱللَّهِ

ishfa` lana `inda allahi

intercede for us before Allah.

يَا أَبَا مُحَمَّدٍ

ya aba muhammadin

O Abu-Muhammad!

يَا حَسَنُ بْنَ عَلِيٍّ

ya hasanu bna `aliyyin

O Hasan the son of `Ali!

أَيُّهَا ٱلزَّكِيُّ ٱلْعَسْكَرِيُّ

ayyuha alzzakiyyu al`askariyyu

O immaculate resident of `Askar [city]!

يَا بْنَ رَسُولِ ٱللَّهِ

yabna rasuli allahi

O son of Allah's Messenger!

يَا حُجَّةَ ٱللَّهِ عَلَىٰ خَلْقِهِ

ya hujjata allahi `ala khalqihi

O Allah's Argument against His creatures!

يَا سَيِّدَنَا وَمَوْلاَنَا

ya sayyidana wa mawlana

O our master and chief!

إِنَّا تَوَجَّهْنَا وَٱسْتَشْفَعْنَا

inna tawajjahana wastashfa`na

we are turning our faces toward you, seeking your intercession

وَتَوَسَّلْنَا بِكَ إِلَىٰ ٱللَّهِ

wa tawassalna bika ila allahi

and your advocacy for us before Allah;

وَقَدَّمْنَاكَ بَيْنَ يَدَيْ حَاجَاتِنَا

wa qaddamnaka bayna yaday hajatina

and we are presenting you [as our intermediary] for the settlement of our needs.

يَا وَجِيهاً عِنْدَ ٱللَّهِ

ya wajihan `inda allahi
O well-esteemed with Allah,

إِشْفَعْ لَنَا عِنْدَ ٱللَّهِ

ishfa` lana `inda allahi
intercede for us before Allah.

يَا وَصِيَّ ٱلْحَسَنِ

ya wasiyya alhasani
O successor of al-Hasan!

وَٱلْخَلَفُ ٱلْحُجَّةُ

walkhalafu alhujjatu
O descendant [of the Infallibles] and Argument [of Allah]

أَيُّهَا ٱلْقَائِمُ ٱلْمُنْتَظَرُ ٱلْمَهْدِيُّ

ayyuha alqa'imu almuntazaru almahdiyyu
O Riser, Awaited, and Well-guided!

يَا بْنَ رَسُولِ ٱللَّهِ

yabna rasuli allahi
O son of Allah's Messenger!

يَا حُجَّةَ ٱللَّهِ عَلَىٰ خَلْقِهِ

ya hujjata allahi `ala khalqihi
O Allah's Argument against His creatures!

يَا سَيِّدَنَا وَمَوْلاَنَا

ya sayyidana wa mawlana
O our master and chief!

إِنَّا تَوَجَّهْنَا وَٱسْتَشْفَعْنَا

inna tawajjahana wastashfa`na
we are turning our faces toward you, seeking your intercession

وَتَوَسَّلْنَا بِكَ إِلَىٰ ٱللَّهِ

wa tawassalna bika ila allahi
and your advocacy for us before Allah;

وَقَدَّمْنَاكَ بَيْنَ يَدَيْ حَاجَاتِنَا

wa qaddamnaka bayna yaday hajatina
and we are presenting you [as our intermediary] for the settlement of our needs.

يَا وَجِيهاً عِنْدَ ٱللَّهِ إِشْفَعْ لَنَا عِنْدَ ٱللَّهِ

ya wajihan `inda allahi ishfa` lana `inda allahi
intercede for us before Allah. O well-esteemed with Allah,

You may now beseech Almighty Allah to grant your needs, and they will be settled, if Allah permits. According to another narration, you may say the following words thereafter:

يَا سَادَتِي وَمَوَالِيَّ

ya sadati wa mawaliyya
O my chiefs and masters!

إِنِّي تَوَجَّهْتُ بِكُمْ

inni tawajjahtu bikum
I am turning my face toward Allah in the names of you [all],

ائِمَّتِي وَعُدَّتِي

a'immati wa `uddati
for you are my leaders and my supporters

لِيَوْمِ فَقْرِي وَحَاجَتِي إِلَىٰ ٱللَّهِ

liyawmi faqri wa hajati ila allahi
on the day of my destitution and neediness before Allah.

وَتَوَسَّلْتُ بِكُمْ إِلَىٰ ٱللَّهِ

wa tawassaltu bikum ila allahi
I am seeking your advocacy for me before Allah

وَٱسْتَشْفَعْتُ بِكُمْ إِلَىٰ ٱللَّهِ

wastashfa`tu bikum ila allahi
and seeking your intercession for me before Allah;

فَٱشْفَعُوا لِي عِنْدَ ٱللَّهِ

fashfa`u li `inda allahi
so, (please) intercede for me before Allah

وَٱسْتَنْقِذُونِي مِنْ ذُنُوبِي عِنْدَ ٱللَّهِ

wastanqidhuni min dhunubi `inda allahi
and save me from my sins before Allah,

فَإِنَّكُمْ وَسِيلَتِي إِلَىٰ ٱللَّهِ

fa'innakum wasilati ila allahi
for you are my means to Allah

وَبِحُبِّكُمْ وَبِقُرْبِكُمْ ارْجُو نَجَاةً مِنَ ٱللَّهِ

wa bihubbikum wa biqurbikum arju najatan mina allahi
and through my love for you and my seeking nearness to you do I hope for salvation from Allah.

فَكُونُوا عِنْدَ ٱللَّهِ رَجَائِي

fakunu `inda allahi raja'i
So, be my hope before Allah.

يَا سَادَتِي يَا اوْلِيَاءَ ٱللَّهِ

ya sadati ya awliya'a allahi
O my masters! O Allah's intimate servants!

صَلَّىٰ ٱللَّهُ عَلَيْهِمْ اجْمَعِينَ

salla allahu `alayhim ajma`ina
May Allah bless you all

وَلَعَنَ ٱللَّهُ اعْدَاءَ ٱللَّهِ ظَالِمِيهِمْ

wa la`ana allahu a`da'a allahi zalimihim
and may Allah curse the enemies of Allah; those who wronged you,

مِنَ ٱلاوَّلِينَ وَٱلآخِرِينَ

mina al-awwalina wal-akhirina
from the past and the last generations.

آمِينَ رَبَّ ٱلْعَالَمِينَ

amina rabba al`alamina
Respond to us, O Lord of the Worlds!

الْحَمْدُ لِلَّهِ رَبِّ ٱلْعَالَمِينَ

alhamdu lillahi rabbi al`alamina
All praise be to Allah the Lord of the worlds.

وَصَلَّىٰ ٱللَّهُ عَلَىٰ سَيِّدِنَا مُحَمَّدٍ نَبِيِّهِ

wa salla allahu `ala sayyidina muhammadin nabiyyihi

May Allah send blessings upon our master Muhammad His Prophet

وَآلِهِ وَسَلَّمَ تَسْلِيماً

wa alihi wa sallama tasliman

and upon his Household and may He salute them with thorough salutation.

AL-AHD

ٱللَّهُمَّ رَبَّ ٱلنُّورِ ٱلْعَظِيمِ

allahumma rabba alnnuri al`azimi

O Allah the Lord of the Great Light,

وَرَبَّ ٱلْكُرْسِيِّ ٱلرَّفِيعِ

wa rabba alkursiyyi alrrafi`i

the Lord of the Elevated Throne,

وَرَبَّ ٱلْبَحْرِ ٱلْمَسْجُورِ

wa rabba albahri almasjuri

the Lord of the swollen ocean,

وَمُنْزِلَ ٱلتَّوْرَاةِ وَٱلإِنْجِيلِ وَٱلزَّبُورِ

wa munzila alttawrati wal-injili wallzzaburi

the Revealer of the Torah, the Gospel, and the Psalms,

وَرَبَّ ٱلظِّلِّ وَٱلْحَرُورِ

wa rabba alzzilli walharuri

the Lord of shade and heat,

وَمُنْزِلَ ٱلْقُرْآنِ ٱلْعَظِيمِ

wa munzila alqur'ani al`azimi

the Revealer of the Great Qur'an,

وَرَبَّ ٱلْمَلاَئِكَةِ ٱلْمُقَرَّبِينَ

wa rabba almala'ikati almuqarrabina

and the Lord of the Archangels,

وَٱلأَنْبِيَاءِ وَٱلْمُرْسَلِينَ

wal-anbiya'i walmursalina

the Prophets, and the Messengers:

ٱللَّهُمَّ إِنِّي أَسْأَلُكَ بِٱسْمِكَ ٱلْكَرِيمِ

allahumma inni as'aluka bismika alkarimi

O Allah, I beseech You in Your Noble Name,

وَبِنُورِ وَجْهِكَ ٱلْمُنِيرِ

wa binuri wajhika almuniri
in the Light of Your Luminous Face

وَمُلْكِكَ ٱلْقَدِيمِ

wa mulkika alqadimi
and Your Eternal Kingdom.

يَا حَيُّ يَا قَيُّومُ

ya hayyu ya qayyumu
O Ever-living! O Self-Subsistent!

أَسْأَلُكَ بِٱسْمِكَ ٱلَّذِي أَشْرَقَتْ بِهِ ٱلسَّمَاوَاتُ وَٱلأَرَضُونَ

as'aluka bismika alladhi ashraqat bihi alssamawatu wal-araduna
I beseech You in the name of Your Name with which the heavens and the earth have lit up

وَبِٱسْمِكَ ٱلَّذِي يَصْلَحُ بِهِ ٱلأَوَّلُونَ وَٱلآخِرُونَ

wa bismika alladhi yasluhu bihi al-awwaluna wal-akhiruna
and in Your Name with which the past and the coming generations have become upright!

يَا حَيّاً قَبْلَ كُلِّ حَيٍّ

ya hayyan qabla kulli hayyin
O He Who has been always alive before the existence of all living things!

وَيَا حَيّاً بَعْدَ كُلِّ حَيٍّ

wa ya hayyan ba`da kulli hayyin
O He Who shall be alive after the extinction of all living things!

وَيَا حَيّاً حِينَ لا حَيٌّ

wa ya hayyan hina la hayyu
O He Who has been always alive even when there was nothing else alive!

يَا مُحْيِيَ ٱلْمَوْتَىٰ وَمُمِيتَ ٱلأَحْيَاءِ

ya muhyiya almawta wa mumita al-ahya'i
O He Who revives the dead ones and causes the living ones to die!

يَا حَيُّ لا إِلٰهَ إِلاَّ أَنْتَ

ya hayyu la ilaha illa anta

O Ever-living! There is no god save You.

اَللَّهُمَّ بَلِّغْ مَوْلاَنَا ٱلإِمَامَ ٱلْهَادِيَ ٱلْمَهْدِيَّ ٱلْقَائِمَ بِأَمْرِكَ

allahumma balligh mawlana al-imama alhadiya almahdiyya alqa'ima bi'amrika

O Allah, convey to our master Imam al-Mahdi, the guide who is to undertake Your orders,

صَلَوَاتُ ٱللَّهِ عَلَيْهِ وَعَلَىٰ آبَائِهِ ٱلطَّاهِرِينَ

salawatu allahi `alayhi wa `ala aba'ihi alttahirina

may Allah's blessings be upon him and upon his immaculate fathers,

عَنْ جَمِيعِ ٱلْمُؤْمِنِينَ وَٱلْمُؤْمِنَاتِ

`an jami`i almu'minina walmu'minati

on behalf of all of the believing men and women

فِي مَشَارِقِ ٱلأَرْضِ وَمَغَارِبِهَا

fi mashariqi al-ardi wa magharibiha

in the east and west of the earth

سَهْلِهَا وَجَبَلِهَا

sahliha wa jabaliha

and in plains, mountains,

وَبَرِّهَا وَبَحْرِهَا

wa barriha wa bahriha

lands, and seas,

وَعَنِّي وَعَنْ وَالِدَيَّ

wa `anni wa `an walidayya

and on behalf of my parents

مِنَ ٱلصَّلَوَاتِ زِنَةَ عَرْشِ ٱللَّهِ

min alssalawati zinata `arshi allahi

(convey to him) blessings that are as weighty as Allah's Throne,

وَمِدَادَ كَلِمَاتِهِ

wa midada kalimatihi
as much as the ink of His Words,

وَمَا أَحْصَاهُ عِلْمُهُ وَأَحَاطَ بِهِ كِتَابُهُ

wa ma ahsahu `ilmuhu wa ahata bihi kitabuhu
and as many as that which is counted by His knowledge and encompassed by His Book.

اَللَّهُمَّ إِنِّي أُجَدِّدُ لَهُ فِي صَبِيحَةِ يَوْمِي هٰذَا

allahumma inni ujaddidu lahu fi sabihati yawmi hadha
O Allah, I update to him in the beginning of this day

وَمَا عِشْتُ مِنْ أَيَّامِي

wa ma `ishtu min ayyami
and throughout the days of lifetime a pledge,

عَهْداً وَعَقْداً وَبَيْعَةً لَهُ فِي عُنُقِي

`ahdan wa `aqdan wa bay`atan lahu fi `unuqi
a covenant, and allegiance to which I commit myself

لا أَحُولُ عنها وَلا أَزُولُ أَبَداً

la ahulu `anhu wa la azulu abadan
and from which I neither convert nor change.

اَللَّهُمَّ ٱجْعَلْنِي مِنْ أَنْصَارِهِ

allahumma ij`alni min ansarihi
O Allah, (please do) make me of his supporters,

وَأَعْوَانِهِ وَٱلذَّابِّينَ عَنْهُ

wa a`wanihi waldhdhabbina `anhu
sponsors, defenders,

وَٱلْمُسَارِعِينَ إِلَيْهِ فِي قَضَاءِ حَوَائِجِهِ

walmusari`ina ilayhi fi qada'i hawa'ijihi
and those who hurry in carrying out his instructions,

وَٱلْمُمْتَثِلِينَ لأَوَامِرِهِ

walmumtathilina li'awamirihi
those who comply with his orders,

وَٱلْمُحَامِينَ عَنْهُ

walmuhamina `anhu

those who uphold him,

وَٱلسَّابِقِينَ إِلَىٰ إِرَادَتِهِ

walssabiqina ila iradatihi

those who precede others to implementing his will,

وَٱلْمُسْتَشْهَدِينَ بَيْنَ يَدَيْهِ

walmustashhadina bayna yadayhi

and those who will be martyred before him.

اَللَّهُمَّ إِنْ حَالَ بَيْنِي وَبَيْنَهُ ٱلْمَوْتُ ٱلَّذِي جَعَلْتَهُ عَلَىٰ عِبَادِكَ حَتْماً مَقْضِيّاً

allahumma in hala bayni wa baynahu almawtu alladhi ja`altahu `ala `ibadika hatman maqdiyyan

O Allah, if death that You have made inevitably and certainly incumbent upon Your servants stands between me and him,

فَأَخْرِجْنِي مِنْ قَبْرِي مُؤْتَزِراً كَفَنِي

fa'akhrijni min qabri mu'taziran kafani

then (please do) take me out of my grave using my shroud as dress,

شَاهِراً سَيْفِي

sharihan sayfi

unsheathing my sword,

مُجَرِّداً قَنَاتِي

mujarridan qanati

holding my lance in my hand,

مُلَبِّياً دَعْوَةَ ٱلدَّاعِي فِي ٱلْحَاضِرِ وَٱلْبَادِي

mulabbiyan da`wata aldda`i filhadiri walbadi

and responding to the call of the Caller who shall announce (his advent) in urban areas and deserts.

اَللَّهُمَّ أَرِنِي ٱلطَّلْعَةَ ٱلرَّشِيدَةَ

allahumma arini alttal`ata alrrashidata

O Allah, (please do) show me his magnificent mien

وَٱلْغُرَّةَ ٱلْحَمِيدَةَ

walghurrata alhamidata

and his praiseworthy forehead,

وَٱكْحُلْ نَاظِرِي بِنَظْرَةٍ مِنِّي إِلَيْهِ

wakhul naziri binazratin minni ilayhi

delight my eyes by letting me have a look at him.

وَعَجِّلْ فَرَجَهُ

wa `ajjil farajahu

And (please) expedite his relief,

وَسَهِّلْ مَخْرَجَهُ

wa sahhil makhrajahu

make his reappearance easy,

وَأَوْسِعْ مَنْهَجَهُ

wa awsi` manhajahu

clear a spacious space for him,

وَٱسْلُكْ بِي مَحَجَّتَهُ

wasluk bi muhajjatahu

guide me to follow his course,

وَأَنْفِذْ أَمْرَهُ

wa anfidh amrahu

give success to his issues,

وَٱشْدُدْ أَزْرَهُ

washdud azrahu

and confirm his strength.

وَٱعْمُرِ ٱللَّهُمَّ بِهِ بِلاَدَكَ

wa`mur allahumma bihi biladaka

O Allah, construct Your lands through him

وَأَحْيِ بِهِ عِبَادَكَ

wa ahyi bihi `ibadaka

and refresh Your servants through him,

فَإِنَّكَ قُلْتَ وَقَوْلُكَ ٱلْحَقُّ

fa'innaka qulta wa qawluka alhaqqu
For You have said, and true are Your words:

ظَهَرَ ٱلْفَسَادُ فِي ٱلْبَرِّ وَٱلْبَحْرِ

zahara alfasadu filbarri walbahri
"Corruption has appeared in the land and the sea

بِمَا كَسَبَتْ أَيْدِي ٱلنَّاسِ

bima kasabat aydi alnnasi
on account of what the hands of men have wrought."

فَأَظْهِرِ ٱللَّهُمَّ لَنَا وَلِيَّكَ

fa'azhir allahumma lana waliyyaka
So, O Allah, (please) show us Your vicegerent,

وَٱبْنَ بِنْتِ نَبِيِّكَ

wabna binti nabiyyika
the son of Your Prophet,

ٱلْمُسَمَّىٰ بِٱسْمِ رَسُولِكَ

almusamma bismi rasulika
and the namesake of Your Messenger,

صَلَّىٰ ٱللَّهُ عَلَيْهِ وَآلِهِ

salla allahu `alayhi wa alihi
peace be upon him and his Household,

حَتَّىٰ لا يَظْفَرَ بِشَيْءٍ مِنَ ٱلْبَاطِلِ إِلاَّ مَزَّقَهُ

hatta la yazfara bishay'in min albatili illa mazzaqahu
so that he shall tear up any wrong item that he will face

وَيُحِقَّ ٱلْحَقَّ وَيُحَقِّقَهُ وَٱجْعَلْهُ

wa yahiqqa alhaqqa wa yuhaqqiqahu waj`alhu
and shall confirm and approve of the truth.

ٱللَّهُمَّ مَفْزَعاً لِمَظْلُومِ عِبَادِكَ

allahumma mafza`an limazlumi `ibadika
O Allah, (please) make him the shelter to whom Your wronged servants shall resort,

وَنَاصِراً لِمَنْ لا يَجِدُ لَهُ نَاصِراً غَيْرَكَ

wa nasiran liman la yajidu lahu nasiran ghayraka

the supporter of those who cannot find any supporter save You,

وَمُجَدِّداً لِمَا عُطِّلَ مِنْ أَحْكَامِ كِتَابِكَ

wa mujaddidan lima `uttila min ahkami kitabika

the reviver of the laws of Your Book that have been suspended,

وَمُشَيِّداً لِمَا وَرَدَ مِنْ أَعْلامِ دِينِكَ وَسُنَنِ نَبِيِّكَ

wa mushayyidan lima warada min a`lami dinika wa sunani nabiyyika

and the constructor of all signs of Your religion and instructions of Your Messenger,

صَلَّىٰ ٱللَّهُ عَلَيْهِ وآلِهِ وَٱجْعَلْهُ

salla allahu `alayhi wa alihi waj`alhu

peace be upon him and his Household, that he will see.

ٱللَّهُمَّ مِمَّنْ حَصَّنْتَهُ مِنْ بَأْسِ ٱلْمُعْتَدِينَ

allahumma mimman hassantahu min ba'si almu`tadina

O Allah, (please) include him with those whom You protect from the domination of the aggressors.

ٱللَّهُمَّ وَسُرَّ نَبِيَّكَ مُحَمَّداً

allahumma wa surra nabiyyaka muhammadan

O Allah, (please) delight Your Prophet Muhammad,

صَلَّىٰ ٱللَّهُ عَلَيْهِ وآلِهِ

salla allahu `alayhi wa alihi

peace be upon him and his Household,

بِرُؤْيَتِهِ وَمَنْ تَبِعَهُ عَلَىٰ دَعْوَتِهِ

biru'yatihi wa man tabi`ahu `ala da`watihi

as well as all those who followed him in his promulgation by making (us) see him,

وَٱرْحَمِ ٱسْتِكَانَتَنَا بَعْدَهُ

warham istikanatana ba`dahu

and (please) have mercy upon our humiliation after him.

اَللَّهُمَّ ٱكْشِفْ هٰذِهِ ٱلْغُمَّةَ عَنْ هٰذِهِ ٱلأُمَّةِ بِحُضُورِهِ

allahumma ikshif hadhihi alghummata `an hadhihi al-ummati bihudurihi

O Allah, (please) relieve this community from the (current) grief through presenting him

وَعَجِّلْ لَنَا ظُهُورَهُ

wa `ajjil lana zuhurahu

and expedite his advent for us:

إِنَّهُمْ يَرَوْنَهُ بَعِيداً وَنَرَاهُ قَرِيباً

innahum yarawnahu ba`idan wa narahu qariban

"Surely, they think it to be far off, and We see it nigh."

بِرَحْمَتِكَ يَا أَرْحَمَ ٱلرَّاحِمِينَ

birahmatika ya arhama alrrahimina

[do all that] In the name of Your mercy; O most merciful of all those who show mercy.

You may then slap your right thigh with your hand three times and, at each time, say the following:

الْعَجَلَ ٱلْعَجَلَ يَامَوْلاَيَ يَا صَاحِبَ ٱلزَّمَانِ

al`ajala al`ajala ya mawlaya ya sahiba alzzaman

(We pray for Your) earliest advent, earliest advent, O Patron of the Age.

MINOR ZIYARAH

This form of ziyarah is acceptable to be recited at all shrines.

اَلسَّلاَمُ عَلَىٰ أَوْلِيَاءِ ٱللَّهِ وَأَصْفِيَائِهِ

alssalamu `ala awliya'i allahi wa asfiya'ihi

Peace be upon Allah's friends and well-chosen ones!

اَلسَّلاَمُ عَلَىٰ أُمَنَاءِ ٱللَّهِ وَأَحِبَّائِهِ

alssalamu `ala umana'i allahi wa ahibba'ihi

Peace be upon Allah's trustees and beloved ones!

اَلسَّلاَمُ عَلَىٰ أَنْصَارِ ٱللَّهِ وَخُلَفَائِهِ

alssalamu `ala ansari allahi wa khulafa'ihi

Peace be upon Allah's supporters and representatives!

اَلسَّلاَمُ عَلَىٰ مَحَالِّ مَعْرِفَةِ ٱللَّهِ

alssalamu `ala mahalli ma`rifati allahi

Peace be upon the centers of the recognition of Allah!

اَلسَّلاَمُ عَلَىٰ مَسَاكِنِ ذِكْرِ ٱللَّهِ

alssalamu `ala masakini dhikri allahi

Peace be upon the places of mentioning Allah

اَلسَّلاَمُ عَلَىٰ مُظْهِرِي أَمْرِ ٱللَّهِ وَنَهْيِهِ

alssalamu `ala muzhiri amri allahi wa nahyihi

Peace be upon the demonstrators of Allah's orders and prohibitions!

اَلسَّلاَمُ عَلَىٰ ٱلدُّعَاةِ إِلَىٰ ٱللَّهِ

alssalamu `ala alddu`ati ila allahi

Peace be upon the callers to Allah!

اَلسَّلاَمُ عَلَىٰ ٱلْمُسْتَقِرِّينَ فِي مَرْضَاتِ ٱللَّهِ

alssalamu `ala almustaqirrina fi mardati allahi

Peace be upon those settling down at Allah's pleasure!

اَلسَّلاَمُ عَلَىٰ ٱلْمُخْلِصِينَ فِي طَاعَةِ ٱللَّهِ

alssalamu `ala almukhlisina fi ta`ati allahi
Peace be upon those obeying Allah sincerely!

اَلسَّلاَمُ عَلَىٰ ٱلأَدِلاَّءِ عَلَىٰ ٱللَّهِ

alssalamu `ala al-adilla'i `ala allahi
Peace be upon those guiding to Allah!

اَلسَّلاَمُ عَلَىٰ ٱلَّذِينَ مَنْ وَالاَهُمْ فَقَدْ وَالَىٰ ٱللَّهَ

alssalamu `ala alladhina man walahum faqad wala allaha
Peace be upon those the loyalty to whom is loyalty to Allah

وَمَنْ عَادَاهُمْ فَقَدْ عَادَىٰ ٱللَّهَ

wa man `adahum faqad `ada allaha
the hostility towards whom is hostility towards Allah

وَمَنْ عَرَفَهُمْ فَقَدْ عَرَفَ ٱللَّهَ

wa man `arafahum faqad `arafa allaha
the recognition of whom is recognition of Allah,

وَمَنْ جَهِلَهُمْ فَقَدْ جَهِلَ ٱللَّهَ

wa man jahilahum faqad jahila allaha
ignorance of whom is ignorance of Allah,

وَمَنِ ٱعْتَصَمَ بِهِمْ فَقَدِ ٱعْتَصَمَ بِٱللَّهِ

wa mani i`tasama bihim faqadi i`tasama billahi
sticking to whom is sticking to Allah,

وَمَنْ تَخَلَّىٰ مِنْهُمْ فَقَدْ تَخَلَّىٰ مِنَ ٱللَّهِ عَزَّ وَجَلَّ

wa man takhalla minhum faqad takhalla min allahi `azza wa jalla
and abandonment of whom is abandonment of Allah the Almighty and All-majestic.

وَأُشْهِدُ ٱللَّهَ أَنِّي سِلْمٌ لِمَنْ سَالَمْتُمْ

wa ushhidu allaha anni silmun liman salamtum
And I call Allah to witness that I am at peace with those with whom you are at peace

وَحَرْبٌ لِمَنْ حارَبْتُمْ

wa harbun liman harabtum

and at war with those with whom you are at war

مُؤْمِنٌ بِسِرِّكُمْ وَعَلاَنِيَتِكُمْ

mu'minun bisirrikum wa `alaniyatikum

I believe in your secret and open affairs

مُفَوِّضٌ فِي ذٰلِكَ كُلِّهِ إِلَيْكُمْ

mufawwidun fi dhalika kullihi ilaykum

and I am relegating all that to you.

لَعَنَ ٱللَّهُ عَدُوَّ آلِ مُحَمَّدٍ

la`ana allahu `aduwa ali muhammadin

May Allah curse the enemy of Muhammad's Household

مِنَ ٱلْجِنِّ وَٱلإِنْسِ

min aljinni wal-insi

including the jinn and mankind

وَأَبْرَأُ إِلَىٰ ٱللَّهِ مِنْهُمْ

wa abra'u ila allahi minhum

and I disavow them in the presence of Allah.

وَصَلَّىٰ ٱللَّهُ عَلَىٰ مُحَمَّدٍ وَآلِهِ

wa salla allahu `ala muhammadin wa alihi

May Allah bless Muhammad and his Household.

GRAND ZIYARAH

This ziyarah (or visitation) is unique in its way of narration and speaks of the incredible status of the Ahl ul-Bayt (peace be upon them) in the eyes of God.

اَلسَّلاَمُ عَلَيْكُمْ يَا أَهْلَ بَيْتِ ٱلنُّبُوَّةِ

alssalamu `alaykum ya ahla bayti alnnubuwwati

Peace be upon you, O Household of Prophethood,

وَمَوْضِعَ ٱلرِّسَالَةِ

wa mawdi`a alrrisalati

location of the Divine mission,

وَمُخْتَلَفَ ٱلْمَلاَئِكَةِ

wa mukhtalafa almala'ikati

frequently visited by the angels,

وَمَهْبِطَ ٱلْوَحْيِ

wa mahbita alwahyi

destination of the Divine revelation,

وَمَعْدِنَ ٱلرَّحْمَةِ

wa ma`dina alrrahmati

core of mercy,

وَخُزَّانَ ٱلْعِلْمِ

wa khuzzana al`ilmi

hoarders of knowledge,

وَمُنْتَهَىٰ ٱلْحِلْمِ

wa muntaha alhilmi

ultimate degree of forbearance,

وَأُصُولَ ٱلْكَرَمِ

wa usula alkarami

origins of generosity,

وَقَادَةَ ٱلْأُمَمِ

wa qadata al-umami
leaders of all nations,

وَأَوْلِيَاءَ ٱلنِّعَمِ

wa awliya'a alnni`ami
sustainers of bounties,

وَعَنَاصِرَ ٱلْأَبْرَارِ

wa `anasira al-abrari
foundations of the dutiful,

وَدَعَائِمَ ٱلْأَخْيَارِ

wa da`a'ima al-akhyari
pillars of the upright,

وَسَاسَةَ ٱلْعِبَادِ

wa sasata al`ibadi
maintainers of the servants (of Allah),

وَأَرْكَانَ ٱلْبِلاَدِ

wa arkana albiladi
props of the lands,

وَأَبْوَابَ ٱلْإِيـمَانِ

wa abwaba al-imani
doors to true faith,

وَأُمَنَاءَ ٱلرَّحْمٰنِ

wa umana'a alrrahmani
trustees of the All-beneficent (Allah),

وَسُلاَلَةَ ٱلنَّبِيِّينَ

wa sulalata alnnabiyyina
descendants of the Prophets,

وَصَفْوَةَ ٱلْمُرْسَلِينَ

wa safwata almursalina
choice of the Messengers,

وَعِتْرَةَ خِيَرَةِ رَبِّ ٱلْعَالَمِينَ

wa `itrata khiyarati rabbi al`alamina
and offspring of the select of the Lord of the worlds.

وَرَحْمَةُ ٱللَّهِ وَبَرَكَاتُهُ

wa rahmatu allahi wa barakatuhu
Allah's mercy and blessings, too, be upon you (all).

اَلسَّلاَمُ عَلَىٰ أَئِمَّةِ ٱلْهُدَىٰ

alssalamu `ala a'immati alhuda
Peace be upon the directors of right guidance,

وَمَصَابِيحِ ٱلدُّجَىٰ

wa masabihi aldduja
the lanterns in darkness,

وَأَعْلاَمِ ٱلتُّقَىٰ

wa a`lami alttuqa
the patterns of piety,

وَذَوِي ٱلنُّهَىٰ

wa dhawi alnnuha
the owners of understanding,

وَأُوْلِي ٱلْحِجَىٰ

wa uli alhija
the endued with thought,

وَكَهْفِ ٱلْوَرَىٰ

wa kahfi alwara
the havens for the peoples,

وَوَرَثَةِ ٱلْأَنْبِيَاءِ

wa warathati al-anbiya'i
the inheritors of the Prophets,

وَٱلْمَثَلِ ٱلْأَعْلَىٰ

walmathali al-a`la
the perfect specimen,

وَٱلدَّعْوَةِ ٱلْحُسْنَىٰ

waldda`wati alhusna
the most excellent call,

وَحُجَجِ ٱللَّهِ عَلَىٰ أَهْلِ ٱلدُّنْيَا

wa hujaji allahi `ala ahli alddunya
and the arguments of Allah against the inhabitants of the world,

وَٱلْآخِرَةِ وَٱلْأُولَىٰ

wal-akhirati wal-ula
the Hereafter, and the former world.

وَرَحْمَةُ ٱللَّهِ وَبَرَكَاتُهُ

wa rahmatu allahi wa barakatuhu
Allah's mercy and blessings, too, be upon you (all).

اَلسَّلاَمُ عَلَىٰ مَحَالِّ مَعْرِفَةِ ٱللَّهِ

alssalamu `ala mahalli ma`rifati allahi
Peace be upon the exponents of the recognition of Allah,

وَمَسَاكِنِ بَرَكَةِ ٱللَّهِ

wa masakini barakati allahi
the centers of Allah's blessing,

وَمَعَادِنِ حِكْمَةِ ٱللَّهِ

wa ma`adini hikmati allahi
the essence of Allah's wisdom,

وَحَفَظَةِ سِرِّ ٱللَّهِ

wa hafazati sirri allahi
the keepers of Allah's secrets,

وَحَمَلَةِ كِتَابِ ٱللَّهِ

wa hamalati kitabi allahi
the bearers of Allah's Book,

وَأَوْصِيَاءِ نَبِيِّ ٱللَّهِ

wa awsiya'i nabiyyi allahi
the successors of Allah's Prophet,

وَذُرِّيَّةِ رَسُولِ ٱللَّهِ

wa dhurriyyati rasuli allahi
and the progeny of Allah's Messenger,

صَلَّىٰ ٱللَّهُ عَلَيْهِ وَآلِهِ

salla allahu `alayhi wa alihi
may Allah send blessings upon him and his Household.

وَرَحْمَةُ ٱللَّهِ وَبَرَكَاتُهُ

wa rahmatu allahi wa barakatuhu
Allah's mercy and blessings, too, be upon them.

اَلسَّلاَمُ عَلَىٰ ٱلدُّعَاةِ إِلَىٰ ٱللَّهِ

alssalamu `ala alddu`ati ila allahi
Peace be upon the callers to Allah,

وَٱلأَدِلاَّءِ عَلَىٰ مَرْضَاتِ ٱللَّهِ

wal-adilla'i `ala mardati allahi
the leaders to Allah's pleasure,

وَٱلْمُسْتَقِرِّينَ فِي أَمْرِ ٱللَّهِ

walmustaqirrina fi amri allahi
the abiders by Allah's decree,

وَٱلتَّامِّينَ فِي مَحَبَّةِ ٱللَّهِ

walttammina fi mahabbati allahi
the perfect in love for Allah,

وَٱلْمُخْلِصِينَ فِي تَوْحِيدِ ٱللَّهِ

walmukhlisina fi tawhidi allahi
the sincere in professing Allah's Oneness,

وَٱلْمُظْهِرِينَ لِأَمْرِ ٱللَّهِ وَنَهْيِهِ

walmuzhirina li'amri allahi wa nahyihi
the manifesters of Allah's orders and prohibitions,

وَعِبَادِهِ ٱلْمُكْرَمِينَ

wa `ibadihi almukramina
and Allah's honored bondmen

ٱلَّذِينَ لَا يَسْبِقُونَهُ بِٱلْقَوْلِ

alladhina la yasbiqunahu bilqawli
who speak not until He has spoken

وَهُمْ بِأَمْرِهِ يَعْمَلُونَ

wa hum bi'amrihi ya`maluna
and act by His command.

وَرَحْمَةُ ٱللَّهِ وَبَرَكَاتُهُ

wa rahmatu allahi wa barakatuhu
Allah's mercy and blessings, too, be upon them.

اَلسَّلاَمُ عَلَىٰ ٱلأَئِمَّةِ ٱلدُّعَاةِ

alssalamu `ala al-a'immati alddu`ati
Peace be upon the Imams, the heralds,

وَٱلْقَادَةِ ٱلْهُدَاةِ

walqadati alhudati
the leaders, the guides,

وَٱلسَّادَةِ ٱلْوُلاَةِ

walssadati alwulati
the chiefs, the authorities,

وَٱلذَّادَةِ ٱلْحُمَاةِ

waldhdhadati alhumati
the defenders, the protectors,

وَأَهْلِ ٱلذِّكْرِ

wa ahli aldhdhikri
the people of the Reminder (i.e. the Qur'an),

وَأُوْلِي ٱلأَمْرِ

wa uli al-amri
the men in authority,

وَبَقِيَّةِ ٱللَّهِ وَخِيَرَتِهِ

wa baqiyyati allahi wa khiyaratihi
the left ones by Allah, His select,

وَحِزْبِهِ وَعَيْبَةِ عِلْمِهِ

wa hizbihi wa `aybati `ilmihi
His party, the case of His knowledge

وَحُجَّتِهِ وَصِرَاطِهِ

wa hujjatihi wa siratihi
His argument, His path,

وَنُورِهِ وَبُرْهَانِهِ

wa nurihi wa burhanihi
His light, and His proof.

وَرَحْمَةُ ٱللَّهِ وَبَرَكَاتُهُ

wa rahmatu allahi wa barakatuhu
Allah's mercy and blessings, too, be upon them.

أَشْهَدُ أَنْ لَا إِلَٰهَ إِلَّا ٱللَّهُ

ashhadu an la ilaha illa allahu
I bear witness that there is no god save Allah;

وَحْدَهُ لَا شَرِيكَ لَهُ

wahdahu la sharika lahu
One and Only and having no partner with Him

كَمَا شَهِدَ ٱللَّهُ لِنَفْسِهِ

kama shahida allahu linafsihi
just as Allah has testified to His Oneness

وَشَهِدَتْ لَهُ مَلاَئِكَتُهُ

wa shahidat lahu mala'ikatuhu
to which His angels

وَأُوْلُو ٱلْعِلْمِ مِنْ خَلْقِهِ

wa ulu al`ilmi min khalqihi
and his knowledgeable creatures testify.

لَا إِلَٰهَ إِلَّا هُوَ ٱلْعَزِيزُ ٱلْحَكِيمُ

la ilaha illa huwa al`azizu alhakimu
There is no god save Him; the Almighty, the All-wise.

وَأَشْهَدُ أَنَّ مُحَمَّداً عَبْدُهُ ٱلْمُنْتَجَبُ

wa ashhadu anna muhammadan `abduhu almuntajabu
I also bear witness that Muhammad is His elect servant

وَرَسُولُهُ ٱلْمُرْتَضَىٰ

wa rasuluhu almurtada
and His approved Messenger.

أَرْسَلَهُ بِٱلْهُدَىٰ وَدِينِ ٱلْحَقِّ

arsalahu bilhuda wa dini alhaqqi
He sent him with right guidance and with the Religion of truth

لِيُظْهِرَهُ عَلَى ٱلدِّينِ كُلِّهِ

liyuzhirahu `ala alddini kullihi

that He may cause it to prevail over all religions

وَلَوْ كَرِهَ ٱلْمُشْرِكُونَ

wa law kariha almushrikuna

however much the idol-worshippers may be averse.

وَأَشْهَدُ أَنَّكُمُ ٱلأَئِمَّةُ ٱلرَّاشِدُونَ

wa ashhadu annakum al-a'immatu alrrashiduna

I also bear witness that you all are the Imams, rightly guiding,

ٱلْمَهْدِيُّونَ ٱلْمَعْصُومُونَ

almahdiyyuna alma`sumuna

well-guided, infallible,

ٱلْمُكَرَّمُونَ ٱلْمُقَرَّبُونَ

almukarramuna almuqarrabuna

highly revered, drawn near (to Allah),

ٱلْمُتَّقُونَ ٱلصَّادِقُونَ

almuttaquna alssadiquna

pious, veracious,

ٱلْمُصْطَفَوْنَ ٱلْمُطِيعُونَ لِلَّهِ

almustafawna almuti`una lillahi

well-chosen, obedient to Allah,

ٱلْقَوَّامُونَ بِأَمْرِهِ

alqawwamuna bi'amrihi

establishing His rule,

ٱلْعَامِلُونَ بِإِرَادَتِهِ

al`amiluna bi'iradatihi

putting into practice His will,

ٱلْفَائِزُونَ بِكَرَامَتِهِ

alfa'izuna bikaramatihi

and winning His honoring.

إِصْطَفَاكُمْ بِعِلْمِهِ

istafakum bi`ilmihi

He chose you on account of His (eternal) knowledge,

وَٱرْتَضَاكُمْ لِغَيْبِهِ

wartadakum lighaybihi

approved of you to maintain His unseen knowledge,

وَٱخْتَارَكُمْ لِسِرِّهِ

wakhtarakum lisirrihi

selected you to keep His secret,

وَٱجْتَبَاكُمْ بِقُدْرَتِهِ

wajtabakum biqudratihi

decided on you by means of His omnipotence,

وَأَعَزَّكُمْ بِهُدَاهُ

wa a`azzakum bihudahu

equipped you with His guidance,

وَخَصَّكُمْ بِبُرْهَانِهِ

wa khassakum biburhanihi

distinguished you with His clear proofs,

وَٱنْتَجَبَكُمْ لِنُورِهِ

wantajabakum linurihi

chose you to hold His Light,

وَأَيَّدَكُمْ بِرُوحِهِ

wa ayyadakum biruhihi

supported you with His Holy spirit,

وَرَضِيَكُمْ خُلَفَاءَ فِي أَرْضِهِ

wa radiyakum khulafa'a fi ardihi
and accepted you as vicegerents in His lands,

وَحُجَجاً عَلَىٰ بَرِيَّتِهِ

wa hujajan `ala bariyyatihi
arguments against His beings,

وَأَنْصَاراً لِدِينِهِ

wa ansaran lidinihi
supporters of His religion,

وَحَفَظَةً لِسِرِّهِ

wa hafazatan lisirrihi
keepers of His secret,

وَخَزَنَةً لِعِلْمِهِ

wa khazanatan li`ilmihi
hoarders of His knowledge,

وَمُسْتَوْدَعاً لِحِكْمَتِهِ

wa mustawda`an lihikmatihi
stores of His wisdom,

وَتَرَاجِمَةً لِوَحْيِهِ

wa tarajimatan liwahyihi
interpreters of His revelation,

وَأَرْكَاناً لِتَوْحِيدِهِ

wa arkanan litawhidihi
pillars of the profession of His Oneness,

وَشُهَدَاءَ عَلَىٰ خَلْقِهِ

wa shuhada'a `ala khalqihi
witnesses on His creatures,

وَأَعْلاَماً لِعِبَادِهِ

wa a`laman li`ibadihi
signs for His servants,

وَمَنَاراً فِي بِلاَدِهِ

wa manaran fi biladihi
torches in His lands,

وَأَدِلاَّءَ عَلَىٰ صِرَاطِهِ

wa adilla'a `ala siratihi
and directors to His path.

عَصَمَكُمُ ٱللَّهُ مِنَ ٱلزَّلَلِ

`asamakum allahu min alzzalali
Allah has preserved you against slips,

وَآمَنَكُمْ مِنَ ٱلْفِتَنِ

wa amanakum min alfitani
secured you against seditious matters,

وَطَهَّرَكُمْ مِنَ ٱلدَّنَسِ

wa tahharakum min alddanasi
purified you from dirt,

وَأَذْهَبَ عَنْكُمُ ٱلرِّجْسَ

wa adhhaba `ankum alrrijsa
removed away from you uncleanness,

وَطَهَّرَكُمْ تَطْهِيراً

wa tahharakum tathiran
and purified you with a thorough purifying.

فَعَظَّمْتُمْ جَلاَلَهُ

fa`azzamtum jalalahu
So, you have glorified His majesty,

وَأَكْبَرْتُمْ شَأْنَهُ

wa akbartum sha'nahu

declared great His magnificence,

وَمَجَّدْتُمْ كَرَمَهُ

wa majjadtum karamahu

glorified His nobility,

وَأَدَمْتُمْ ذِكْرَهُ

wa adamtum dhikrahu

perpetuated mentioning Him,

وَوَكَّدْتُمْ مِيثَاقَهُ

wa wakkadtum mithaqahu

consolidated His covenant,

وَأَحْكَمْتُمْ عَقْدَ طَاعَتِهِ

wa ahkamtum `aqda ta`atihi

made firm your pledge of obedience to Him,

وَنَصَحْتُمْ لَهُ فِي ٱلسِّرِّ وَٱلْعَلاَنِيَةِ

wa nasahtum lahu fi alssirri wal`alaniyati

acted sincerely to Him privately and publicly,

وَدَعَوْتُمْ إِلَىٰ سَبِيلِهِ

wa da`awtum ila sabilihi

called unto His way

بِٱلْحِكْمَةِ وَٱلْمَوْعِظَةِ ٱلْحَسَنَةِ

bilhikmati walmaw`izati alhasanati

with wisdom and fair admonition,

وَبَذَلْتُمْ أَنْفُسَكُمْ فِي مَرْضَاتِهِ

wa badhaltum anfusakum fi mardatihi

sacrificed yourselves for the sake of attaining His pleasure,

وَصَبَرْتُمْ عَلَىٰ مَا أَصَابَكُمْ فِي جَنْبِهِ

wa sabartum `ala ma asabakum fi janbihi
acted patiently towards what has befallen you for His sake,

وَأَقَمْتُمُ ٱلصَّلاَةَ

wa aqamtum alssalata
performed the prayers,

وَآتَيْتُمُ ٱلزَّكَاةَ

wa ataytum alzzakata
defrayed the poor-rate,

وَأَمَرْتُمْ بِٱلْمَعْرُوفِ

wa amartum bilma`rufi
enjoined the right,

وَنَهَيْتُمْ عَنِ ٱلْمُنْكَرِ

wa nahaytum `an almunkari
forbade the wrong,

وَجَاهَدْتُمْ فِي ٱللَّهِ حَقَّ جِهَادِهِ

wa jahadtum fi allahi haqqa jihadihi
and strived in the way of Allah as exactly as striving should be

حَتَّىٰ أَعْلَنْتُمْ دَعْوَتَهُ

hatta a`lantum da`watahu
until you made known His call,

وَبَيَّنْتُمْ فَرَائِضَهُ

wa bayyantum fara'idahu
rendered clear His obligations,

وَأَقَمْتُمْ حُدُودَهُ

wa aqamtum hududahu
executed His provisions,

وَنَشَرْتُمْ شَرَائِعَ أَحْكَامِهِ

wa nashartum shara'i`a ahkamihi

propagated for the enacted laws of Him,

وَسَنَنْتُمْ سُنَّتَهُ

wa sanantum sunnatahu

acted out His rules,

وَصِرْتُمْ فِي ذٰلِكَ مِنْهُ إِلَىٰ ٱلرِّضَا

wa sirtum fi dhalika minhu ila alrrida

attained His pleasure through carrying out all these matters,

وَسَلَّمْتُمْ لَهُ ٱلْقَضَاءَ

wa sallamtum lahu alqada'a

surrendered to His will,

وَصَدَّقْتُمْ مِنْ رُسُلِهِ مَنْ مَضَىٰ

wa saddaqtum min rusulihi man mada

and confirmed the truth of the past Messengers of Him.

فَٱلرَّاغِبُ عَنْكُمْ مَارِقٌ

falrraghibu `ankum mariqun

Therefore, whoever forsakes you is apostate,

وَٱللاَّزِمُ لَكُمْ لاَحِقٌ

wallazimu lakum lahiqun

whoever adheres to you will attain the destination,

وَٱلْمُقَصِّرُ فِي حَقِّكُمْ زَاهِقٌ

walmuqassiru fi haqqikum zahiqun

and whoever fails to carry out the duties towards you will perish.

وَٱلْحَقُّ مَعَكُمْ وَفِيكُمْ

walhaqqu ma`akum wa fikum

Verily, the truth is always with you, amid you,

وَمِنْكُمْ وَإِلَيْكُمْ

wa minkum wa ilaykum

from you, and to you.

وَأَنْتُمْ أَهْلُهُ وَمَعْدِنُهُ

wa antum ahluhu wa ma`dinuhu

You are the people and the core of it (i.e. the truth).

وَمِيرَاثُ ٱلنُّبُوَّةِ عِنْدَكُمْ

wa mirathu alnnubuwwati `indakum

The inheritance of Prophethood is with you.

وَإِيَابُ ٱلْخَلْقِ إِلَيْكُمْ

wa iyabu alkhalqi ilaykum

The ultimate destination of the creatures is to you.

وَحِسَابُهُمْ عَلَيْكُمْ

wa hisabuhum `alaykum

Calling them to account is your mission.

وَفَصْلُ ٱلْخِطَابِ عِنْدَكُمْ

wa faslu alkhitabi `indakum

Decisive speech is with you.

وَآيَاتُ ٱللَّهِ لَدَيْكُمْ

wa ayatu allahi ladaykum

The verses of Allah is in your possession.

وَعَزَائِمُهُ فِيكُمْ

wa `aza'imuhu fikum

His unavoidable decrees rely upon you.

وَنُورُهُ وَبُرْهَانُهُ عِنْدَكُمْ

wa nuruhu wa burhanuhu `indakum

His light and proof are with you.

وَأَمْرُهُ إِلَيْكُمْ

wa amruhu ilaykum

His authority is to you.

مَنْ وَالاكُمْ فَقَدْ وَالَى ٱللَّهَ

man walakum faqad wala allaha

Whoever declares loyalty to you has in fact declared loyalty to Allah,

وَمَنْ عَادَاكُمْ فَقَدْ عَادَىٰ ٱللَّهَ

wa man `adakum faqad `ada allaha

whoever shows enmity towards you has in fact shown enmity towards Allah,

وَمَنْ أَحَبَّكُمْ فَقَدْ أَحَبَّ ٱللَّهَ

wa man ahabbakum faqad ahabba allaha

whoever loves you has in fact loved Allah,

وَمَنْ أَبْغَضَكُمْ فَقَدْ أَبْغَضَ ٱللَّهَ

wa man abghadakum faqad abghada allaha

whoever hates you has in fact hated Allah,

وَمَنِ ٱعْتَصَمَ بِكُمْ فَقَدِ ٱعْتَصَمَ بِٱللَّهِ

wa man i`tasama bikum faqad i`tasama billahi

and whoever holds fast to you has in fact held fast to Allah.

أَنْتُمُ ٱلصِّرَاطُ ٱلأَقْوَمُ

antumu alssiratu al-aqwamu

You are the most straight path

وَشُهَدَاءُ دَارِ ٱلْفَنَاءِ

wa shuhada'u dari alfana'i

the witnesses of this abode of extinction,

وَشُفَعَاءُ دَارِ ٱلْبَقَاءِ

wa shufa`a'u dari albaqa'i

the intercessors in the abode of permanence,

وَٱلرَّحْمَةُ ٱلْمَوْصُولَةُ

walrrahmatu almawsulatu
the connected mercy,

وَٱلآيَةُ ٱلْمَخْزُونَةُ

wal-ayatu almakhzunatu
the stored sign,

وَٱلأَمَانَةُ ٱلْمَحْفُوظَةُ

wal-amanatu almahfuzatu
the safeguarded deposit,

وَٱلْبَابُ ٱلْمُبْتَلَىٰ بِهِ ٱلنَّاسُ

walbabu almubtala bihi alnnasu
and the door with which people are put to test.

مَنْ أَتَاكُمْ نَجَا

man atakum naja
Whoever comes to will have been saved

وَمَنْ لَمْ يَأْتِكُمْ هَلَكَ

wa man lam ya'tikum halaka
but whoever refrains from joining you will have perished.

إِلَىٰ ٱللَّهِ تَدْعُونَ

ila allahi tad`una
To Allah do you invite people,

وَعَلَيْهِ تَدُلُّونَ

wa `alayhi tadulluna
towards him do you show the way,

وَبِهِ تُؤْمِنُونَ

wa bihi tu'minuna
in Him do you believe,

وَلَهُ تُسَلِّمُونَ

wa lahu tusallimuna
to Him do you submit,

وَبِأَمْرِهِ تَعْمَلُونَ

wa bi'amrihi ta`maluna
upon His command do you act,

وَإِلَىٰ سَبِيلِهِ تُرْشِدُونَ

wa ila sabilihi turshiduna
to His path do you direct,

وَبِقَوْلِهِ تَحْكُمُونَ

wa biqawlihi tahkumuna
and according to His saying do you judge.

سَعَدَ مَنْ وَالاكُمْ

sa`ada man walakum
Happy is he who is loyal to you,

وَهَلَكَ مَنْ عَادَاكُمْ

wa halaka man `adakum
desolate is he who forsakes you,

وَخَابَ مَنْ جَحَدَكُمْ

wa khaba man jahadakum
disappointed is he who denies you,

وَضَلَّ مَنْ فَارَقَكُمْ

wa dalla man faraqakum
straying off is he who separates himself from you

وَفَازَ مَنْ تَمَسَّكَ بِكُمْ

wa faza man tamassaka bikum
winner is he who adheres to you,

وَأَمِنَ مَنْ لَجَأَ إِلَيْكُمْ

wa amina man laja' ilaykum

secured is he who resorts to you,

وَسَلِمَ مَنْ صَدَّقَكُمْ

wa salima man saddaqakum

saved is he who gives credence to you,

وَهُدِيَ مَنِ ٱعْتَصَمَ بِكُمْ

wa hudiya man i`tasama bikum

and rightly guided is he who takes shelter in you

مَنِ ٱتَّبَعَكُمْ فَٱلْجَنَّةُ مَأْوَاهُ

man ittaba`akum faljannatu ma'wahu

As to whoever follows you, Paradise will be his abode.

وَمَنْ خَالَفَكُمْ فَٱلنَّارُ مَثْوَاهُ

wa man khalafakum falnnaru mathwahu

As to whoever dissents you, Hellfire will be his dwelling.

وَمَنْ جَحَدَكُمْ كَافِرٌ

wa man jahadakum kafirun

He who denies you is unbeliever,

وَمَنْ حَارَبَكُمْ مُشْرِكٌ

wa man harabakum mushrikun

he who makes war against you is polytheist,

وَمَنْ رَدَّ عَلَيْكُمْ فِي أَسْفَلِ دَرْكٍ مِنَ ٱلْجَحِيمِ

wa man radda `alaykum fi asfali darakin min aljahimi

and he who objects to you will be in the lowest tier of the burning fire.

أَشْهَدُ أَنَّ هٰذَا سَابِقٌ لَكُمْ فِيمَا مَضَىٰ

ashhadu anna hadha sabiqun lakum fima mada

I bear witness that all the previous was pre-decided for you

وَجَارٍ لَكُمْ فِيمَا بَقِيَ

wa jarin lakum fima baqiya

and it will continue in the future;

وَأَنَّ أَرْوَاحَكُمْ وَنُورَكُمْ

wa anna arwahakum wa nurakum

and that your souls, your light,

وَطِينَتَكُمْ وَاحِدَةٌ

wa tinatakum wahidatun

and your form are the same;

طَابَتْ وَطَهُرَتْ

tabat wa tahurat

blessed and purified,

بَعْضُهَا مِنْ بَعْضٍ

ba`duha min ba`din

and one of the other.

خَلَقَكُمُ ٱللَّهُ أَنْوَاراً

khalaqakum allahu anwaran

Allah created you as lights;

فَجَعَلَكُمْ بِعَرْشِهِ مُحْدِقِينَ

faja`alakum bi`arshihi muhdiqina

He then made you observe from His Thron

حَتَّىٰ مَنَّ عَلَيْنَا بِكُمْ

hatta manna `alayna bikum

until He endued us with the favor of your existence (among us)

فَجَعَلَكُمْ فِي بُيُوتٍ

faja`alakum fi buyutin

and then placed you in houses

أَذِنَ ٱللَّهُ أَنْ تُرْفَعَ

adhina allahu an turfa`a
that He allowed to be raised

وَيُذْكَرَ فِيهَا ٱسْمُهُ

wa yudhkara fiha ismuhu
and to have His Name mentioned therein.

وَجَعَلَ صَلَوَاتِنَا عَلَيْكُمْ

wa ja`ala salatana `alaykum
He also decided our invocation of blessings upon you

وَمَا خَصَّنَا بِهِ مِنْ وِلاَيَتِكُمْ

wa ma khassana bihi min wilayatikum
and our loyalty to yo

طِيباً لِخَلْقِنَا

tiban likhalqina
to be immaculacy of our creation,

وَطَهَارَةً لأَنْفُسِنَا

wa taharatan li'anfusina
purity of our souls,

وَتَزْكِيَةً لَنَا

wa tazkiyatan lana
refinement of our manners,

وَكَفَّارَةً لِذُنُوبِنَا

wa kaffaratan lidhunubina
and forgiveness of our sins.

فَكُنَّا عِنْدَهُ مُسَلِّمِينَ بِفَضْلِكُمْ

fakunna `indahu musallimina bifadlikum
We have thus become, with Him, of those believing in your precedence

وَمَعْرُوفِينَ بِتَصْدِيقِنَا إِيَّاكُمْ

wa ma`rufina bitasdiqina iyyakum
and of those known for their giving credence to you.

فَبَلَغَ ٱللَّهُ بِكُمْ أَشْرَفَ مَحَلِّ ٱلْمُكَرَّمِينَ

fabalagha allahu bikum ashrafa mahalli almukarramina
Thus, Allah has raised you to the most principled place of the honored ones,

وَأَعْلَىٰ مَنَازِلِ ٱلْمُقَرَّبِينَ

wa a`la manazili almuqarrabina
the highest station of those drawn near to Him,

وَأَرْفَعَ دَرَجَاتِ ٱلْمُرْسَلِينَ

wa arfa`a darajati almursalina
and the loftiest ranks of the Messengers

حَيْثُ لَا يَلْحَقُهُ لاَحِقٌ

haythu la yalhaquhu lahiqun
where none can ever reach you,

وَلاَ يَفُوقُهُ فَائِقٌ

wa la yafuquhu fa'iqun
nor can anyone ever surpass you,

وَلاَ يَسْبِقُهُ سَابِقٌ

wa la yasbiquhu sabiqun
nor can anyone ever precede you,

وَلاَ يَطْمَعُ فِي إِدْرَاكِهِ طَامِعٌ

wa la yatma`u fi idrakihi tami`un
no can anyone ever look forward to reaching your positions;

حَتَّىٰ لَا يَبْقَىٰ مَلَكٌ مُقَرَّبٌ

hatta la yabqa malakun muqarrabun
therefore, no archangel,

وَلاَ نَبِيٌّ مُرْسَلٌ

wa la nabiyyun mursalun
commissioned Prophet,

وَلاَ صِدِّيقٌ وَلاَ شَهِيدٌ

wa la siddiqun wa la shahidun
a veracious one, a martyr

وَلاَ عَالِمٌ وَلاَ جَاهِلٌ

wa la `alimun wa la jahilun
a knowledgeable one, an ignorant one,

وَلاَ دَنِيٌّ وَلاَ فَاضِلٌ

wa la daniyyun wa la fadilun
an inferior, a superior,

وَلاَ مُؤْمِنٌ صَالِحٌ

wa la mu'minun salihun
a righteous believer,

وَلاَ فَاجِرٌ طَالِحٌ

wa la fajirun talihun
a wicked sinner,

وَلاَ جَبَّارٌ عَنِيدٌ

wa la jabbarun `anidun
an obstinate tyrant,

وَلاَ شَيْطَانٌ مَرِيدٌ

wa la shaytanun maridun
a devilish rebel,

وَلاَ خَلْقٌ فِيمَا بَيْنَ ذٰلِكَ شَهِيدٌ

wa la khalqun fima bayna dhalika shahidun
or any other witnessing being among these classes—all of those

إِلاَّ عَرَّفَهُمْ جَلاَلَةَ أَمْرِكُمْ

illa `arrafahum jalalata amrikum
were informed by Allah about the majesty of your issue,

وَعِظَمَ خَطَرِكُمْ

wa `izama khatarikum
the importance of your standing,

وَكِبَرَ شَأْنِكُمْ

wa kibara sha'nikum
the greatness of your prestige,

وَتَمَامَ نُورِكُمْ

wa tamama nurikum
the thoroughness of your illumination,

وَصِدْقَ مَقَاعِدِكُمْ

wa sidqa maqa`idikum
the honesty of your position,

وَثَبَاتَ مَقَامِكُمْ

wa thabata maqamikum
the firmness of your stance,

وَشَرَفَ مَحَلِّكُمْ وَمَنْزِلَتِكُمْ عِنْدَهُ

wa sharafa mahallikum wa manzilatikum `indahu
the honor of your station and position with Him,

وَكَرَامَتَكُمْ عَلَيْهِ

wa karamatakum `alayhi
your upstanding reputation with Him,

وَخَاصَّتَكُمْ لَدَيْهِ

wa khassatakum ladayhi
your special position with Him,

وَقُرْبَ مَنْزِلَتِكُمْ مِنْهُ

wa qurba manzilatikum minhu

and your close location to Him.

بِأَبِي أَنْتُمْ وَأُمِّي

bi'abi antum wa ummi

May my father, my mother,

وَأَهْلِي وَمَالِي وَأُسْرَتِي

wa ahli wa mali wa usrati

my kin, my property, and my family be ransoms for you.

أُشْهِدُ ٱللَّهَ وَأُشْهِدُكُمْ

ushhidu allaha wa ushhidukum

I beseech Allah and I beseech you all to witness for me

أَنِّي مُؤْمِنٌ بِكُمْ وَبِمَا آمَنْتُمْ بِهِ

anni mu'minun bikum wa bima amantum bihi

that I believe in you all and in that in which you believe,

كَافِرٌ بِعَدُوِّكُمْ وَبِمَا كَفَرْتُمْ بِهِ

kafirun bi`aduwwikum wa bima kafartum bihi

I renounce your enemies and whatever you renounce,

مُسْتَبْصِرٌ بِشَأْنِكُمْ

mustabsirun bisha'nikum

I am fully aware of your matter

وَبِضَلاَلَةِ مَنْ خَالَفَكُمْ

wa bidalalati man khalafakum

and of the deviation of those who oppose you,

مُوَالٍ لَكُمْ وَلأَوْلِيَائِكُمْ

muwalin lakum wa li'awliya'ikum

I am loyalist to you and to your loyalists,

مُبْغِضٌ لأَعْدَائِكُمْ وَمُعَادٍ لَهُمْ

mubghidun li'a`da'ikum wa mu`adin lahum

I hate your enemies and I show enmity towards them,

سِلْمٌ لِمَنْ سَالَمَكُمْ

silmun liman salamakum

I am at peace with those who make peace with you,

وَحَرْبٌ لِمَنْ حَارَبَكُمْ

wa harbun liman harabakum

I take the field against those who march against you,

مُحَقِّقٌ لِمَا حَقَّقْتُمْ

muhaqqiqun lima haqqaqtum

I accept as true that which you have decided as true,

مُبْطِلٌ لِمَا أَبْطَلْتُمْ

mubtilun lima abtaltum

I prove false that which you have decided as false,

مُطِيعٌ لَكُمْ

muti`un lakum

I am obedient to you,

عَارِفٌ بِحَقِّكُمْ

`arifun bihaqqikum

I recognize your right,

مُقِرٌّ بِفَضْلِكُمْ

muqirrun bifadlikum

I confess of your superiority,

مُحْتَمِلٌ لِعِلْمِكُمْ

muhtamilun li`ilmikum

I preserve your knowledge,

مُحْتَجِبٌ بِذِمَّتِكُمْ

muhtajibun bidhimmatikum
I take refuge under your protective shelter,

مُعْتَرِفٌ بِكُمْ

mu`tarifun bikum
I profess you,

مُؤْمِنٌ بِإِيَابِكُمْ

mu'minun bi'iyabikum
I believe in your coming back (to this world),

مُصَدِّقٌ بِرَجْعَتِكُمْ

musaddiqun biraj`atikum
I give credence to your return,

مُنْتَظِرٌ لأَمْرِكُمْ

muntazirun li'amrikum
I am awaiting your issue,

مُرْتَقِبٌ لِدَوْلَتِكُمْ

murtaqibun lidawlatikum
I am expecting your rule,

آخِذٌ بِقَوْلِكُمْ

akhidhun biqawlikum
I take in your sayings,

عَامِلٌ بِأَمْرِكُمْ

`amilun bi'amrikum
I carry out your orders,

مُسْتَجِيرٌ بِكُمْ

mustajirun bikum
I take shelter in you,

زَائِرٌ لَكُمْ

za'irun lakum
I make visits to you

لَائِذٌ عَائِذٌ بِقُبُورِكُمْ

la'idhun `a'idhun biquburikum
I resort to and seek protection in your graves,

مُسْتَشْفِعٌ إِلَىٰ ٱللَّهِ عَزَّ وَجَلَّ بِكُمْ

mustashfi`un ila allahi `azza wa jalla bikum
I seek your intercession for me with Allah the Almighty and All-majestic,

وَمُتَقَرِّبٌ بِكُمْ إِلَيْهِ

wa mutaqarribun bikum ilayhi
I seek nearness to Him in your names

وَمُقَدِّمُكُمْ أَمَامَ طَلِبَتِي

wa muqaddimukum amama talibati
I provide you as my means for seeking fulfillment of my desires,

وَحَوَائِجِي وَإِرَادَتِي

wa hawa'iji wa iradati
needs, and wishes,

فِي كُلِّ أَحْوَالِي وَأُمُورِي

fi kulli ahwali wa umuri
in all of my manners and affairs

مُؤْمِنٌ بِسِرِّكُمْ وَعَلاَنِيَتِكُمْ

mu'minun bisirrikum wa `alaniyatikum
I believe in your invisibility, visibility,

وَشَاهِدِكُمْ وَغَائِبِكُمْ

wa shahidikum wa gha'ibikum
presence, absence,

وَأَوَّلِكُمْ وَآخِرِكُمْ

wa awwalikum wa akhirikum
first, and last of you;

وَمُفَوِّضٌ فِي ذٰلِكَ كُلِّهِ إِلَيْكُمْ

wa mufawwidun fi dhalika kullihi ilaykum
and I confide all that to you

وَمُسَلِّمٌ فِيهِ مَعَكُمْ

wa musallimun fihi ma`akum
and submit to all of it with you

وَقَلْبِي لَكُمْ مُسَلِّمٌ

wa qalbi lakum musallimun
My heart is subservient to you,

وَرَأْيِي لَكُمْ تَبَعٌ

wa ra'yi lakum taba`un
my opinion is following yours,

وَنُصْرَتِي لَكُمْ مُعَدَّةٌ

wa nusrati lakum mu`addatun
and my support to you is all set

حَتَّىٰ يُحْيِيَ ٱللَّهُ تَعَالَىٰ دِينَهُ بِكُمْ

hatta yuhyiya allahu ta`ala dinahu bikum
until Allah the All-exalted restores His religion to life through you,

وَيَرُدَّكُمْ فِي أَيَّامِهِ

wa yaruddakum fi ayyamihi
brings you back again in His days,

وَيُظْهِرَكُمْ لِعَدْلِهِ

wa yuzhirakum li`adlihi
allows you to appear for (establishing) His justice,

وَيُمَكِّنَكُمْ فِي أَرْضِهِ

wa yumakkinakum fi ardihi

and gives you power to rule in His land.

فَمَعَكُمْ مَعَكُمْ

fama`akum ma`akum

So, I am (always) with you, with you

لاَ مَعَ غَيْرِكُمْ

la ma`a ghayrikum

but not with any one other than you.

آمَنْتُ بِكُمْ

amantu bikum

I have full faith in you

وَتَوَلَّيْتُ آخِرَكُمْ بِمَا تَوَلَّيْتُ بِهِ أَوَّلَكُمْ

wa tawallaytu akhirakum bima tawallaytu bihi awwalakum

and I declare my loyalty to the last of you just as I declared it to the first of you.

وَبَرِئْتُ إِلَىٰ ٱللَّهِ عَزَّ وَجَلَّ

wa bari'tu ila allahi `azza wa jalla

In the presence of Allah the Almighty and All-majestic, I repudiate

مِنْ أَعْدَائِكُمْ

min a`da'ikum

your enemies,

وَمِنَ ٱلْجِبْتِ وَٱلطَّاغُوتِ

wa min aljibti walttaghuti

all idols, false deities

وَٱلشَّيَاطِينِ وَحِزْبِهِمُ ٱلظَّالِمِينَ لَكُمُ

walshshayatini wa hizbihim alzzalimina lakumu

the devils, and their party who have wronged you,

ٱلْجَاحِدِينَ لِحَقِّكُمْ

aljahidina lihaqqikum
denied your rights,

وَٱلْمَارِقِينَ مِنْ وِلاَيَتِكُمْ

walmariqina min wilayatikum
apostatized from your (divinely commissioned) leadership,

وَٱلْغَاصِبِينَ لإِرْثِكُمْ

walghasibina li'irthikum
usurped your inheritance,

ٱلشَّاكِّينَ فِيكُمْ

alshshakkina fikum
arisen doubts about you

ٱلْمُنْحَرِفِينَ عَنْكُمْ

almunharifina `ankum
and deviated from you,

وَمِنْ كُلِّ وَلِيجَةٍ دُونَكُمْ

wa min kulli walijatin dunakum
and (I repudiate) any adherence to anyone other than you,

وَكُلِّ مُطَاعٍ سِوَاكُمْ

wa kulli muta`in siwakum
any obeyed one save you

وَمِنَ ٱلأَئِمَّةِ ٱلَّذِينَ يَدْعُونَ إِلَىٰ ٱلنَّارِ

wa min al-a'immati alladhina yad`una ila alnnari
and the leaders who call to Hellfire

فَثَبَّتَنِيَ ٱللَّهُ أَبَداً مَا حَيِيتُ

fathabbataniya allahu abadan ma hayitu
May Allah make me firm forever as long as I am alive

عَلَىٰ مُوَالاَتِكُمْ

`ala muwalatikum
on loyalty to you,

وَمَحَبَّتِكُمْ وَدِينِكُمْ

wa mahabbatikum wa dinikum
love for you, and on your religion

وَوَفَّقَنِي لِطَاعَتِكُمْ

wa waffaqani lita`atikum
May He grant me success in obedience to you,

وَرَزَقَنِي شَفَاعَتَكُمْ

wa razaqani shafa`atakum
endue me with your intercession,

وَجَعَلَنِي مِنْ خِيَارِ مَوَالِيكُمْ

wa ja`alani min khiyari mawalikum
make me of the best of your loyalists

ٱلتَّابِعِينَ لِمَا دَعَوْتُمْ إِلَيْهِ

alttabi`ina lima da`awtum ilayhi
who carry out all that to which you have called,

وَجَعَلَنِي مِمَّنْ يَقْتَصُّ آثَارَكُمْ

wa ja`alani mimman yaqtassu atharakum
and make me of those who are tracking your footsteps,

وَيَسْلُكُ سَبِيلَكُمْ

wa yasluku sabilakum
taking your path,

وَيَهْتَدِي بِهُدَاكُمْ

wa yahtadi bihudakum
following your guidance,

وَيُحْشَرُ ي زُمْرَتِكُمْ

wa yuhsharu fi zumratikum

(and those who are) resurrected in your group

وَيَكِرُّ فِي رَجْعَتِكُمْ

wa yakirru fi raj`atikum

given the chance to appear again in your Return,

وَيُمَلَّكُ فِي دَوْلَتِكُمْ

wa yumallaku f dawlatikum

given authority in your administration,

وَيُشَرَّفُ فِي عَافِيَتِكُمْ

wa yusharrafu fi `afiyatikum

honored to live under your sound supervision,

وَيُمَكَّنُ فِي أَيَّامِكُمْ

wa yumakkanu fi ayyamikum

given power in your days,

وَتَقِرُّ عَيْنُهُ غَداً بِرُؤْيَتِكُمْ

wa taqirru `aynuhu ghadan biru'yatikum

and having their eyes delighted by seeing you in the morrow.

بِأَبِي أَنْتُمْ وَأُمِّي

bi'abi antum wa ummi

May my father, mother,

وَنَفْسِي وَأَهْلِي وَمَالِي

wa nafsi wa ahli wa mali

soul, family, and possessions be ransoms for you.

مَنْ أَرَادَ ٱللَّهَ بَدَأَ بِكُمْ

man arada allaha bada'a bikum

Whoever desires for Allah should begin with you,

وَمَنْ وَحَّدَهُ قَبِلَ عَنْكُمْ

wa man wahhadahu qabila `ankum

whoever professes His Oneness should accept your instructions,

وَمَنْ قَصَدَهُ تَوَجَّهَ بِكُمْ

wa man qasadahu tawajjaha bikum

and whoever heads for Him should make you the means to Him.

مَوَالِيَّ لَا أُحْصِي ثَنَاءَكُمْ

mawaliyya la uhsi thana'akum

O my masters, I cannot count your merits

وَلاَ أَبْلُغُ مِنَ ٱلْمَدْحِ كُنْهَكُمْ

wa la ablughu min almadhi kunhakum

and I cannot attain the utmost of praise of you

وَمِنَ ٱلْوَصْفِ قَدْرَكُمْ

wa min alwasfi qadrakum

and the utmost of the description of your actual value,

وَأَنْتُمْ نُورُ ٱلأَخْيَار

wa antum nuru al-akhyari

since you are the light of the upright ones,

وَهُدَاةُ ٱلأَبْرَار

wa hudatu al-abrari

the guides of the pious ones,

وَحُجَجُ ٱلْجَبَّار

wa hujaju aljabbari

and the arguments of the Supreme Lord.

بِكُمْ فَتَحَ ٱللَّهُ

bikum fataha allahu

With you has Allah begun Creation

وَبِكُمْ يَخْتِمُ

wa bikum yakhtimu
and with you will He seal it.

وَبِكُمْ يُنَزِّلُ ٱلْغَيْثَ

wa bikum yunazzilu alghaytha
For your sake does He pour down rain,

وَبِكُمْ يُمْسِكُ ٱلسَّمَاءَ أَنْ تَقَعَ عَلَىٰ ٱلأَرْضِ إِلاَّ بِإِذْنِهِ

wa bikum yumsiku alssama'a an taqa`a `ala al-ardi illa bi'idhnihi
for your sake does He withhold the heavens from falling on the earth except by His permission

وَبِكُمْ يُنَفِّسُ ٱلْهَمَّ

wa bikum yunaffisu alhamma
and out of consideration for you does He dismiss agonie

وَيَكْشِفُ ٱلضُّرَّ

wa yakshifu alddurra
and relieves harms.

وَعِنْدَكُمْ مَا نَزَلَتْ بِهِ رُسُلُهُ

wa `indakum ma nazalat bihi rusuluhu
In your possession is all that which His Messengers brought down

وَهَبَطَتْ بِهِ مَلاَئِكَتُهُ

wa habatat bihi mala'ikatuhu
and with which His angels descended.

وَإِلَىٰ جَدِّكُمْ بُعِثَ ٱلرُّوحُ الأَمِينُ

wa ila jaddikum bu`itha alrruhu al-aminu
To your forefather( ) was the Honest Spirit sent.

آتَاكُمُ ٱللَّهُ مَا لَمْ يُؤْتِ أَحَداً مِنَ ٱلْعَالَمِينَ

atakum allahu ma lam yu'ti ahadan min al`alamina
Allah has given you that which He has not given to any one all over the worlds

طَأْطَأَ كُلُّ شَرِيفٍ لِشَرَفِكُمْ

ta'ta'a kullu sharifin lisharafikum
All highborn ones nod down their heads before your noble lineage,

وَبَخَعَ كُلُّ مُتَكَبِّرٍ لِطَاعَتِكُمْ

wa bakha`a kullu mutakabbirin lita`atikum
all arrogant ones submit to the obedience to you,

وَخَضَعَ كُلُّ جَبَّارٍ لِفَضْلِكُمْ

wa khada`a kullu jabbarin lifadlikum
all insolent oppressors succumb to your excellence,

وَذَلَّ كُلُّ شَيْءٍ لَكُمْ

wa dhalla kullu shay'in lakum
all things are humiliated before you

وَأَشْرَقَتِ ٱلأَرْضُ بِنُورِكُمْ

wa ashraqat al-ardu binurikum
the earth has been lit up with your light

وَفَازَ ٱلْفَائِزُونَ بِوِلاَيَتِكُمْ

wa faza alfa'izuna biwilayatikum
and the winners have attained triumph due to their loyalty to you.

بِكُمْ يُسْلَكُ إِلَىٰ ٱلرِّضْوَانِ

bikum yuslaku ila alrridwani
Through you can the way to Paradise be taken

وَعَلَىٰ مَنْ جَحَدَ وِلاَيَتَكُمْ غَضَبُ ٱلرَّحْمٰنِ

wa `ala man jahada wilayatakum ghadabu alrrahmani
and the ire of the All-beneficent is poured on whoever has denied your (divinely commissioned) leadership

بِأَبِي أَنْتُمْ وَأُمِّي

bi'abi antum wa ummi
May my father, mother,

وَنَفْسِي وَأَهْلِي وَمَالِي

wa nafsi wa ahli wa mali

soul, family, and possessions be ransoms for you.

ذِكْرُكُمْ فِي ٱلذَّاكِرِينَ

dhikrukum fi aldhdhakirina

your mention is within the mention of others.

وَأَسْمَاؤُكُمْ فِي ٱلْأَسْمَاءِ

wa asma'ukum fi al-asma'i

Your names are called along with other names.

وَأَجْسَادُكُمْ فِي ٱلْأَجْسَادِ

wa ajsadukum fi al-ajsadi

Your figures appear among other figures.

وَأَرْوَاحُكُمْ فِي ٱلْأَرْوَاحِ

wa arwahukum fi al-arwahi

Your souls are among other souls.

وَأَنْفُسُكُمْ فِي ٱلنُّفُوسِ

wa anfusukum fi alnnufusi

Your selves are among other selves.

وَآثَارُكُمْ فِي ٱلآثَارِ

wa atharukum fi al-athari

Your traditions are among other traditions.

وَقُبُورُكُمْ فِي ٱلْقُبُورِ

wa quburukum fi alquburi

Your graves are among other graves.

فَمَا أَحْلَىٰ أَسْمَاءَكُمْ

fama ahla asma'akum

But how gracious your names are!

وَأَكْرَمَ أَنْفُسَكُمْ

wa akrama anfusakum
How noble your souls are!

وَأَعْظَمَ شَأْنَكُمْ

wa a`zama sha'nakum
How superior your affairs are!

وَأَجَلَّ خَطَرَكُمْ

wa ajalla khatarakum
How majestic your stations are!

وَأَوْفَىٰ عَهْدَكُمْ

wa awfa `ahdakum
How dependable your covenants are!

وَأَصْدَقَ وَعْدَكُمْ

wa asdaqa wa`dakum
How truthful your promises are!

كَلاَمُكُمْ نُورٌ

kalamukum nurun
Your words are illumination.

وَأَمْرُكُمْ رُشْدٌ

wa amrukum rushdun
Your affairs are (leading to) orthodoxy.

وَوَصِيَّتُكُمُ ٱلتَّقْوَىٰ

wa wasiyyatukum alttaqwa
Your precepts are piety.

وَفِعْلُكُمُ ٱلْخَيْرُ

wa fi`lukum alkhayru
Your deeds are all good.

وَعَادَتُكُمُ ٱلإِحْسَانُ

wa `adatukum al-ihsanu
Your habits are charity

وَسَجِيَّتُكُمُ ٱلْكَرَمُ

wa sajiyyatukum alkaramu
Your nature is generosity.

وَشَأْنُكُمُ ٱلْحَقُّ

wa sha'nukum alhaqqu
Your issue is truth,

وَٱلصِّدْقُ وَٱلرِّفْقُ

walssidqu walrrifqu
honesty, and lenience.

وَقَوْلُكُمْ حُكْمٌ وَحَتْمٌ

wa qawlukum hukmun wa hatmun
Your words are judgments and decisiveness.

وَرَأْيُكُمْ عِلْمٌ وَحِلْمٌ وَحَزْمٌ

wa ra'yukum `ilmun wa hilmun wa hazmun
Your views are (based upon) knowledge, temperance, and forethought.

إِنْ ذُكِرَ ٱلْخَيْرُ كُنْتُمْ أَوَّلَهُ

in dhukira alkhayru kuntum awwalahu
Whenever goodness is mentioned, you are its initiation,

وَأَصْلَهُ وَفَرْعَهُ

wa aslahu wa far`ahu
origin, branch,

وَمَعْدِنَهُ وَمَأْوَاهُ وَمُنْتَهَاهُ

wa ma`dinahu wa ma'wahu wa muntahahu
essence, center, and ultimate

بِأَبِي أَنْتُمْ وَأُمِّي وَنَفْسِي

bi'abi antum wa ummi wa nafsi

May my father, mother, and soul be ransoms for you

كَيْفَ أَصِفُ حُسْنَ ثَنَائِكُمْ

kayfa asifu husna thana'ikum

How shall I describe the excellence of your merit

وَأُحْصِي جَمِيلَ بَلاَئِكُمْ

wa uhsi jamila bala'ikum

and define the beauty of your conferrals

وَبِكُمْ أَخْرَجَنَا ٱللَّهُ مِنَ ٱلذُّلِّ

wa bikum akhrajana allahu min aldhdhulli

It is on account of you that Allah has pulled us out of degradation,

وَفَرَّجَ عَنَّا غَمَرَاتِ ٱلْكُرُوبِ

wa farraja `anna ghamarati alkurubi

removed from us the clutches of hardships,

وَأَنْقَذَنَا مِنْ شَفَا جُرُفِ ٱلْهَلَكَاتِ

wa anqadhana min shafa jurufi alhalakati

and saved us from the brink of the pit of perditions

وَمِنَ ٱلنَّارِ

wa min alnnari

and from the Fire

بِأَبِي أَنْتُمْ وَأُمِّي وَنَفْسِي

bi'abi antum wa ummi wa nafsi

May my father, mother, and soul be ransoms for you

بِمُوَالاَتِكُمْ عَلَّمَنَا ٱللَّهُ مَعَالِمَ دِينِنَا

bimuwalatikum `allamana allahu ma`alima dinina

Through our loyalty to your leadership, Allah has taught us the features of our religion

وَأَصْلَحَ مَاكَانَ فَسَدَ مِنْ دُنْيَانَا

wa aslaha ma kana fasada min dunyana
and has set aright the spoiled items of our worldly lives

وَبِمُوَالاَتِكُمْ تَمَّتِ ٱلْكَلِمَةُ

wa bimuwalatikum tammat alkalimatu
Through our loyalty to your leadership, the Word has been perfected,

وَعَظُمَتِ ٱلنِّعْمَةُ

wa `azumat alnni`matu
the grace has become great

وَائْتَلَفَتِ ٱلْفُرْقَةُ

wa'talafat alfurqatu
and the discord has turned into alliance,

وَبِمُوَالاَتِكُمْ تُقْبَلُ ٱلطَّاعَةُ ٱلْمُفْتَرَضَةُ

wa bimuwalatikum tuqbalu altta`atu almuftaradatu
Through our loyalty to your leadership, the obligatory obedience (to Allah) is accepted.

وَلَكُمُ ٱلْمَوَدَّةُ ٱلْوَاجِبَةُ

wa lakum almawaddatu alwajibatu
To you alone are the obligatory affection,

وَٱلدَّرَجَاتُ ٱلرَّفِيعَةُ

walddarajatu alrrafi`atu
the elevated ranks

وَٱلْمَقَامُ ٱلْمَحْمُودُ

walmaqamu almahmudu
the praiseworthy standing,

وَٱلْمَكَانُ ٱلْمَعْلُومُ عِنْدَ ٱللَّهِ عَزَّ وَجَلَّ

walmakanu alma`lumu `inda allahi `azza wa jalla
the renowned station with Allah the Almighty and All-majestic,

وَٱلْجَاهُ ٱلْعَظِيمُ

waljahu al`azimu
the topmost prestige,

وَٱلشَّأْنُ ٱلْكَبِيرُ

walshsha'nu alkabiru
the supreme station

وَٱلشَّفَاعَةُ ٱلْمَقْبُولَةُ

walshshafa`atu almaqbulatu
and the admitted intercession.

رَبَّنَا آمَنَّا بِمَا أَنْزَلْتَ

rabbana amanna bima anzalta
O our Lord, we believe in that which You have sent down

وَٱتَّبَعْنَا ٱلرَّسُولَ

wattaba`na alrrasula
and we follow the Messenger;

فَٱكْتُبْنَا مَعَ ٱلشَّاهِدِينَ

faktubna ma`a alshshahidina
so, write our names among those who bear witness.

رَبَّنَا لَا تُزِغْ قُلُوبَنَا بَعْدَ إِذْ هَدَيْتَنَا

rabbana la tuzigh qulubana ba`da idh hadaytana
Our Lord, cause not our hearts to stray after You have guided us,

وَهَبْ لَنَا مِنْ لَدُنْكَ رَحْمَةً

wa hab lana min ladunka rahmatan
and bestow upon us mercy from Your Presence

إِنَّكَ أَنْتَ ٱلْوَهَّابُ

innaka anta alwahhabu
Lo! You, only You, are the Bestower.

سُبْحَانَ رَبِّنَا

subhana rabbina
Glory be to our Lord

إِنْ كَانَ وَعْدُ رَبِّنَا لَمَفْعُولاً

in kana wa`du rabbina lamaf`ulan
for in fact the promise of our Lord immediately takes effect.

يَا وَلِيَّ ٱللَّهِ

ya waliyya allahi
O vicegerent of Allah!( )

إِنَّ بَيْنِي وَبَيْنَ ٱللَّهِ عَزَّ وَجَلَّ ذُنُوباً

inna bayni wa bayna allahi `azza wa jalla dhunuban
There stand between me and Allah the Almighty and All-majestic, sins

لاَ يَأْتِي عَلَيْهَا إِلاَّ رِضَاكُمْ

la ya'ti `alayha illa ridakum
that cannot be demolished except by attaining your satisfaction.

فَبِحَقِّ مَنِ ٱئْتَمَنَكُمْ عَلَىٰ سِرِّهِ

fabihaqqi man i'tamanakum `ala sirrihi
Therefore, [I beseech you] in the name of the One Who has entrusted you with His secret,

وَٱسْتَرْعَاكُمْ أَمْرَ خَلْقِهِ

wastar`akum amra khalqihi
assigned you to supervise the affairs of His creatures,

وَقَرَنَ طَاعَتَكُمْ بِطَاعَتِهِ

wa qarana ta`atakum bita`atihi
and attached the obedience to Him with the obedience to you,

لَمَّا ٱسْتَوْهَبْتُمْ ذُنُوبِي

lamma istawhabtum dhunubi
to (please) endue me with the favor of absolving my sins

وَكُنْتُمْ شُفَعَائِي

wa kuntum shufa`a'i
and to be my intercessors

فَإِنِّي لَكُمْ مُطِيعٌ

fa'inni lakum muti`un
for I am obedient to you.

مَنْ أَطَاعَكُمْ فَقَدْ أَطَاعَ ٱللَّهَ

man ata`akum faqd ata`a allaha
He who obeys you has in fact obeyed Allah,

وَمَنْ عَصَاكُمْ فَقَدْ عَصَىٰ ٱللَّهَ

wa man `asakum faqad `asa allaha
he who disobeys you has in fact disobeyed Allah

وَمَنْ أَحَبَّكُمْ فَقَدْ أَحَبَّ ٱللَّهَ

wa man ahabbakum faqad ahabba allaha
he who loves you has in fact loved Allah,

وَمَنْ أَبْغَضَكُمْ فَقَدْ أَبْغَضَ ٱللَّهَ

wa man abghadakum faqad abghada allaha

and he who hates you has in fact hated Allah.

اَللَّهُمَّ إِنِّي لَو وَجَدْتُ شُفَعَاءَ

allahumma inni law wajadtu shufa`a'a
O Allah, had I known interceder

أَقْرَبَ إِلَيْكَ مِنْ مُحَمَّدٍ وَأَهْلِ بَيْتِهِ

aqraba ilayka min muhammadin wa ahli baytihi
that are closer to You than Muhammad and his Household

ٱلْأَخْيَارِ ٱلْأَئِمَّةِ ٱلْأَبْرَارِ

al-akhyari al-a'immati al-abrari
the virtuous and pious Imams

لَجَعَلْتُهُمْ شُفَعَائِي

laja`altuhum shufa`a'i

I would have chosen them as my intercessors

فَبِحَقِّهِمُ ٱلَّذِي أَوْجَبْتَ لَهُمْ عَلَيْكَ

fabihaqqihim alladhi awjabta lahum `alayka

So, [I beseech You] in the name of their Right that You have made obligatory upon You

أَسْأَلُكَ أَنْ تُدْخِلَنِي فِي جُمْلَةِ ٱلْعَارِفِينَ بِهِمْ وَبِحَقِّهِمْ

as'aluka an tudkhilani fi jumlati al`arifina bihim wa bihaqqihim

(please) include me with the group of those who recognize their Right and them

وَفِي زُمْرَةِ ٱلْمَرْحُومِينَ بِشَفَاعَتِهِمْ

wa fi zumrati almarhumina bishafa`atihim

and with the assembly of those who are shown mercy owing to their (i.e. Muhammad and his Household) intercession

إِنَّكَ أَرْحَمُ ٱلرَّاحِمِينَ

innaka arhamu alrrahimina

Verily, You are the most merciful of all those who show mercy.

وَصَلَّىٰ ٱللَّهُ عَلَىٰ مُحَمَّدٍ وَآلِهِ ٱلطَّاهِرِينَ

wa salla allahu `ala muhammadin wa alihi alttahirina

May Allah send blessings upon Muhammad and his immaculate Household

وَسَلَّمَ تَسْلِيماً كَثِيراً

wa sallama tasliman kathiran

and send His thorough peace upon them.

وَحَسْبُنَا ٱللَّهُ وَنِعْمَ ٱلْوَكِيلُ

wa hasbuna allahu wa ni`ma alwakilu

Allah is Sufficient for us! Most Excellent is He in Whom we trust.

ZIYARAH ASHURAA

اَلسَّلاَمُ عَلَيْكَ يَا أَبَا عَبْدِ ٱللَّهِ

alssalamu `alayka ya aba `abdillahi
Peace be upon you, O Abu-`Abdullah.

اَلسَّلاَمُ عَلَيْكَ يَا بْنَ رَسُولِ ٱللَّهِ

alssalamu `alayka yabna rasuli allahi
Peace be upon you, O son of Allah's Messenger.

اَلسَّلاَمُ عَلَيكَ يَا خِيَرَةَ ٱللَّهِ وَٱبْنَ خِيَرَتِهِ

alssalamu `alayka ya khiyarata allahi wabna khiyaratihi
Peace be upon you, O choicest of Allah and son of His choicest.

اَلسَّلاَمُ عَلَيْكَ يَا بْنَ أَمِيرِ ٱلْمُؤْمِنِينَ

alssalamu `alayka yabna amiri almu'minina
Peace be upon you, O son of the Commander of the Faithful

وَٱبْنَ سَيِّدِ ٱلْوَصِيِّينَ

wabna sayyidi alwasiyyina
and son of the chief of the Prophets' successors.

اَلسَّلاَمُ عَلَيْكَ يَا بْنَ فَاطِمَةَ

alssalamu `alayka yabna fatimata
Peace be upon you, O son of Fatimah

سَيِّدَةِ نِسَاءِ ٱلْعَالَمِينَ

sayyidati nisa'i al`alamina
the doyenne of the women of the worlds.

اَلسَّلاَمُ عَلَيْكَ يَا ثَارَ ٱللَّهِ وَٱبْنَ ثَارِهِ وَٱلْوِتْرَ ٱلْمَوْتُورَ

alssalamu `alayka ya thara allahi wabna tharihi walwitra almawtura
Peace be upon you, O vengeance of Allah, son of His vengeance, and the unavenged so far.

اَلسَّلاَمُ عَلَيْكَ وَعَلَىٰ ٱلأَرْوَاحِ ٱلَّتِي حَلَّتْ بِفِنَائِكَ

alssalamu `alayka wa `ala al-arwahi allati hallat bifina'ika
Peace be upon you and upon the souls that resided in your courtyard.

عَلَيْكُمْ مِنِّي جَمِيعاً سَلاَمُ ٱللَّهِ أَبَداً

`alaykum minni jami`an salamu allahi abadan

Peace of Allah be upon all of you from me forever

مَا بَقِيتُ وَبَقِيَ ٱللَّيْلُ وَٱلنَّهَارُ

ma baqitu wa baqiya allaylu walnnaharu

as long as I am existent and as long as there are day and night.

يَا أَبَا عَبْدِ ٱللَّهِ

ya aba `abdillahi

O Abu-`Abdullah,

لَقَدْ عَظُمَتِ ٱلرَّزِيَّةُ

laqad `azumat alrraziyyatu

unbearable is the sorrow

وَجَلَّتْ وَعَظُمَتِ ٱلْمُصِيبَةُ بِكَ

wa jallat wa `azumat almusibatu bika

and excruciating and unbearable is the misfortune of you

عَلَيْنَا وَعَلَىٰ جَمِيعِ أَهْلِ ٱلإِسْلاَمِ

`alayna wa `ala jami`i ahli al-islami

for us and for all the people of Islam.

وَجَلَّتْ وَعَظُمَتْ مُصِيبَتُكَ

wa jallat wa `azumat musibatuka

Excruciating and unbearable has been your misfortune

فِي ٱلسَّمَاوَاتِ عَلَىٰ جَمِيعِ أَهْلِ ٱلسَّمَاوَاتِ

fi alssamawati `ala jami`i ahli alssamawati

in the heavens for all the inhabitants of the heavens.

فَلَعَنَ ٱللَّهُ أُمَّةً أَسَّسَتْ أَسَاسَ ٱلظُّلْمِ وَٱلْجَوْرِ عَلَيْكُمْ أَهْلَ ٱلْبَيْتِ

fala`ana allahu ummatan assasat asasa alzzulmi waljawri `alaykum ahla albayti

So, may Allah curse the people who laid the basis of persecution and wronging against you, O Members of the Household.

وَلَعَنَ ٱللَّهُ أُمَّةً دَفَعَتْكُمْ عَنْ مَقَامِكُمْ

wa la`ana allahu ummatan dafa`atkum `an maqamikum
May Allah curse the people who drove you away from your position

وَأَزَالَتْكُمْ عَنْ مَرَاتِبِكُمُ ٱلَّتِي رَتَّبَكُمُ ٱللَّهُ فِيهَا

wa azalatkum `an maratibikum allati rattabakum allahu fiha
and removed you away from your ranks that Allah has put you in.

وَلَعَنَ ٱللَّهُ أُمَّةً قَتَلَتْكُمْ

wa la`ana allahu ummatan qatalatkum
May Allah curse the people who slew you.

وَلَعَنَ ٱللَّهُ ٱلْمُمَهِّدِينَ لَهُمْ

wa la`ana allahu almumahhidina lahum
May Allah curse those who paved the way for them to do so

بِٱلتَّمْكِينِ مِنْ قِتَالِكُمْ

bilttamkini min qitalikum
and who made possible for them to fight against you.

بَرِئْتُ إِلَىٰ ٱللَّهِ وَإِلَيْكُمْ مِنْهُمْ

bari'tu ila allahi wa ilaykum minhum
I repudiate them in the presence of Allah and You

وَمِنْ أَشْيَاعِهِمْ وَأَتْبَاعِهِمْ وَأَوْلِيَائِهِمْ

wa min ashya`ihim wa atba`ihim wa awliya'ihim
and I repudiate their devotees, followers, and loyalists.

يَا أَبَا عَبْدِ ٱللَّهِ

ya aba `abdillahi
O Abu-`Abdullah,

إِنِّي سِلْمٌ لِمَنْ سَالَمَكُمْ

inni silmun liman salamakum
I am at peace with those who are at peace with you

وَحَرْبٌ لِمَنْ حَارَبَكُمْ إِلَىٰ يَوْمِ ٱلْقِيَامَةِ

wa harbun liman harabakum ila yawmi alqiyamati

and I am at war against those who have fought against you up to the Resurrection Day.

وَلَعَنَ ٱللَّهُ آلَ زِيَادٍ وَآلَ مَرْوَانَ

wa la`ana allahu ala ziyadin wa ala marwana

May Allah also curse the family of Ziyad and the family of Marwan.

وَلَعَنَ ٱللَّهُ بَنِي أُمَيَّةَ قَاطِبَةً

wa la`ana allahu bani umayyata qatibatan

May Allah also curse the descendants of Umayyah altogether.

وَلَعَنَ ٱللَّهُ ٱبْنَ مَرْجَانَةَ

wa la`ana allahu ibna marjanata

May Allah also curse the son of Marjanah.

وَلَعَنَ ٱللَّهُ عُمَرَ بْنَ سَعْدٍ

wa la`ana allahu `umara bna sa`din

May Allah also curse `Umar the son of Sa`d.

وَلَعَنَ ٱللَّهُ شِمْرًا

wa la`ana allahu shimran

May Allah also curse Shimr.

وَلَعَنَ ٱللَّهُ أُمَّةً أَسْرَجَتْ وَأَلْجَمَتْ

wa la`ana allahu ummatan asrajat wa aljamat

May Allah also curse the people who saddled up, gave reins to their horses,

وَتَنَقَّبَتْ لِقِتَالِكَ

wa tanaqqabat liqitalika

and masked their faces in preparation for fighting against you.

بِأَبِي أَنْتَ وَأُمِّي

bi'abi anta wa ummi

May my father and mother be ransoms for you.

لَقَدْ عَظُمَ مُصَابِي بِكَ

laqad `azuma musabi bika

Extremely insufferable is my commiserations with you;

فَأَسْأَلُ ٱللَّهَ ٱلَّذِي أَكْرَمَ مَقَامَكَ وَأَكْرَمَنِي بِكَ

fa'as'alu allaha alladhi akrama maqamaka wa akramani bika

so, I beseech Allah Who has honored your position and honored me because of you

أَنْ يَرْزُقَنِي طَلَبَ ثَأْرِكَ

an yarzuqani talaba tha'rika

to endue me with the chance to avenge you

مَعَ إِمَامٍ مَنْصُورٍ مِنْ أَهْلِ بَيْتِ مُحَمَّدٍ

ma`a imamin mansurin min ahli bayti muhammadin

with a (Divinely) supported leader from the Household of Muhammad,

صَلَّىٰ ٱللَّهُ عَلَيْهِ وَآلِهِ

salla allahu `alayhi wa alihi

peace of Allah be upon him and his Household.

ٱللَّهُمَّ ٱجْعَلْنِي عِنْدَكَ وَجِيهاً

allahumma ij`alni `indaka wajihan

O Allah, (please) make me illustrious in Your sight

بِٱلْحُسَيْنِ عَلَيْهِ ٱلسَّلاَمُ فِي ٱلدُّنْيَا وَٱلآخِرَةِ

bilhusayni `alayhi alssalamu fi alddunya wal-akhirati

in the name of al-Husayn, peace be upon him, in this world and in the Hereafter.

يَا أَبَا عَبْدِ ٱللَّهِ

ya aba `abdillahi

O Abu-`Abdullah,

إِنِّي أَتَقَرَّبُ إِلَىٰ ٱللَّهِ وَإِلَىٰ رَسُولِهِ

inni ataqarrabu ila allahi wa ila rasulihi

I do seek nearness to Allah, to His Messenger,

وَإِلَىٰ أَمِيرِ ٱلْمُؤْمِنِينَ وَإِلَىٰ فَاطِمَةَ

wa ila amiri almu'minina wa ila fatimata

to the Commander of the Faithful, to Fatimah,

وَإِلَىٰ ٱلْحَسَنِ وَإِلَيْكَ بِمُوَالاَتِكَ

wa ila alhasani wa ilayka bimuwalatika

to al-Hasan, and to you by means of loyalty to you

وَبِٱلْبَرَاءَةِ مِمَّنْ قَاتَلَكَ

wa bilbara'ati (mimman qatalaka

and by means of repudiation of those who fought against you

وَنَصَبَ لَكَ ٱلْحَرْبَ

wa nasaba laka alharba

and incurred your hostility,

وَبِٱلْبَرَاءَةِ مِمَّنْ أَسَّسَ أَسَاسَ ٱلظُّلْمِ وَٱلْجَوْرِ عَلَيْكُمْ

wa bilbara'ati mimman assasa asasa alzzulmi waljawri `alaykum

and repudiation of those who laid the basis of persecution and wronging against you all.

وَأَبْرَأُ إِلَىٰ ٱللَّهِ وَإِلَىٰ رَسُولِهِ(

wa abra'u ila allahi wa ila rasulihi)

I also repudiate, in the presence of Allah and His Messenger,

مِمَّنْ أَسَّسَ أَسَاسَ ذٰلِكَ

mimman assasa asasa dhalika

those who laid the basis of all that,

وَبَنَىٰ عَلَيْهِ بُنْيَانَهُ

wa bana `alayhi bunyanahu

established their foundations on it,

وَجَرَىٰ فِي ظُلْمِهِ وَجَوْرِهِ عَلَيْكُمْ وَعلىٰ أَشْيَاعِكُمْ

wa jara fi zulmihi wa jawrihi `alaykum wa `ala ashya`ikum

and continued in wronging and persecuting you and your adherents.

بَرِئْتُ إِلَىٰ ٱللَّهِ وَإِلَيْكُمْ مِنْهُمْ

bari'tu ila allahi wa ilaykum minhum
In the presence of Allah and you all do I repudiate these.

وَأَتَقَرَّبُ إِلَىٰ ٱللَّهِ ثُمَّ إِلَيْكُمْ

wa ataqarrabu ila allahi thumma ilaykum
And I seek nearness to Allah and then to you all

بِمُوَالاَتِكُمْ وَمُوَالاَةِ وَلِيِّكُمْ

bimuwalatikum wa muwalati waliyyikum
by means of declaring loyalty to you and to your loyalists

وَبِٱلْبَرَاءَةِ مِنْ أَعْدَائِكُمْ

wa bilbara'ati min a`da'ikum
and declaring repudiation of your enemies

وَٱلنَّاصِبِينَ لَكُمُ ٱلْحَرْبَ

walnnasibina lakum alharba
and those who incur animosity of you

وَبِٱلْبَرَاءَةِ مِنْ أَشْيَاعِهِمْ وَأَتْبَاعِهِمْ

wa bilbara'ati min ashya`ihim wa atba`ihim
and repudiation of their adherents and followers.

إِنِّي سِلْمٌ لِمَنْ سَالَمَكُمْ

inni silmun liman salamakum
I am verily at peace with those who have been at peace with you,

وَحَرْبٌ لِمَنْ حَارَبَكُمْ

wa harbun liman harabakum
I am at war against those who fought against you,

وَوَلِيٌّ لِمَنْ وَالاَكُمْ

wa waliyyun liman walakum
loyalist to those who have been loyalist to you,

وَعَدُوٌّ لِمَنْ عَادَاكُمْ

wa `aduwwun liman `adakum

and enemy of those who have shown enmity towards you.

فَأَسْأَلُ ٱللَّهَ ٱلَّذِي أَكْرَمَنِي بِمَعْرِفَتِكُمْ

fa'as'alu allaha alladhi akramani bima`rifatikum

So, I beseech Allah Who has endued me with the honor of recognizing you

وَمَعْرِفَةِ أَوْلِيَائِكُمْ

wa ma`rifati awliya'ikum

and recognizing your loyalists

وَرَزَقَنِيَ ٱلْبَرَاءَةَ مِنْ أَعْدَائِكُمْ

wa razaqani albara'ata min a`da'ikum

and Who conferred upon me with repudiation of your enemies,

أَنْ يَجْعَلَنِي مَعَكُمْ فِي ٱلدُّنْيَا وَٱلآخِرَةِ

an yaj`alani ma`akum fi alddunya wal-akhirati

to include me with you in this world and in the Hereafter

وَأَنْ يُثَبِّتَ لِي عِنْدَكُمْ قَدَمَ صِدْقٍ

wa an yuthabbita li `indakum qadama sidqin

and to make firm step of honesty for me with you

فِي ٱلدُّنْيَا وَٱلآخِرَةِ

fi alddunya wal-akhirati

in this world and in the Hereafter.

وَأَسْأَلُهُ أَنْ يُبَلِّغَنِيَ ٱلْمَقَامَ ٱلْمَحْمُودَ لَكُمْ عِنْدَ ٱللَّهِ

wa as'aluhu an yuballighani almaqama almahmuda lakum `inda allahi

I also beseech Him to make me attain the praiseworthy status that you enjoy with Allah

وَأَنْ يَرْزُقَنِي طَلَبَ ثَأْرِي

wa an yarzuqani talaba tha'ri

and to bestow upon me with the chance to take my own vengeance

مَعَ إِمَامِ هُدىً ظَاهِرٍ

ma`a imami hudan zahirin

with a leader of true guidance who is (Divinely) sustained

نَاطِقٍ بِٱلْحَقِّ مِنْكُمْ

natiqin bilhaqqi minkum

and expressing the truth from among you.

وَأَسْأَلُ ٱللَّهَ بِحَقِّكُمْ

wa as'alu allaha bihaqqikum

I also beseech Allah in your names

وَبِٱلشَّأْنِ ٱلَّذِي لَكُمْ عِنْدَهُ

wa bilshsha'ni alladhi lakum `indahu

and in the name of the standing that you enjoy with Him

أَنْ يُعْطِيَنِي بِمُصَابِي بِكُمْ

an yu`tiyani bimusabi bikum

to recompense me for my commiserations for you

أَفْضَلَ مَا يُعْطِي مُصَاباً بِمُصِيبَتِهِ

afdala ma yu`ti musaban bimusibatihi

with the most favorite thing that He ever gives as compensation for misfortunes that has afflicted anyone.

مُصِيبَةً مَا أَعْظَمَهَا

musibatan ma a`zamaha

(Your) misfortune has been so astounding

وَأَعْظَمَ رَزِيَّتَهَا فِي ٱلإِسْلاَمِ

wa a`zama raziyyataha fi al-islami

and so catastrophic for Islam

وَفِي جَمِيعِ ٱلسَّمَاوَاتِ وَٱلأَرْضِ

wa fi jami`i alssamawati wal-ardi

and for all the heavens and the entire earth.

اَللَّهُمَّ ٱجْعَلْنِي فِي مَقَامِي هٰذَا

allahumma ij`alni fi maqami hadha

O Allah, (please) make me in this situation of mine

مِمَّنْ تَنَالُهُ مِنْكَ صَلَوَاتٌ وَرَحْمَةٌ وَمَغْفِرَةٌ

mimman tanaluhu minka salawatun wa rahmatun wa maghfiratun

one of those who receive blessings, mercy, and forgiveness from You.

اَللَّهُمَّ ٱجْعَلْ مَحْيَايَ مَحْيَا مُحَمَّدٍ وَآلِ مُحَمَّدٍ

allahumma ij`al mahyaya mahya muhammadin wa ali muhammadin

O Allah, (please) make me live my lifetime in the same way as Muhammad and Muhammad's Household lived

وَمَمَاتِي مَمَاتَ مُحَمَّدٍ وَآلِ مُحَمَّدٍ

wa mamati mamata muhammadin wa ali muhammadin

and make me die on the same principles on which Muhammad and Muhammad's Household died.

اَللَّهُمَّ إِنَّ هٰذَا يَوْمٌ

allahumma inna hadha yawmun

O Allah, this day

تَبَرَّكَتْ بِهِ بَنُو أُمَيَّةَ

tabarrakat bihi banu umayyata

has been regarded as blessed day by the descendants of Umayyah

وَٱبْنُ آكِلَةِ ٱلأَكْبَادِ

wabnu akilati al-akbadi

and by the son of the liver-eater woman,

اَللَّعِينُ ٱبْنُ ٱللَّعِينِ

alla`inu ibnu alla`ini

the accursed and son of the accursed

عَلَىٰ لِسَانِكَ وَلِسَانِ نَبِيِّكَ

`ala lisanika wa lisani nabiyyika

by the tongue of You and by the tongue of Your Prophet,

صَلَّىٰ ٱللَّهُ عَلَيْهِ وَآلِهِ

salla allahu `alayhi wa alihi
Allah's peace be upon him,

فِي كُلِّ مَوْطِنٍ وَمَوْقِفٍ

fi kulli mawtinin wa mawqifin
on every occasion and in every situation,

وَقَفَ فِيهِ نَبِيُّكَ صَلَّىٰ ٱللَّهُ عَلَيْهِ وَآلِهِ

waqafa fihi nabiyyuka salla allahu `alayhi wa alihi
which Your Prophet, Allah's peace be upon him, attended.

ٱللَّهُمَّ ٱلْعَنْ أَبَا سُفْيَانَ وَمُعَاوِيَةَ وَيَزِيدَ بْنَ مُعَاوِيَةَ

allahumma il`an aba sufyana wa mu`awiyata wa yazida bna mu`awiyata
O Allah, pour curses upon Abu-Sufyan, Mu`awiyah, and Yazid son of Mu`awiyah.

عَلَيْهِمْ مِنْكَ ٱللَّعْنَةُ أَبَدَ ٱلآبِدِينَ

`alayhim minka alla`natu abada al-abidina
May Your curse be upon them incessantly and everlastingly.

وَهٰذَا يَوْمٌ فَرِحَتْ بِهِ آلُ زِيَادٍ وَآلُ مَرْوَانَ

wa hadha yawmun farihat bihi alu ziyadin wa alu marwana
This is the day on which the family of Ziyad and the family of Marwan gloated

بِقَتْلِهِمُ ٱلْحُسَيْنَ صَلَوَاتُ ٱللَّهِ عَلَيْهِ

biqatlihim alhusayna salawatu allahi `alayhi
because they had killed al-Husayn, Allah's blessings be upon him.

ٱللَّهُمَّ فَضَاعِفْ عَلَيْهِمُ ٱللَّعْنَ مِنْكَ

allahumma fada`if `alayhim alla`na minka
So, O Allah, pour frequent curses upon them

وَٱلْعَذَابَ ٱلأَلِيمَ

wal`adhaba (al-alima)
and double for them the painful chastisement.

اَللَّهُمَّ إِنِّي أَتَقَرَّبُ إِلَيْكَ فِي هٰذَا ٱلْيَوْمِ

allahumma inni ataqarrabu ilayka fi hadha alyawmi
O Allah, I do seek nearness to You on this day,

وَفِي مَوْقِفِي هٰذَا

wa fi mawqifi hadha
on this occasion,

وَأَيَّامِ حَيَاتِي

wa ayyami hayati
and on all the days of my lifetime,

بِٱلْبَرَاءَةِ مِنْهُمْ وَٱللَّعْنَةِ عَلَيْهِمْ

bilbara'ati minhum walla`nati `alayhim
by repudiating these and invoking Your curses upon them,

وَبِٱلْمُوَالاَةِ لِنَبِيِّكَ وَآلِ نَبِيِّكَ

wa bilmuwalati linabiyyika wa ali nabiyyika
and by declaring loyalty to Your Prophet and Your Prophet's Household,

عَلَيْهِ وَعَلَيْهِمُ ٱلسَّلاَمُ

`alayhi wa `alayhim alssalamu
peace be upon him and them.

You may then repeat the following statement one hundred times:

اَللَّهُمَّ ٱلْعَنْ أَوَّلَ ظَالِمٍ

allahumma il`an awwala zalimin
O Allah, pour curses upon the foremost persecutor

ظَلَمَ حَقَّ مُحَمَّدٍ وَآلِ مُحَمَّدٍ

zalama haqqa muhammadin wa ali muhammadin
who usurped the right of Muhammad and Muhammad's Household

وَآخِرَ تَابِعٍ لَهُ عَلَىٰ ذٰلِكَ

wa akhira tabi`in lahu `ala dhalika

and the last follower who acceded to his deed.

اَللَّهُمَّ ٱلْعَنِ ٱلْعِصَابَةَ ٱلَّتِي جَاهَدَتِ ٱلْحُسَيْنَ

allahumma il`an al`isabata allati jahadat alhusayna

O Allah, pour curses upon the gang that struggled against al-Husayn

وَشَايَعَتْ وَبَايَعَتْ وَتَابَعَتْ عَلَىٰ قَتْلِهِ

wa shaya`at wa baya`at wa taba`at `ala qatlihi

and who supported each other against him, paid homage to his enemies, and participated in slaying him.

اَللَّهُمَّ ٱلْعَنْهُمْ جَمِيعاً

allahumma il`anhum jami`an

O Allah, pour curses upon all of them.

You may then repeat the following one hundred times:

اَلسَّلاَمُ عَلَيْكَ يَا أَبَا عَبْدِ ٱللَّهِ

alssalamu `alayka ya aba `abdillahi

Peace be upon you, O Abu-`Abdullah

وَعَلَىٰ ٱلأَرْوَاحِ ٱلَّتِي حَلَّتْ بِفِنَائِكَ

wa `ala al-arwahi allati hallat bifina'ika

and upon the souls that gathered in your courtyard.

عَلَيْكَ مِنِّي سَلاَمُ ٱللَّهِ أَبَداً

`alayka minni salamu allahi abadan

Peace of Allah be upon you from me forever

مَا بَقِيتُ وَبَقِيَ ٱللَّيْلُ وَٱلنَّهَارُ

ma baqitu wa baqiya allaylu walnnaharu

as long as I am existent and as long as there are day and night.

وَلاَ جَعَلَهُ ٱللَّهُ آخِرَ ٱلْعَهْدِ مِنِّي لِزِيَارَتِكُمْ

wa la ja`alahu allahu akhira al`ahdi minni liziyaratikum

May Allah not cause this (visit) to be the last of my visit to you (all).

اَلسَّلاَمُ عَلَىٰ ٱلْحُسَيْنِ

alssalamu `ala alhusayni
Peace be upon al-Husayn,

وَعَلَىٰ عَلِيِّ بْنِ ٱلْحُسَيْنِ

wa `ala `aliyyi bni alhusayni
upon `Ali ibn al-Husayn,

وَعَلَىٰ أَوْلاَدِ ٱلْحُسَيْنِ

wa `ala awladi alhusayni
upon the sons of al-Husayn,

وَعَلَىٰ أَصْحَابِ ٱلْحُسَيْنِ

wa `ala ashabi alhusayni
and upon the companions of al-Husayn.

You may then say the following words:

اَللَّهُمَّ خُصَّ أَنْتَ أَوَّلَ ظَالِمٍ بِٱللَّعْنِ مِنِّي

allahumma khussa anta awwala zalimin billa`ni minni
O Allah, pour special curses on the foremost persecutor

وَٱبْدَأْ بِهِ أَوَّلاً

wabda' bihi awwalan
and begin with him first,

ثُمَّ ٱلْعَنِ ٱلثَّانِيَ وَٱلثَّالِثَ وَٱلرَّابِعَ

thumma il`an alththaniya walththalitha walrrabi`a
and then pour curses on the second, the third, and the fourth.

اَللَّهُمَّ ٱلْعَنْ يَزِيدَ خَامِساً

allahumma il`an yazida khamisan
O Allah, curse Yazid fifthly,

وَٱلْعَنْ عُبَيْدَ ٱللَّهِ بْنَ زِيَادٍ وَٱبْنَ مَرْجَانَةَ

wal`an `ubaydallahi bna ziyadin wabna marjanata
and curse `Ubaydullah ibn Ziyad, the son of Marjanah,

وَعُمَرَ بْنَ سَعْدٍ وَشِمْراً

wa `umara bna sa`din wa shimran
`Umar ibn Sa`d, Shimr,

وَآلَ أَبِي سُفْيَانَ وَآلَ زِيَادٍ وَآلَ مَرْوَانَ

wa ala abi sufyana wa ala ziyadin wa ala marwana
the family of Abu-Sufyan, the family of Ziyad, and the family of Marwan

إِلَىٰ يَوْمِ ٱلْقِيَامَةِ

ila yawmi alqiyamati
up to the Resurrection Day.

You may then prostrate yourself and say the following words meanwhile:

ٱللَّهُمَّ لَكَ ٱلْحَمْدُ

allahumma laka alhamdu
O Allah, all praise be to You;

حَمْدَ ٱلشَّاكِرِينَ لَكَ عَلَىٰ مُصَابِهِمْ

hamda alshshakirina laka `ala musabihim
the praise of those who thank You for their misfortunes.

ٱلْحَمْدُ لِلَّهِ عَلَىٰ عَظِيمِ رَزِيَّتِي

alhamdu lillahi `ala `azimi raziyyati
All praise be to Allah for my great misfortune.

ٱللَّهُمَّ ٱرْزُقْنِي شَفَاعَةَ ٱلْحُسَيْنِ يَوْمَ ٱلْوُرُودِ

allahumma irzuqni shafa`ata alhusayni yawma alwurudi
O Allah, (please) grant me the intercession of al-Husayn on the Day of Coming (to You)

وَثَبِّتْ لِي قَدَمَ صِدْقٍ عِنْدَكَ

wa thabbit li qadama sidqin `indaka
and make for me with You a firm step of honesty

مَعَ ٱلْحُسَيْنِ وَأَصْحَابِ ٱلْحُسَيْنِ

ma`a alhusayni wa ashabi alhusayni

with al-Husayn and the companions of al-Husayn

ٱلَّذِينَ بَذَلُوٓاْ مُهَجَهُمْ دُونَ ٱلْحُسَيْنِ عَلَيْهِ ٱلسَّلاَمُ

alladhina badhalu muhajahum duna alhusayni

who sacrificed their souls in defense of al-Husayn, peace be upon him.

Printed in Great Britain
by Amazon

52323346R10169